Salesforce Platform App Builder Certification Handbook

A handy guide that covers the most essential topics for Salesforce Platform App Builder Certification in an easy-to-understand format

Siddhesh Kabe

BIRMINGHAM - MUMBAI

Salesforce Platform App Builder Certification Handbook

First published: April 2016

Production reference: 1220416

Published by Packt Publishing Ltd.
Livery Place
35 Livery Street
Birmingham B3 2PB, UK.

ISBN 978-1-78528-369-7

www.packtpub.com

Credits

Author
Siddhesh Kabe

Reviewer
Doug Ayers

Acquisition Editor
Sonali Vernekar

Content Development Editor
Mayur Pawanikar

Technical Editor
Naveenkumar Jain

Copy Editor
Rashmi Sawant

Project Coordinator
Nidhi Joshi

Proofreader
Safis Editing

Indexer
Hemangini Bari

Graphics
Kirk D'Penha

Production Coordinator
Shantanu N. Zagade

Cover Work
Shantanu N. Zagade

About the Author

Siddhesh Kabe calls himself the monk who sold his computer for the cloud. He has had a rock-solid career in consulting, training, designing, developing, and advocating the Force.com platform for 8 years. He has five certifications in Salesforce. He likes to break into things—code and gadgets—and believes that, given enough coffee, anything can be hacked into.

His other published work includes a science-fiction satire called Ragnarok and a fantasy graphic novel entitled Agatya. Apart from this, he is an active member of the Force.com community and owns an active blog (`http://force.siddheshkabe.co.in`). He is also the leader of the Force.com Pune Users Group.

Acknowledgments

When I first started writing the *Force.com Developer Certification Handbook (DEV401), Packt Publishing* in 2012, the goal was clear—how can you make the Salesforce development easy, accessible, and simple. You don't realize how daunting a task is, until you actually start it. But in the infamous words of Brian Tracy, you eat a large frog one bite at a time. And so the little bites started and the book finally released almost 4 years ago. When the team from Packt Publishing asked me to write a revised edition of the book, we all thought it would be easy.

With Salesforce, it hardly is. The pioneers of cloud computing are known for one thing—they change fast and for better. The exam had changed, the syllabus was different, and there were tons of new features coming in. When it comes to publishing, we cannot always tackle things quickly, not with a book as massive as this. Hence, while working with this book, I had to accommodate as many new features as I could before the book went live. The lessons learned from my previous experience and the feedback received on social media, in person and via e-mails, are all included in this book, and an extra effort has been made to make the book error-free.

One cannot trot forward without the undying support system and I would like to take this opportunity to thank some of those who were there for me. First and foremost, I would like to thank Govind and Shobhana Kabe, my parents and mentors, who insisted very vocally that I take computer engineering as a career. I cannot thank my wife, Deepika, enough and if I start enlisting all the ways she supports me, this acknowledgment will fill more pages than the book itself. My brother, Chaitanya Kabe, for being there with me always.

A special thanks to Doug Ayers for painstakingly going through the content and giving a honest and valuable feedback.

I would like to thank the team at Packt Publishing for being patient and keeping up with me as I kept missing deadline after deadline. A special thanks to the content editor, Mayur Pawanikar, for not losing patience as he kept chasing me for the content. Thanks to the technical editor, Naveenkumar Jain, for helping with the content and to Sonali Vernekar for initiating this project.

I would like to thank the mentors I met on this journey of the Salesforce platform, who helped and guided me at different stages of my career. Without their guidance, I would not be where I am today. No book on the Salesforce platform can be complete without mentioning the amazing developer community and the Salesforce developers team itself; thank you for the great cloud platform and the developer events that have helped us from time to time.

About the Reviewer

Doug Ayers has over 9 years of experience leading teams to build reliable web apps and enterprise services with agile engineering practices on Salesforce and Java platforms. He holds multiple Salesforce developer certifications and is pursuing the Technical Architect certification. He enjoys the rich ecosystem of open source software and contributes to the community on GitHub, `https://github.com/DouglasCAyers`, Twitter, `https://twitter.com/DouglasCAyers`, and his technology blog, `http://douglascayers.com`.

As someone who is continually learning and trying new approaches, he enjoys collaborating with and mentoring others. He volunteers as a coach for the VetForce Program, `https://veterans.force.com`, and leads and speaks at the Nashville Salesforce Developers Group.

www.PacktPub.com

eBooks, discount offers, and more

Did you know that Packt offers eBook versions of every book published, with PDF and ePub files available? You can upgrade to the eBook version at `www.PacktPub.com` and as a print book customer, you are entitled to a discount on the eBook copy. Get in touch with us at `customercare@packtpub.com` for more details.

At `www.PacktPub.com`, you can also read a collection of free technical articles, sign up for a range of free newsletters and receive exclusive discounts and offers on Packt books and eBooks.

`https://www2.packtpub.com/books/subscription/packtlib`

Do you need instant solutions to your IT questions? PacktLib is Packt's online digital book library. Here, you can search, access, and read Packt's entire library of books.

Why subscribe?

- Fully searchable across every book published by Packt
- Copy and paste, print, and bookmark content
- On demand and accessible via a web browser

Instant updates on new Packt books

Get notified! Find out when new books are published by following `@PacktEnterprise` on Twitter or the *Packt Enterprise* Facebook page.

Table of Contents

Preface

This book will assist you in building a strong foundation in Force.com to prepare for the Platform App Builder Certification Exam. It will help you to design, build, and implement custom applications using the declarative customization capabilities of the Force.com platform.

What this book covers

Chapter 1, Getting Started with Force.com, helps you understand the application life cycle of an application build using Force.com.

Chapter 2, Creating a Database on Force.com, helps you start with building a database model to support our application.

Chapter 3, User Interface, focuses on how to create user interfaces and user experiences.

Chapter 4, Implementing Business Logic, focuses on the declarative syntax used to write business logic and connect our database to the user experience.

Chapter 5, Data Management, covers the cloud-based import wizard and the utility data loader to import data. It also gives a brief overview of automatic data loading.

Chapter 6, Analytics and Reporting, teaches you how to generate reports and display maximum information using colorful charts.

Chapter 7, Application Administration, discusses how to configure the application for multiple users.

Chapter 8, Exam Guide and Practice Test, helps you understand the exam and answer the frequently asked questions. This chapter also includes a practice test that will help refresh the skills we have learned throughout the book.

What you need for this book

The Salesforce online application can run on any computer with an Internet connection and supports the following browsers:

- Google Chrome™, most recent stable version.
- Mozilla® Firefox®, most recent stable version.
- Microsoft® Internet Explorer® versions 9, 10, and 11. If you use Internet Explorer, use the latest version that Salesforce supports. Apply all Microsoft software updates.
- Apple® Safari® Versions 5.x, 6.x, and 7.x on Mac OSX.

Who this book is for

This book is intended for Salesforce developers who are preparing for the Salesforce Certified Platform App Builder exam. This book provides an introduction to the Force.com platform if you are new to the platform and don't know where to start.

Conventions

You will also find a number of text styles that distinguish between different kinds of information. Here are some examples of these styles and an explanation of their meaning.

Code words in text, database table names, folder names, filenames, file extensions, pathnames, dummy URLs, user input, and Twitter handles are shown as follows: "You may notice that we used the Unix command `rm` to remove the `Drush` directory rather than the DOS `del` command."

A block of code is set as follows:

```
If(TODAY()>BookIssueDate__c,TODAY() - BookIssueDate__c,0);
```

New terms and **important words** are shown in bold. Words that you see on the screen, in menus or dialog boxes for example, appear in the text like this: "As shown in the following screenshot, and click on **Reset Security Token**."

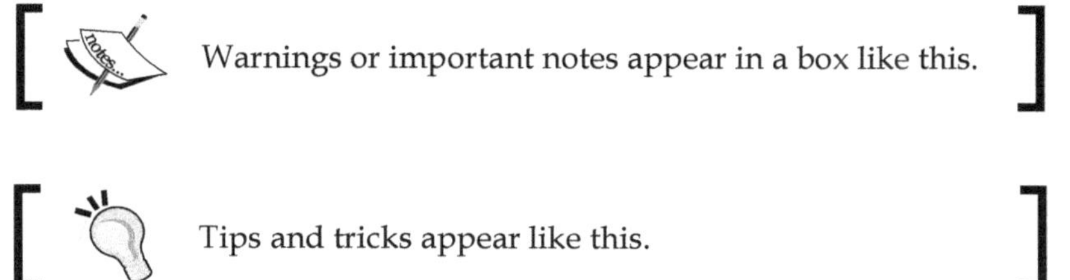

Warnings or important notes appear in a box like this.

Tips and tricks appear like this.

Reader feedback

Feedback from our readers is always welcome. Let us know what you think about this book—what you liked or disliked. Reader feedback is important for us as it helps us develop titles that you will really get the most out of.

To send us general feedback, simply e-mail `feedback@packtpub.com`, and mention the book's title in the subject of your message.

If there is a topic that you have expertise in and you are interested in either writing or contributing to a book, see our author guide at `www.packtpub.com/authors`.

Customer support

Now that you are the proud owner of a Packt book, we have a number of things to help you to get the most from your purchase.

Downloading the color images of this book

We also provide you with a PDF file that has color images of the screenshots/diagrams used in this book. The color images will help you better understand the changes in the output. You can download this file from: `https://www.packtpub.com/sites/default/files/downloads/SalesforcePlatformAppBuilderCertificationHandbook_ColorImages.pdf`.

Errata

Although we have taken every care to ensure the accuracy of our content, mistakes do happen. If you find a mistake in one of our books—maybe a mistake in the text or the code—we would be grateful if you could report this to us. By doing so, you can save other readers from frustration and help us improve subsequent versions of this book. If you find any errata, please report them by visiting `http://www.packtpub.com/submit-errata`, selecting your book, clicking on the **Errata Submission Form** link, and entering the details of your errata. Once your errata are verified, your submission will be accepted and the errata will be uploaded to our website or added to any list of existing errata under the Errata section of that title.

To view the previously submitted errata, go to `https://www.packtpub.com/books/content/support` and enter the name of the book in the search field. The required information will appear under the **Errata** section.

Piracy

Piracy of copyrighted material on the Internet is an ongoing problem across all media. At Packt, we take the protection of our copyright and licenses very seriously. If you come across any illegal copies of our works in any form on the Internet, please provide us with the location address or website name immediately so that we can pursue a remedy.

Please contact us at `copyright@packtpub.com` with a link to the suspected pirated material.

We appreciate your help in protecting our authors and our ability to bring you valuable content.

Questions

If you have a problem with any aspect of this book, you can contact us at `questions@packtpub.com`, and we will do our best to address the problem.

1
Getting Started with Force.com

This chapter will introduce you to the Force.com platform. We will understand the life cycle of an application build using Force.com. We will define a multi-tenant architecture and understand how it will impact the data of organizations stored on the cloud. And finally, we will build our first application on Force.com.

We will cover the following topics in this chapter:

- The multi-tenant architecture of Force.com
- Understanding the Force.com platform
- Application development on the Force.com platform
- Discussing the maintenance and releases schedule by Salesforce.com
- Types of Force.com applications
- Discussing when to use point-and-click customization and when to use code
- Discussing Salesforce.com IDs
- Developer resources

So, let's get started and step into the cloud.

The cloud computing model of Force.com

Force.com is a cloud computing platform used to build enterprise applications. The end user does not have to worry about networks, hardware, software licenses, or any other things. The data saved is completely secure in the cloud.

The following features of Force.com make it a 100 percent cloud-based system:

- **The multi-tenant architecture**: The multi-tenant architecture is a way of serving multiple clients on the single software instance. Each client gets their own full version of the software configuration and data. They cannot utilize the other instance resources. The software is virtually partitioned into different instances. The basic structure of the multi-tenant architecture is shown in the following figure:

  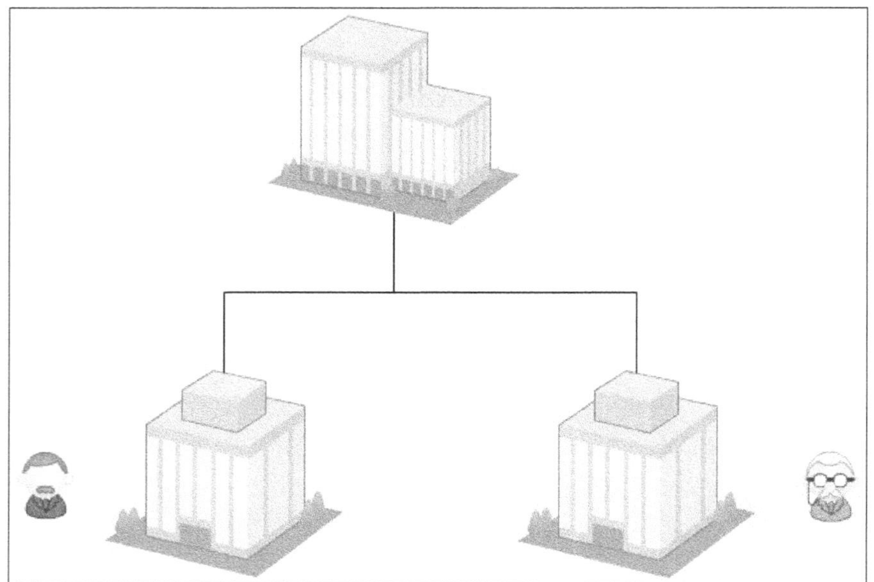

  Just like how tenants in a single building share the resources of electricity and water, in the multi-tenant system tenants share common resources and databases.

In a multi-tenant system, such as Salesforce.com, different organizations use the same shared database system that is separated by a secure virtual partition. Special programs keep the data separated and make sure that no single organization monopolizes the resources.

- **Automatic upgrades**: In a cloud computing system, all the new updates are automatically released to its subscribers. Any developments or customizations made during the previous version are automatically updated to the latest version without any manual modification to the code. This results in all instances of Salesforce staying up to date and on the same version.
- **Subscription model**: Force.com is distributed under the subscription model. The user can purchase a few licenses and build the system. After the system is up and successful, further user licenses can be purchased from Salesforce. This model ensures that there are no large startup fees and we pay as we go, which adds fixed, predictable costs in the future.

  The subscription model can be visualized like the electricity distribution system. We pay for whatever electricity we use and not the complete generator and the infrastructure.
- **Scalability**: The multi-tenant kernel is already tested and runs for many users simultaneously. If the organization is growing, there is always room for scaling the application with new users without worrying about load balancing and data limitation. Force.com provides data storage on a per-user basis, which means that the data storage increases with the number of users added to the organization.
- **Upgrades and maintenance**: Force.com releases three updated versions every year. The new releases consist of feature updates to Salesforce.com and the Force.com platform with selected top ideas from IdeaExchange. IdeaExchange is the community of Salesforce users where the users submit ideas and the community votes for them. The most popular ideas are considered by Salesforce in their next release.

All instances hosted on the servers are upgraded with no additional cost. The Salesforce maintenance outage during a major release is only 5 minutes.

The sandboxes are upgraded early so there can be testing for compatibility with the new release. The new releases are backward-compatible with previous releases, thus the old code will work with new versions. The upgrades are taken care of by Force.com and the end user gets the latest-version running application.

Understanding the new model of the Salesforce1 platform

In the earlier edition of this book, we discussed the Force.com platform in detail. In the last couple of years, Salesforce has introduced a new **Salesforce1 platform**. It encompasses all the existing features of the Force.com platform but also includes the new powerful tools for mobile development. The new Salesforce1 platform is built mobile-first and all the existing features of cloud development are automatically available for mobiles. From Winter 16, Salesforce has also introduced the lighting experience. The lighting experience is another extension to the existing platform. It provides a brand new set of design and development library that let developers build applications that work on mobiles as well as the Web.

Let's take a detailed look at the services that form the platform offered by Force.com. The following section provides us with an overview of the Force.com platform.

Force.com platform

Force.com is the world's first cloud application development platform where end users can build, share, and run an application directly on the cloud. While most cloud computing systems provide the ability to deploy the code from the local machine, Force.com lets us directly write the code in the cloud.

The Force.com platform runs in a hosted multi-tenant environment, which gives the end users freedom to build their custom application without hardware purchases, database maintenance, and maintaining a software license. Salesforce.com provides the following main products:

- Sales force Automation, Sales Cloud
- Service and Support Center, Service Cloud
- The Exact Target Marketing Cloud
- Collaboration Cloud, Chatter

The following screenshot shows the Force.com platform:

The application built on Force.com is automatically hosted on the cloud platform. It can be used separately (without the standard Sales, Service, and Marketing cloud) or can be used in parallel with the existing Salesforce application.

The users can access the application using a browser from any mobile, computer, tablet, and any of the operating system such as Windows, UNIX, Mac, and so on, giving them complete freedom of location.

For a complete list of supported browsers, visit:

`https://help.salesforce.com/apex/HTViewHelpDoc?id=getstart_browser_overview.htm`

Model-View-Controller architecture

The most efficient way to build an enterprise application is to clearly separate out the model: the data, the code (the controller), and the UI (the View). By separating the three, we can make sure that each area is handled by an expert. The business logic is separated from the backend database and the frontend user interface.

It is also easy to upgrade a part of the system without disturbing the entire structure. The following diagram illustrates the model-view-controller of Force.com:

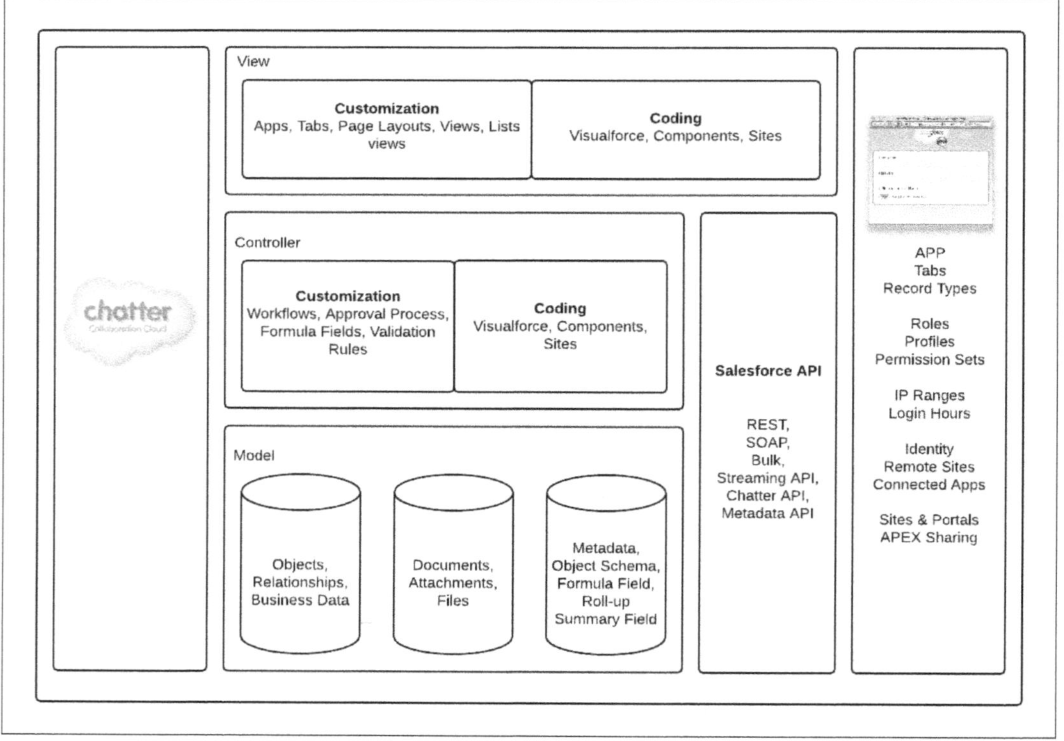

We will be looking in detail at each layer in the MVC architecture in subsequent chapters.

Key technologies behind the Force.com platform

Force.com is a hosted multi-tenant service used to build a custom cloud computing application. It is a 100 percent cloud platform where we pay no extra cost for the hardware and network. Any application built on Force.com is directly hosted on the cloud and can be accessed using a simple browser from a computer or a mobile.

The Force.com platform runs on some basic key technologies.

The multi-tenant kernel

The base of the platform forms a multi-tenant kernel where all users share a common code base and physical infrastructure. The multiple tenants, who are hosted on a shared server, share the resources under governor limits to prevent a single instance monopolizing the resources. The custom code and data are separated by software virtualization and users cannot access each other's code.

The multi-tenant kernel ensures that all the instances are updated to the latest version of the software simultaneously. The updates are applied automatically without any patches or software download.

The multi-tenant architecture is already live for one million users. This helps developers easily scale the applications from one to a million users with little or no modification at all. The following figure illustrates the multi-tenant architecture:

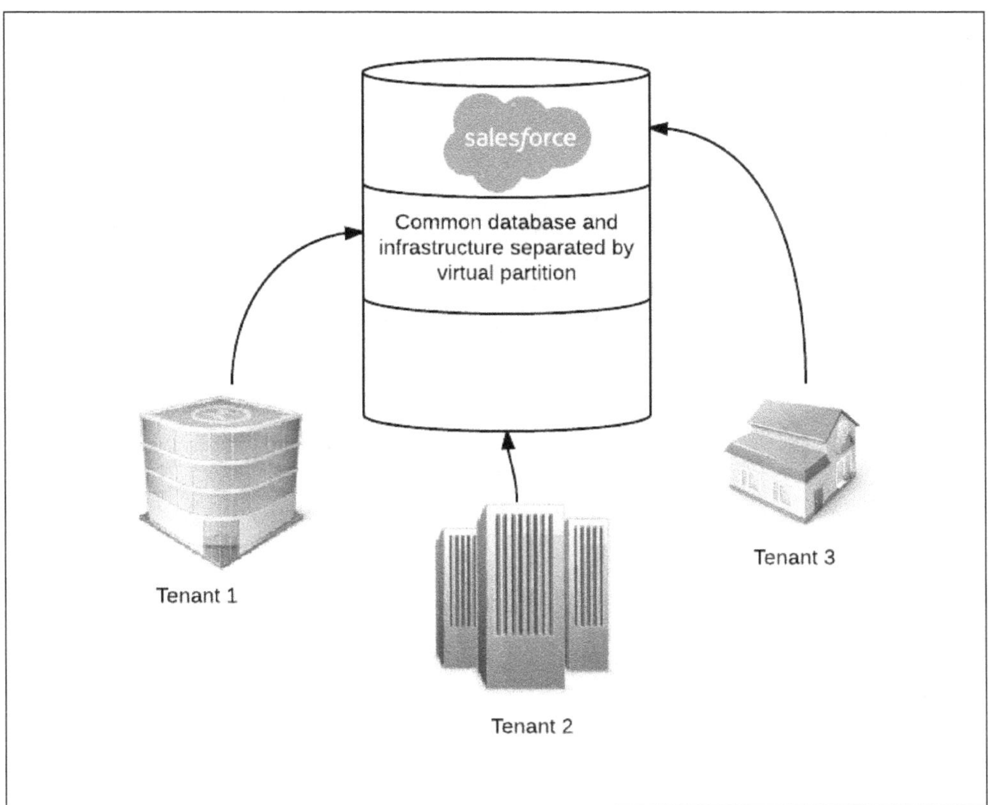

Traditional software systems are hosted on a single-tenant system, usually a client-server-based enterprise application. With the multi-tenant architecture, the end user does not have to worry about the hardware layer or software upgrades and patches. The software system deployed over the Internet can be accessed using a browser from any location possible, even wide ranges of mobile devices.

The multi-tenant architecture also allows the applications to be low-cost, quick to deploy, and open to innovation. Other examples of software using the multi-tenant architecture are webmail systems (such as `www.gmail.com` and `www.yahoo.com`) and online storage systems, such as `www.dropbox.com`, or note-taking applications, such as Evernote, Springpad, and so on.

Force.com metadata

Force.com is entirely metadata-driven. The metadata is defined in XML and can be extracted and imported. We will look into metadata in detail later in this chapter.

Force.com Webservice API

The data and the metadata stored on the Force.com server can be accessed programmatically through the Webservice API. This enables the developers to extend the functionality to virtually any language, operating system, and platform possible.

The web services are based on open web standards, such as SOAP, XML, and JSON REST, and are directly compatible with other technologies, such as .Net, Java, SAP, and Oracle. We can easily integrate the Force.com application with the current business application without rewriting the entire code.

Apex and Visualforce

Apex is the world's first on-demand language introduced by Salesforce. It is an object-oriented language very similar to C# or Java. Apex is specially designed to process bulk data for business applications. Apex is used to write the controller in the MVC architecture.

Salesforce Object Query Language (**SOQL**) gives developers an easy and declarative query language that can fetch and process a large amount of data in an easy, human-readable query language. For those who have used other relational database systems, such as Oracle, SQL Server, and so on, it is similar to SQL but does not support advanced capabilities, such as joins.

Apex and SOQL together give developers powerful tools to manage data and processes for their application, leaving the rest of the overhead on the Force.com platform.

The following screenshot shows the page editor for Visualforce. It is easy to use and splits a page into two parts: the one at the bottom is for development and the other shows the output:

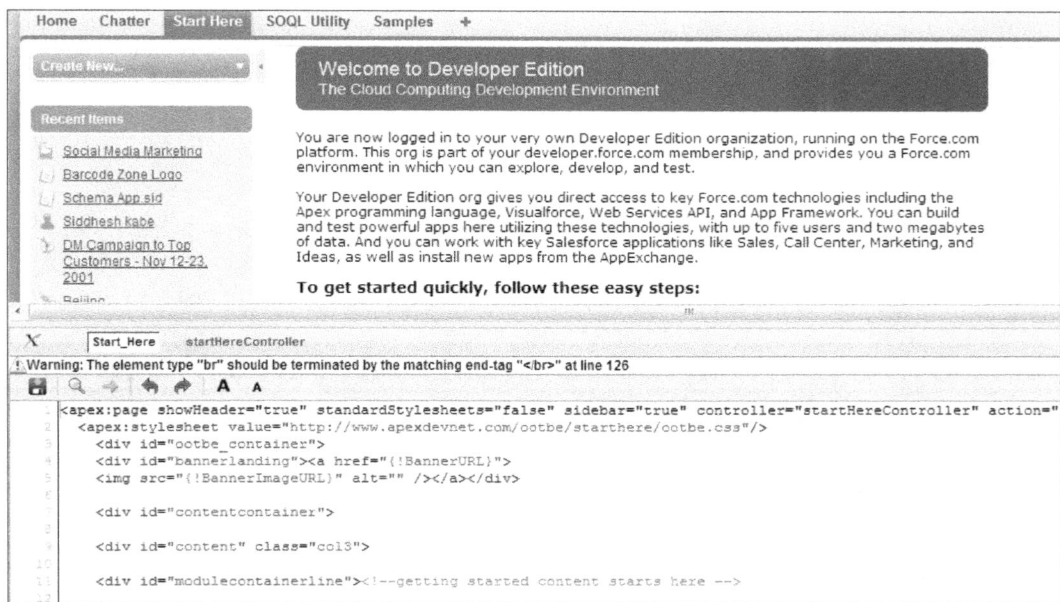

Visualforce is an easy-to-use, yet powerful framework used to create rich user interfaces, thus extending the standard tabs and forms to any kind of interfaces imaginable. Visualforce ultimately renders into HTML, and hence we can use any HTML code alongside the Visualforce markup to create a powerful and rich UI to manage business applications.

Apart from the UI, Visualforce provides very easy and direct access to the server-side data and metadata from Apex. This powerful combination of a rich UI with access to the Salesforce metadata makes Visualforce the ultimate solution to build powerful business applications on Salesforce.

As the Salesforce.com Certified Force.com Developer Certification does not include Apex and Visualforce, we won't be going into Apex and Visualforce in detail.

The Developer Console

The Developer Console is an Integrated Development Environment (IDE) for tools to help write code, run tests, and debug the system. The developer console provides an editor for writing code. It also provides a UI to monitor and debug Unit test classes, as shown in the following screenshot:

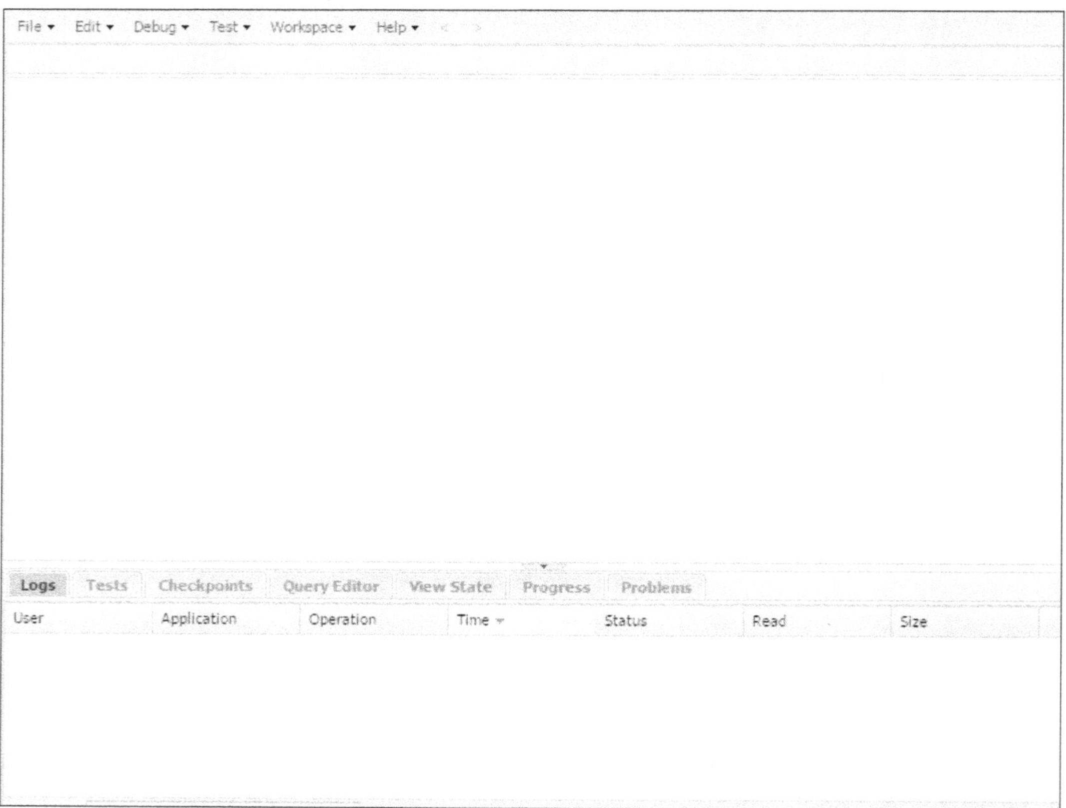

AppExchange

AppExchange is a directory of applications built on the Force.com platform. Developers can **choose** to submit their developed applications on `AppExchange`. The applications extend the functionality of Force.com beyond CRM with many ready-made business applications available to download and use.

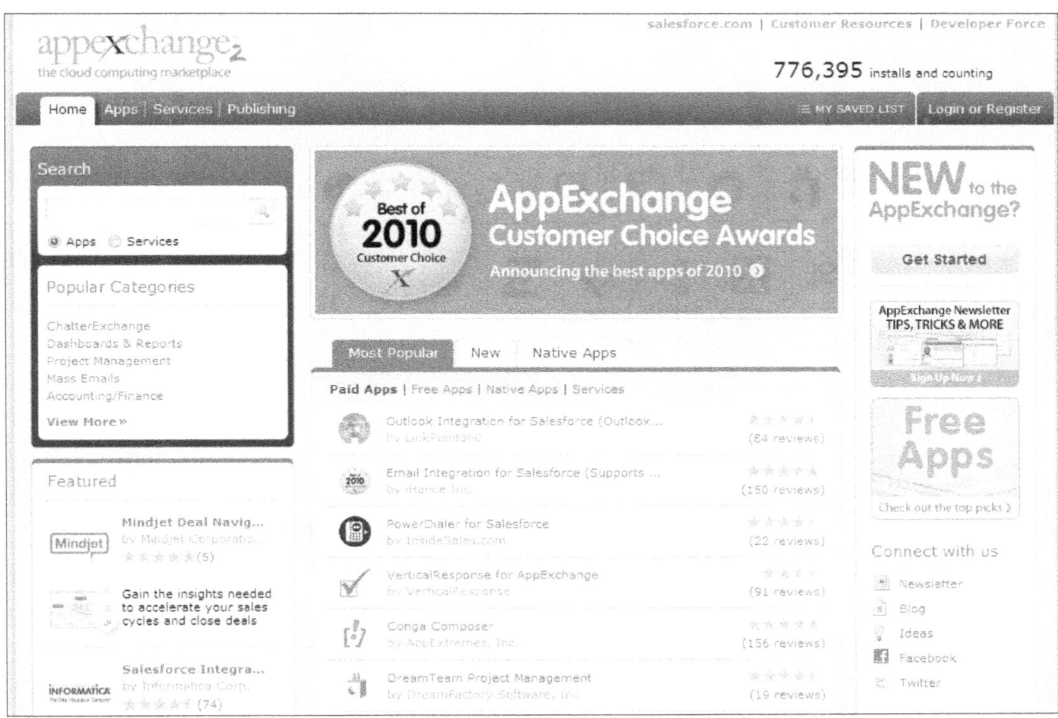

AppExchange is available at `http://appexchange.salesforce.com`.

Force.com sites

Using Force.com sites or site.com, we can build public-facing websites that use the existing Salesforce data and browser technologies, such as HTML, JavaScript, CSS, Angular JS, Bootstrap, and so on. The sites can have an external login for sensitive data or a no-login public portal that can be linked to the corporate website as well.

Site.com helps create websites using drag-and-drop controls. Users with little or no HTML knowledge can build websites using the site.com editor.

Force.com development

Like any other traditional software development process, the Force.com platform offers tools used to define data, business processes, logic, and rich UIs for the business application. Many of these tools are built-in, point-and-click tools simplified for users without any development skills. Any user with no programming knowledge can build applications suitable for their business on Force.com.

The point-and-click tools are easy to use, but they have limitations. To extend the platform beyond these limitations, we use Apex and Visualforce.

Let's now compare the tools used for traditional software development with Force.com:

	Java	**Dot Net**	**Force.com**
Building the database	Oracle, MS-Access, SQL, or any third-party database setup	Oracle, MS-Access, SQL, or any third-party database setup	Salesforce metadata (now database.com)
Connection to the database	JDBC	Ado.net	Salesforce metadata API
Developing the IDE	NetBeans, Eclipse, and so on	Visual Studio	Online Page Editor and App Setup, Force.com IDE, Maven's Mate, and Aside.io
Controlled environment for development and testing	Local servers, remote test servers	Local servers, remote test servers	Force.com real-time sandboxes

Force.com metadata

Everything on Force.com such as data models, objects, forms, tabs, and workflows are defined by metadata. The definitions or metadata are made in XML and can be extracted and imported. The metadata-driven development also helps users with no prior development experience to build business applications without any need to code. We can define the objects, tabs, and forms in the UI using point-and-click.

All changes made to the metadata in `App-Setup` are tracked. Alternatively, developers can customize every part of Salesforce using XML files that control the organization's metadata. The files are downloaded using the Eclipse IDE or Force.com IDE.

To customize metadata on Salesforce UI, go to **Setup** | **Build**:

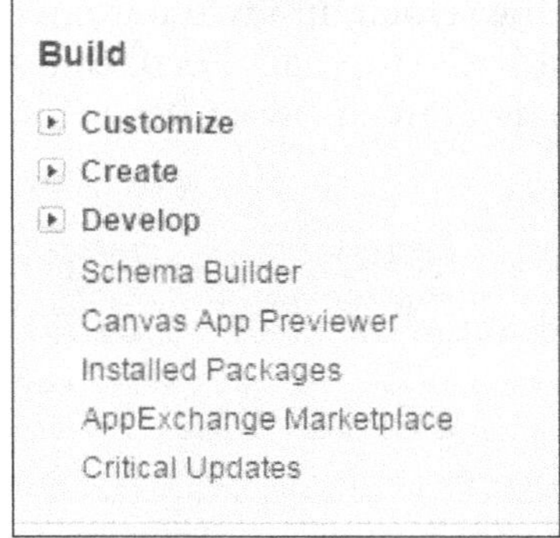

As Force.com Developer Certification is about using point-and-click, we will explore setup details in upcoming chapters.

Metadata API

The metadata API provides easy access to the organization data, business logic, and the user interface. We can modify the metadata in a controlled test organization called the **sandbox**. Finally, the tested changes can be deployed to a live production environment edition. The production environment is the live environment that is used by the users and contains live data. The production instance does not allow developers to code in them directly; this ensures that only debugged and tested code reaches the live organization.

Online page editor and the Eclipse Force.com IDE

Force.com provides a built-in online editor that helps edit Visualforce pages in real time. The online editor can be enabled by checking the **Development Mode** checkbox on the user profile, as shown in the following screenshot:

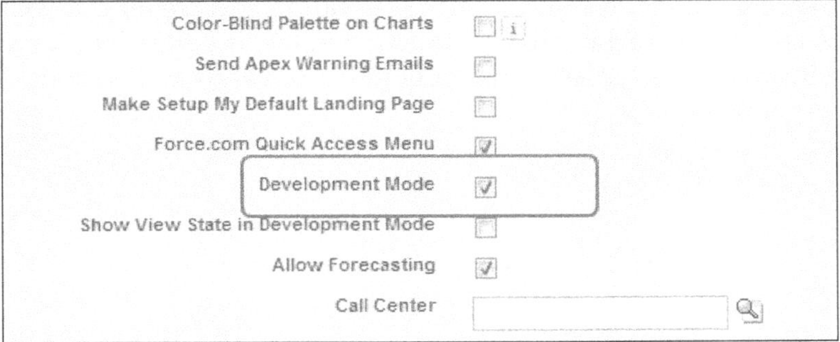

The online page editor splits the screen into two parts with live code in the bottom half and the final page output in the top half. Force.com also provides an inline editor for editing the Apex code in the browser itself.

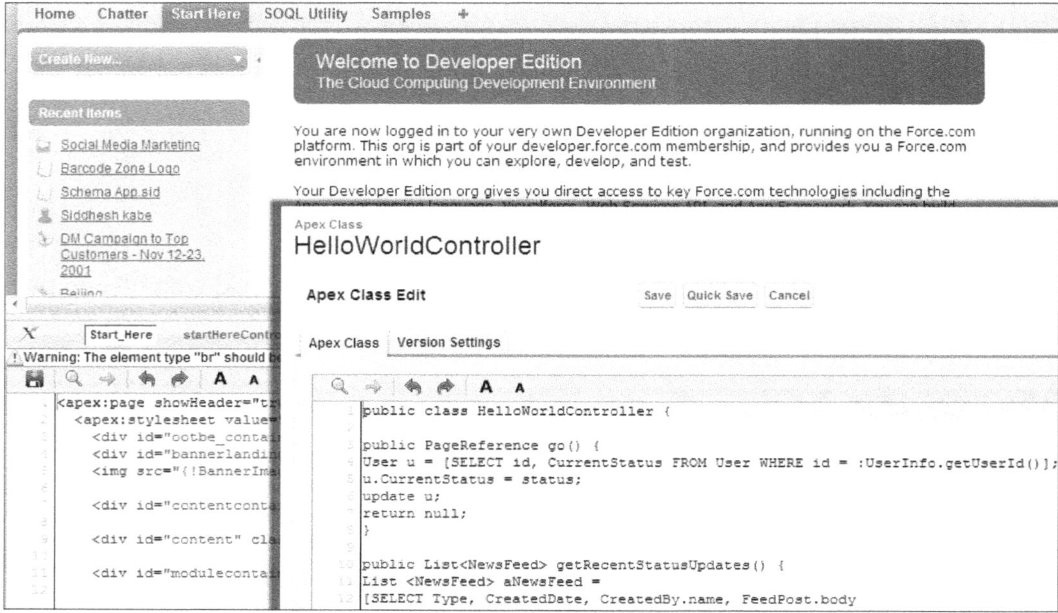

Force.com IDE is an IDE built over Eclipse. It provides an easy environment to write code and offline saving. It also comes with a schema browser and a query generator, which helps in generating simple queries (`select` statements) by selecting fields and objects. The code is auto-synced with the organization.

Sandboxes

Force.com provides a real-time environment to develop, test, and train people in the organization. It is a safe and isolated environment where any changes made will not affect the production data or application. These sandboxes are used to experiment on new features without disturbing live production in the organization. Separating the test and `dev` instances also ensures that only the tested and verified code reaches the production organization.

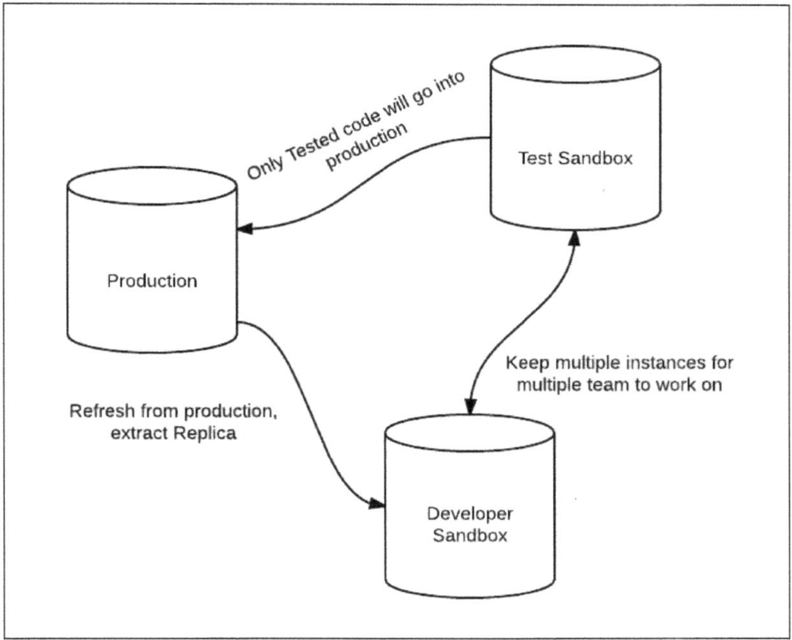

There are four types of sandbox:

- **Developer sandbox**: This environment is specially used to code and test the environment by a single developer. As with the configuration-only sandbox, this also copies the entire customization of the production organization, excluding the data. An added feature of a developer sandbox is that it allows Apex and Visualforce coding.
- **Developer pro sandbox**: Developer pro sandboxes are similar to developer sandboxes but with larger storage. This sandbox is mostly used to handle more developer and quality-assurance tasks. With a larger sandbox, we can store more data and run more efficient tasks.
- **Partial copy sandbox**: This is used as a testing environment. This environment copies the full metadata of the production environment and a subset of production data that can be set using a template.
- **Full copy sandbox**: This copies the entire production organization and all its data records, documents, and attachments. This is usually used to develop and test a new application until it is ready to be shared with users. Full copy sandbox has the same IDs of the records as that of production only when it has been freshly created.

Force.com application types

There are some common types of applications that are required to automate an enterprise process. They are as follows:

- **Content-centric applications**: These applications enable organizations to share and version content across different levels. They consist of file sharing systems, versioning systems, and content management systems.
- **Transaction-centric applications**: These applications focus on transactions. They are banking systems, online payment systems, and so on.
- **Process-centric applications**: These applications focus on automating the organization's business process in the organization such as a bug tracking systems, procurement processes, approval processes, and so on. Force.com is suitable for building these kinds of applications.
- **Data-centric applications**: These applications are built around a powerful database. Many of the organizations use spreadsheets for these applications. Some examples include CRM, HRM, and so on. Force.com is suitable for building these kinds of applications.

Developing on the Force.com platform

There are two ways to develop on Force.com: one is to use point-and-click without a single line of coding, called the **declarative** development. The other way is to develop an application using code, called **programmatic** development. Let's take a look at the two types of development in detail.

Declarative development

The declarative type of development is done by point-and-click using a browser. We use ready-to-use components and modify their configuration to build applications. We can add new objects, define their standard views, and create input forms with simple point-and-link with no coding knowledge. The declarative framework allows the rapid development and deployment of applications.

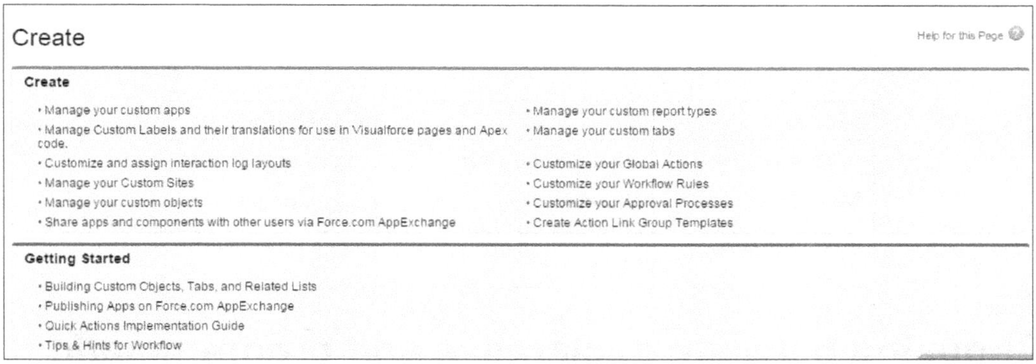

Create

Help for this Page

Create

- Manage your custom apps
- Manage Custom Labels and their translations for use in Visualforce pages and Apex code.
- Customize and assign interaction log layouts
- Manage your Custom Sites
- Manage your custom objects
- Share apps and components with other users via Force.com AppExchange
- Manage your custom report types
- Manage your custom tabs
- Customize your Global Actions
- Customize your Workflow Rules
- Customize your Approval Processes
- Create Action Link Group Templates

Getting Started

- Building Custom Objects, Tabs, and Related Lists
- Publishing Apps on Force.com AppExchange
- Quick Actions Implementation Guide
- Tips & Hints for Workflow

The declarative development also follows the MVC architecture in development. The MVC components in the declarative development using Force.com are mentioned in the following table:

Model	View	Controller
Objects	Applications	Workflow rules
Fields	Tabs	Validation rules
Relationships	Page layouts	Assignment rules
	Record types	

Programmatic development

Programmatic development requires prior coding knowledge. This method allows us to extend the Force.com platform beyond declarative capabilities. This method gives us the control and flexibility over the application we build.

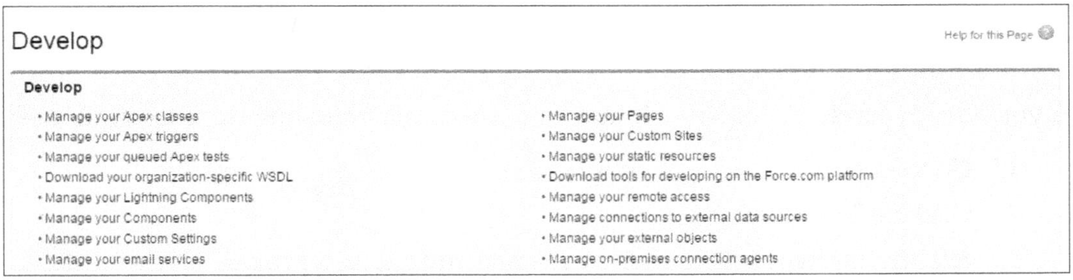

Develop

Help for this Page

Develop

- Manage your Apex classes
- Manage your Apex triggers
- Manage your queued Apex tests
- Download your organization-specific WSDL
- Manage your Lightning Components
- Manage your Components
- Manage your Custom Settings
- Manage your email services
- Manage your Pages
- Manage your Custom Sites
- Manage your static resources
- Download tools for developing on the Force.com platform
- Manage your remote access
- Manage connections to external data sources
- Manage your external objects
- Manage on-premises connection agents

The programmatic development also uses the MVC architecture, as shown in the following table:

Model	View	Controller
Web services API Metadata API External object	Visualforce pages Visualforce component Sites	Apex controllers Apex triggers Web service API

Choosing between declarative and programmatic solutions

There is no hard and fast rule to help us choose between declarative and programmatic solutions.

Declarative solutions supply ease of development and maintenance. They are automatically upgraded with new releases of Salesforce. They are not subject to governor limits. They are faster and cheaper to build.

However, not all declarative features are capable of building specialized and complex business processes. We cannot build highly customizable user interfaces and click-through them with declarative methods.

You can also prefer to build Salesforce solutions without code first, and then, use the code to extend it beyond its limitations.

Exercise – creating a developer account

The easiest way to get your hands on Salesforce is to log in through a developer account. Developer editions are free, two-user-only accounts that can be used for exercises.

If you already have one, log in to it now or perform the following steps to create one:

1. Go to `http://developer.Force.com`.
2. Click on **Join now**.
3. Fill out the form and validate the e-mail address you provided.

Salesforce editions

In addition to the free developer editions, there are different paid editions that Salesforce offers. The four common types of edition are as follows:

- **Starter**: The starter edition is for up to five users.
- **Professional**: The professional edition provides limited customization and enhancement opportunities. It is used as a basic CRM with no facility to extend it beyond what is provided out of the box.

- **Enterprise**: This is the most commonly used edition. It provides the ability to extend Salesforce CRM with code.
- **Unlimited**: This is the advanced version of the Enterprise edition is mostly used by large organizations, which require a lot of data space. It provides unlimited customizations.

Authentication on Force.com

We can log in to Force.com from any standard web browser or third-party application. As a security measure, Salesforce tries to prevent unauthorized access to your account as it requires verification whenever you log in from a new IP address. The user is authenticated using the username, password, and the IP address of the system. The IP address where account is created is automatically white-listed for the user:

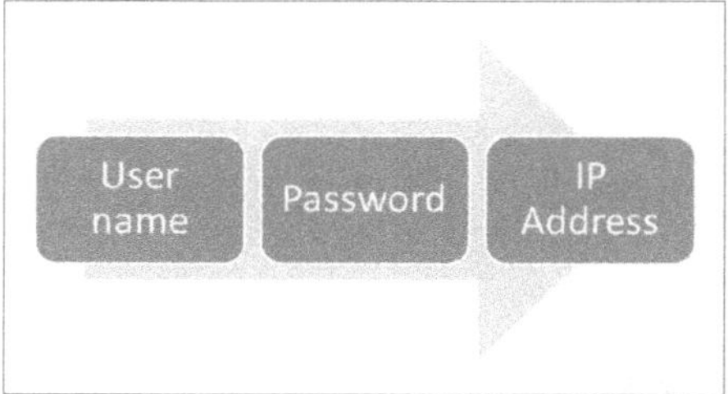

Every time the user logs in from a separate IP address, the application verifies the IP by sending an e-mail to the registered e-mail address in the personal profile. Alternatively, the system administrator can enable access by setting the trusted IP ranges. Users who log in from the white-listed IP ranges are not asked to validate their IP address or the security token.

The Force.com username is in the format of an e-mail address: `xyz@abc.com`; the username is unique across the global organization of Salesforce. If you already have a developer organization with `abc@hotmail.com`, you won't be able to create another one in with the same username. You can give a separate username (`someone@something.com`) and a valid e-mail (`abc@hotmail.com`) in this case.

Exercise – adding trusted IP addresses

Use the following steps to whitelist an IP address:

1. Go to **Setup** | **Administer** | **Security Controls** | **Network Access**.
2. Add your IP address to **Trusted IP Ranges**, as shown in the following screenshot:

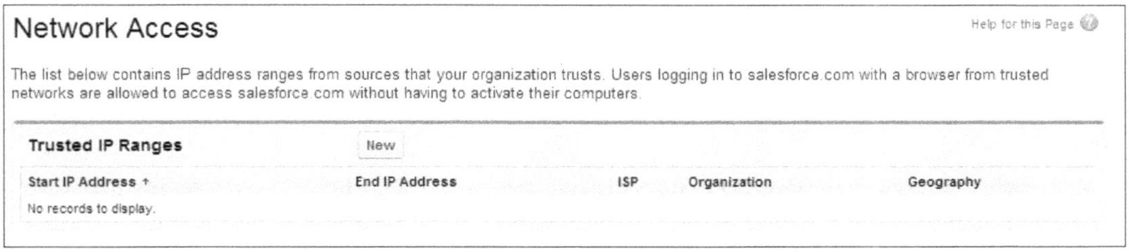

Network Access

Help for this Page

The list below contains IP address ranges from sources that your organization trusts. Users logging in to salesforce.com with a browser from trusted networks are allowed to access salesforce.com without having to activate their computers.

Trusted IP Ranges New

Start IP Address ↑	End IP Address	ISP	Organization	Geography
No records to display.				

If you are within a LAN network of your office, university, and so on, the IP address given by the `ipconfig` command in DOS will give you the internal network-specific IP. This IP address is not seen by Force.com; you need the public domain IP address to whitelist the address. To find your public domain IP address, you can visit `http://www.whatismyip.com`.

Whitelisting the IP address has its own pros and cons; the main benefit is that when logging in via the API, such as with Data Loader or the Force.com IDE, you aren't challenged to provide the security token. The disadvantage is that the security token challenge and IP address verification challenge are not enforced, thus lowering the security threshold of a malicious login attempt.

When you log in to Force.com from a third-party tool, such as the Force.com IDE, Outlook Edition, Data Loader, or the API, you need an additional security token along with a username and password. Every login user gets a security token tied to the password. We need to reset the security token the first time. It is automatically reset whenever the password is changed.

Exercise – resetting security tokens

Reset your security token in the new org.

To reset your security token, navigate to **Your Name** | **My Settings** | **Personal** | **Reset My Security Token**, as shown in the following screenshot, and click on **Reset Security Token**:

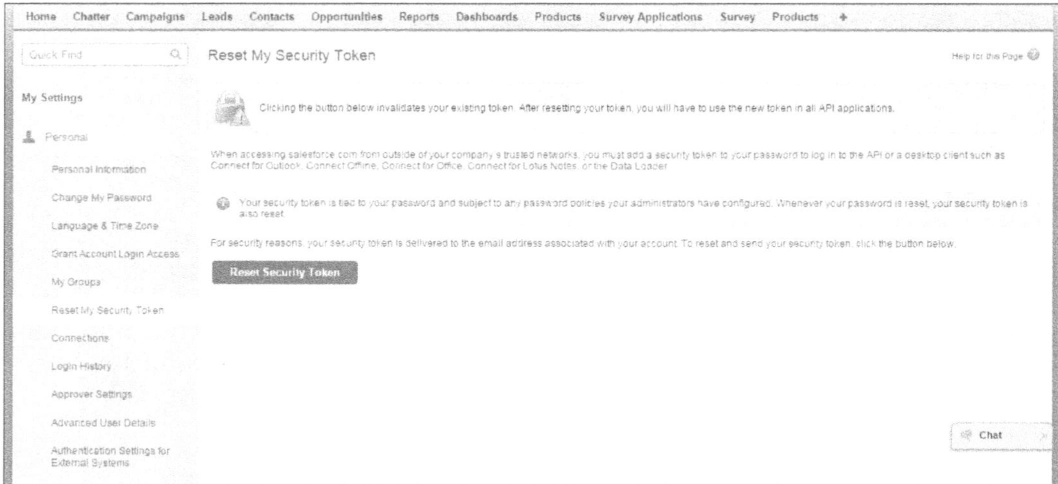

DeveloperForce.com

Along with a developer account, `http://developer.Force.com` provides additional resources for developers. The developer website is your one-stop place to learn more about Salesforce and its features.

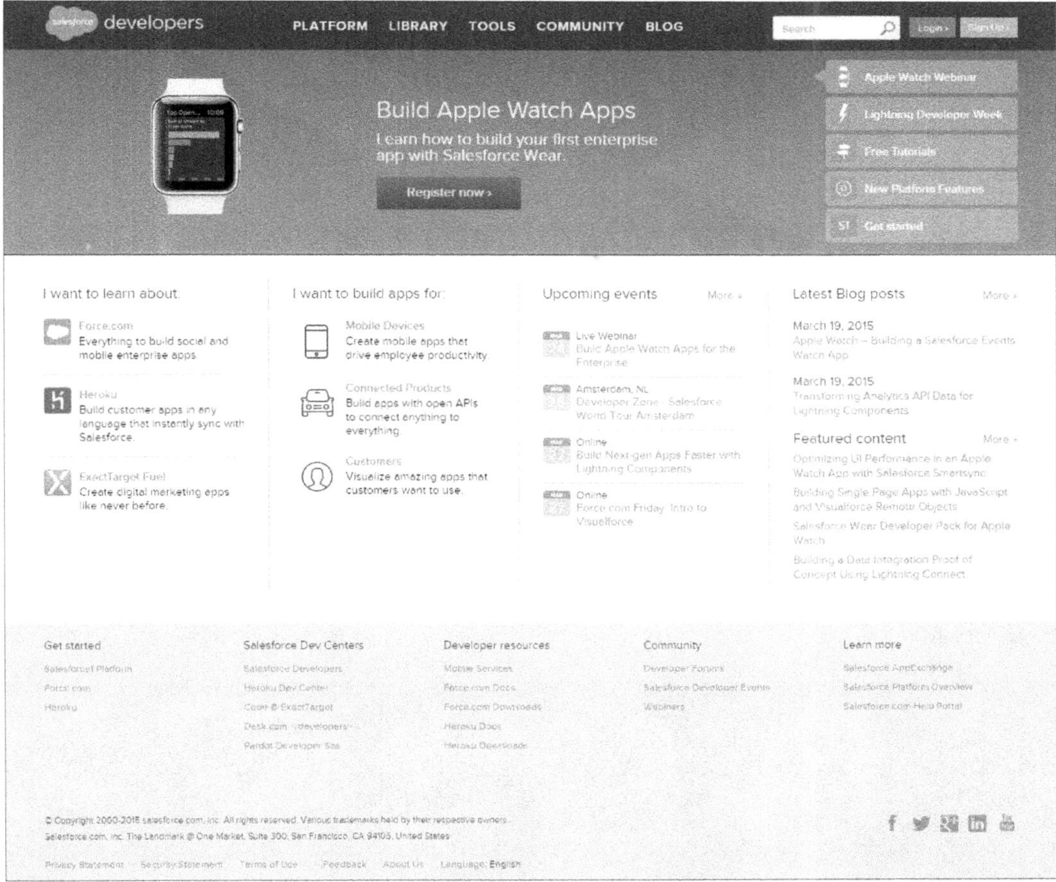

It provides the following features:

- Additional documentation
- Online forums
- Code share

All these resources can be accessed free of charge with a single developer account. Additional community blogs and recourses are available in the final chapter of this book.

> The first place to get help is from the developer forums available at `https://developer.salesforce.com/forums`.
>
> If you are on Twitter, additional help can be found using the `#AskForce` hashtag with the Salesforce Community. You may also address the Tweet to `@sforceNinja`.

Trailhead

One of the coolest new learning resources provided by Salesforce is the Trailhead. It provides free training, tutorials, and interactive learning paths through the basic building blocks of the Salesforce1 platform. We can test our knowledge while earning points and badges to celebrate our achievements.

To begin your learning journey, visit `https://developer.salesforce.com/trailhead`:

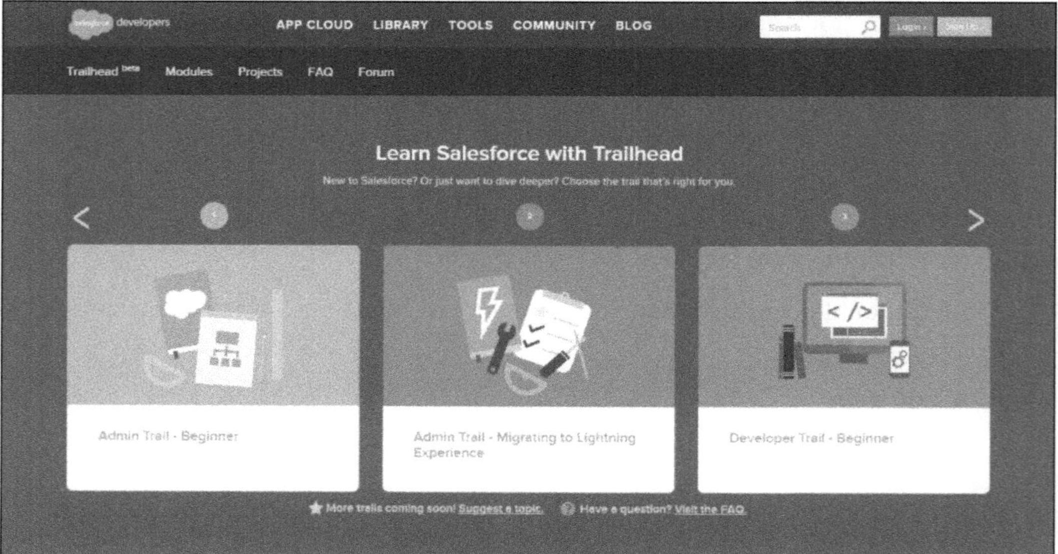

Summary

In this chapter, we became familiar with the Force.com platform. We have seen the life cycle of an application build using Force.com. We saw the multi-tenant architecture and how it is different from the web hosting server.

We have a fresh new developer account, and now in further chapters we will be using it to build an application on Force.com.

Test your knowledge

Answer the following questions:

Q1 Out of the following tasks, which can be done using the Force.com platform? (Select two)

1. Data warehousing
2. Creating applications via point and click and not code
3. Applications can be upgraded without loss of customization
4. Using a code version control system

Q2 Which of the following statements are true concerning e-mail activation? (Select one)

1. The e-mail activation feature requires that the user click on an activation link before logging in from a new computer
2. The e-mail activation feature cannot be disabled
3. The e-mail activation feature can be disabled by sending a request to Salesforce.com support
4. The e-mail activation feature can be disabled through the UI

Q3 A security token is required for API access when connecting from an IP address within the list of trusted networks.

1. True
2. False

Q4 Out of the following, which applications are suitable for Force.com? (Choose)

1. Time card application
2. Word processor
3. Online auction management
4. Inventory management

Q5 Which of the following refer to the data model of Salesforce? (Choose 2)

1. The Force.com API
2. Force.com metadata API
3. Sandbox
4. The Force.com IDE

Q6 What paid Salesforce editions are available?

1. Enterprise edition
2. Unlimited edition
3. Trial edition
4. Developer edition

Q7 Where are Force.com IDs identical?

1. Production and full copy sandbox only
2. Production and dev sandbox only
3. Two developer orgs
4. Two sandbox org

2
Creating a Database on Force.com

Now that we have defined the types of applications that can be built with Force.com and created a developer account, we can move deeper into application development. In this chapter, we are going to:

- Create objects
- Create fields
- Create relationships

The exercises covered in this chapter will be useful for you till the time you are working on the Force.com platform.

So, let's begin.

Objects

Force.com is an object-oriented relational database system. An object is the background of any application built on Force.com. An object is like a database table that allows you to store data in different formats. It also gives you options to create a UI in order to enter, modify, or delete records.

Force.com doesn't give you the option to create database tables using code. To create a table, we need to define the object using the UI. The UI not only allows you to define the object definition but also comes with unique built-in features, including recording activities (such as logging a call, sending an e-mail, and so on) and the ability to add notes and attachments. The platform automatically creates a standard UI for the object thus defined and adds basic features, such as create, update, and delete.

Note

An object in Salesforce is like a worksheet in Excel or a table in the database. A field in an object is similar to a column in an Excel sheet or a table, and the record of the object is similar to a row in an Excel sheet or a database.

Before we define a new object, let's explore what Force.com offers us initially.

Standard objects

Standard objects are part of Salesforce CRM Cloud. These objects are offered as is, and while we can extend them and add new attributes to them, we cannot modify the existing attributes unless permitted; for example, while we can add new values to `Status Picklist`, we cannot change the name of the `Picklist` value.

The following are important objects that are part of the Sales Cloud:

- **Accounts**: The entire CRM Universe revolves around `Accounts` (and `Contacts`). An individual account is an organization that is associated with your business. It could be your `Customer`, `Competitor`, or `Partner`.
- **Contacts**: A contact complements an `Account` by acting as a contact manager or an address book.
- **Leads**: A lead is the contact information for a prospect or an opportunity.
- **Opportunity**: An opportunity is a pending sale or a deal.
- **Other** supporting Objects: Along with the top four objects mentioned previously, there are many other supporting objects, such as `Products`, `Orders`, and so on.

The following are objects from the Service Cloud offering:

- **Case**: This is a customer issue such as a customer's feedback, problem, or question.
- **Solutions**: These store the detailed description of a customer's issue and the resolution of that issue. These objects and others come with the packaged CRM offering. Along with them, we have built-in processes, for example, Leads can be converted into **Contacts and Accounts**. We can create **Case from Email**. We can rename the standard objects based on the business process; for example, we can rename **Accounts** to **Customers** and **Leads** to **Prospects**. The other ways to customize the standard application is to extend it by adding custom fields or modifying the **Picklist** values.

Custom objects

Apart from the standard objects defined earlier and others that come built-in with the Salesforce CRM package, we can extend the Force.com platform by building our own set of custom objects.

Let's explore custom objects in detail.

Exercise – creating your first custom object

The public library needs to store information regarding its customers, its workers, the physical locations of its branches, and the media stored in those locations.

It specializes in lending out two types of media: books and videos. The library must keep track of the attributes of each media item, its location, status, descriptive attributes, and cost for losses and late returns.

Books will be identified by their ISBN and videos by their title and year. In order to allow multiple copies of the same book or video, each media item will have a unique ID number.

The following diagram shows a basic E-R diagram of the **Library Management System**:

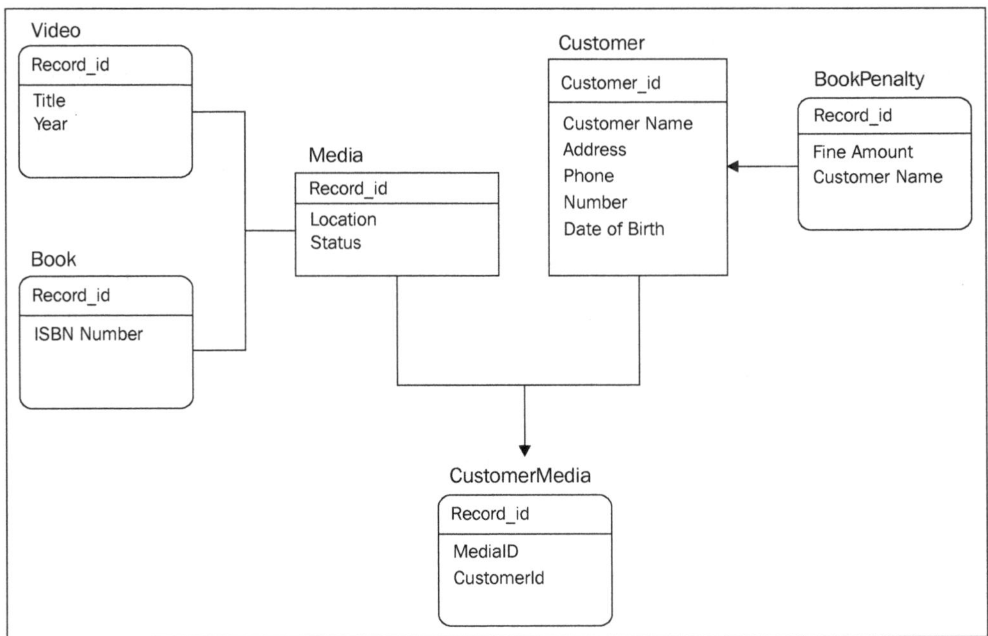

The library customers will provide their name, address, phone number, and date of birth when signing up for a library card. They will then be assigned a unique ID number. Checkout operations will require a UID number as well as requests to put media on hold. Each library card will store its own dues. The late fees for returning the media items will be stored in a separate penalty object. These penalties will be summed up for the master object.

Employees will work at a specific branch of the library. They receive a paycheck, but they can also have library cards; therefore, the same information that is collected from the customers should be collected from the employees as well.

The object structure of the Library Management can be summarized in the following table:

Object name	Related to (Relationship)	Comments
Media	CustomerMedia (Detail object of Media)	The media object is the master table used to store the collection of media. Books and videos are separated by the record type to show different types of media.
Customer	CustomerMedia (Detail Object of Customer) Book Penalty (Detail object of Member)	The Customer object stores the customer information. It also stores the total fine paid by the customer as a roll-up field.
CustomerMedia	Customer, Media (Master Object)	The CustomerMedia object stores the customer and media in a junction object and is used during the checkout and checkin function of the Library Management System.
Book Penalty	Customer	This is a child object of the Customer object and stores the amount of late fees paid by the customer.

The Library Management System

For the purpose of this exercise, we need to create all the four objects for the Library Management System, so let's start with the Customer object.

The steps to create a custom object are as follows:

1. Go to **Setup** | **Build** | **Create** | **Objects**.
2. Click on the **New custom** object.
3. Enter the details in the object. The following screenshot shows the Custom Object wizard:

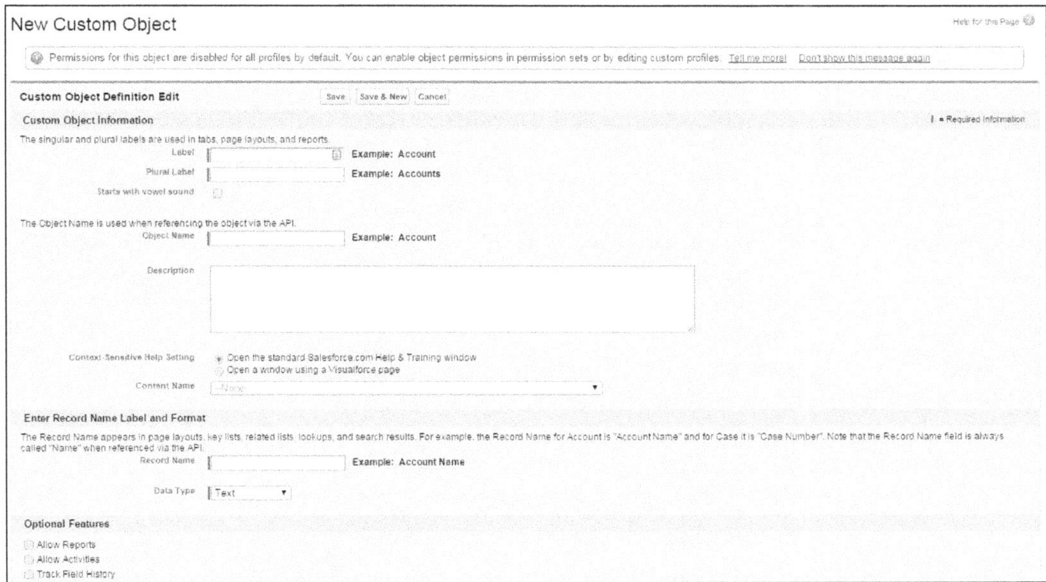

The wizard consists of the following fields:

Field	Description
Label	The label of the object is seen on the user interface. This will be used everywhere on reports, UI pages, and records. For example, Customer and Media.
Plural label	This is used when we are creating the tab of the object. For Example, Customers and Media.
Starts with a vowel sound	This checks whether the label should be preceded by an instead of a.

Field	Description
Object name	This is a unique name used to refer to the object when using the Force.com API; hence it is also called the API name. The label is seen on the frontend and the UI of the application while the API name is used to refer to the object from the backend. The **Object Name** field can contain only underscores and alphanumeric characters. It must be unique, begin with a letter, not include spaces, not end with an underscore, and must not contain two consecutive underscores. For example, customer. Note: Force.com automatically appends a `__c` (a double underscore c) to every object name. This is not seen in the UI form but is stored in the database with the name. This is how Force.com distinguishes between standard objects and custom objects. The API name of the Custom Account object becomes `Custom_Account__c`.
Description	An optional description of the object. The description saves us the trouble of remembering why we created the object in the first place when we are viewing the list of all the objects. This is extremely helpful when working with a team.
Context-sensitive help setting	If we are using a custom help system for applications built for customers, we select the custom help Visualforce page or S-control here.
Record Name	The record name used in page layouts, list views, related lists, and search results. For example, Customer Name, Customer Number, or UID. For the purpose of the example, we can name the record name UID. Note: Irrespective of what the record name is, the API name of the field is always *name* and is consistent across all standard and custom objects.
Data Type	This determines the type of field (text or auto number) for the record name. An auto number is a unique number assigned automatically. If the data type is an auto number, it is a read-only field. For the purpose of the exercise, we can create the data type as an auto number. This will be the UID of the media.

Field	Description

Display Format	For a Record Name of the auto number type, enter a display format. The display format can be of the following types:
	Format
	Displayed values
	{0}
	Incremental single-digit values, for example, 0, 2, 3, and so on.
	{000}
	Incremental three-digit values, for example, 000, 002, 003, and so on.
	`Customer- {00000}`
	`Customer - 00003, Customer -123, and so on`
	`UID- {00} {MM} {DD} {YY}`
	`UID -02 011410, UID -123 071910`
	`Customer #{0} {MM}-{DD}-{YYYY}`
	`Customer #02 01-14-2010, Customer #123 07-19-2010`

Starting Number	For a record name of the auto number type, this is the number from where the counting starts.
Allow Reports	This makes the data in the custom object records available for reporting purposes. We will discuss reports later in detail.
Allow Activities	This allows users to associate tasks and scheduled calendar events related to custom object records. The related lists of activities are directly added when this checkbox is enabled.
Track Field History	This checkbox helps you record the field changes made to the object, such as who changed the value of a field, when it was changed, and what the value of the field was before and after the edit. We can maintain a history of 20 fields for a maximum of 18 months. We can easily create audit trail reports when this feature is enabled. Note: Following the Spring 15 release, we can purchase the `Field Audit Trail Add-on` to track more than 20 fields.
Deployment Status	The custom object won't be visible to any users unless it is deployed. The best practice is to always create objects in Sandbox and deploy them in production, but if you need to develop in production then you can keep the object hidden by marking it as in-development.
Add Notes & Attachments	This allows users to attach notes and attachments to custom object records. This allows you to attach external documents to any object record, in the same way in which you can add a PDF or photo as an attachment to an e-mail. This option is only available when you are creating a new object. We can add or remove the *Notes & Attachment*-related list from the page layout.

Field	Description
Launch the New Custom Tab Wizard	Checking this option will launch the custom tab wizard for the object immediately. We will go through this wizard later in this chapter. For now, do not launch the custom tab wizard. We can at any time go to **Setup** | **Build** | **Create** | **Tabs** to create a new custom object tab.

Fill the form with the values for the Customer object. Label the object as Customer; the plural is Customers. Fill the other values according to the description.

4. Save the page.

Fields

We have successfully created the Customer object. We are going to take a look at some major types of custom fields on Force.com. Let's create the fields for the Customer object.

When we create a new field, we have to go through four steps. Let's take a look at each one of them in detail.

Standard fields

Custom objects include some standard fields that are included automatically. When we create a new custom object, it automatically has five standard fields. To capture additional data in the object, we need to add more fields to it. The standard fields include audit fields such as:

- Created By
- Last Modified By
- Owner
- CreatedDate
- ModifiedDate

Apart from the owner field, the other fields cannot be edited from the UI. The owner field is automatically assigned to the person who created the record and can be changed by transferring the record to another user.

Custom fields

The Force.com platform provides us with some good and unconventional custom data types. These custom data types are directly aligned with business use cases and come packed with unique properties and validation rules. For example, the `Email` field comes automatically with e-mail validation, the `URL` field automatically checks whether the input is a valid URL, the `Phone` field automatically formats the phone number in the local format. One of the latest additions to the custom fields is `geolocation compound fields` that come bundled with functions to calculate the distance between two locations.

We can change the data type of a custom field in some cases; however, it is not recommended as it can result in data loss. For example, we can change a text area to a text field; this may result in loss of data (truncate) if the field length is also decreased.

To begin with, let's create a few custom fields and take a look at the custom field wizard.

Choosing the field type

The first step to create custom fields is to choose the right field type that can capture the correct data.

Let's take a detailed look at all the custom field types.

Text fields

Text fields are used to capture free-flowing text. They are used to capture alphanumeric data. The five types of text fields are used to capture different lengths of data:

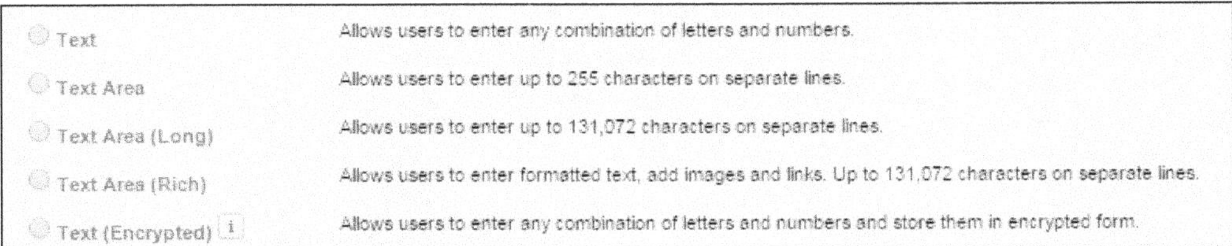

Text
Allows users to enter any combination of letters and numbers.
Text Area
Allows users to enter up to 255 characters on separate lines.
Text Area (Long)
Allows users to enter up to 131,072 characters on separate lines.
Text Area (Rich)
Allows users to enter formatted text, add images and links. Up to 131,072 characters on separate lines.
Text (Encrypted)
Allows users to enter any combination of letters and numbers and store them in encrypted form.

There are four types of basic text fields, which are as follows:

- Text (maximum 255 characters, only single-line characters)
- Text area (maximum 255 characters, allows multiple lines and paragraphs)
- Long text area (maximum 131,072 characters on multiple lines and big paragraphs)
- Rich text area (maximum 131,072 characters on multiple lines, accepts rich text formatting also; accepts images and links via the special editor)

Picklists

Picklist is a type of predefined text field. It can be used to prevent spelling mistakes and grammatical errors while entering the data. Picklist is rendered as a drop-down select list on the UI, but it is stored as text in the database. It can store predetermined values, such as `City names`, `State names`, and `Status`:

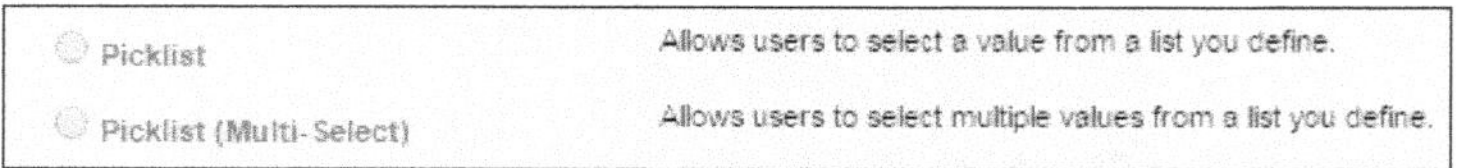

Picklist (Multi-select) is a special type of picklist that can allow the users to select multiple values at the same time.

General fields

Let's take a look at the other general data fields:

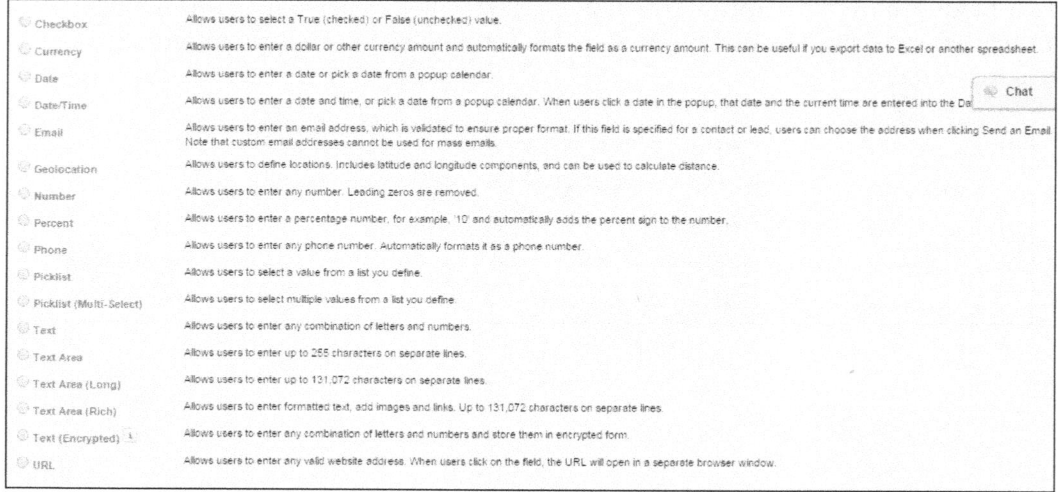

Checkbox
Allows users to select a True (checked) or False (unchecked) value.
Currency
Allows users to enter a dollar or other currency amount and automatically formats the field as a currency amount. This can be useful if you export data to Excel or another spreadsheet.
Date
Allows users to enter a date or pick a date from a popup calendar.
Date/Time
Allows users to enter a date and time, or pick a date from a popup calendar. When users click a date in the popup, that date and the current time are entered into the Da
Chat
Email
Allows users to enter an email address, which is validated to ensure proper format. If this field is specified for a contact or lead, users can choose the address when clicking Send an Email. Note that custom email addresses cannot be used for mass emails.
Geolocation
Allows users to define locations. Includes latitude and longitude components, and can be used to calculate distance.
Number
Allows users to enter any number. Leading zeros are removed.
Percent
Allows users to enter a percentage number, for example, '10' and automatically adds the percent sign to the number.
Phone
Allows users to enter any phone number. Automatically formats it as a phone number.
Picklist
Allows users to select a value from a list you define.
Picklist (Multi-Select)
Allows users to select multiple values from a list you define.
Text
Allows users to enter any combination of letters and numbers.
Text Area
Allows users to enter up to 255 characters on separate lines.
Text Area (Long)
Allows users to enter up to 131,072 characters on separate lines.
Text Area (Rich)
Allows users to enter formatted text, add images and links. Up to 131,072 characters on separate lines.
Text (Encrypted)
Allows users to enter any combination of letters and numbers and store them in encrypted form.
URL
Allows users to enter any valid website address. When users click on the field, the URL will open in a separate browser window.

Checkbox: This field stores values as true or false. On the page layout or Visualforce, the field is rendered as a checked box for true and an unchecked box for false.

Date: This field captures the date based on a data picker. The Salesforce platform stores the date/time values in the GMT time zone, but the values that are displayed are based on the **Locale & Time Zone preferences** in **My Settings**:

Date/Time: This is similar to the date but also captures the time along with the date.

Email: This captures and validates the e-mail values.

Number: This field is used to capture numeric values. We can specify the number of digits before and after the decimal point.

Percent: This field captures the percent data. The values are stored as decimals, such as 0=0%, 0.5=50%, 1=100%, and so on.

Phone: When we enter the phone number through the Salesforce UI, it is auto-formatted as Phone. If we use a third-party softphone with Salesforce, the phone number fields are auto click-to-dial-enabled.

URL: This captures the URL and makes it a clickable link.

Geolocation field

Geolocation is a compound field that allows us to identify the location using the latitude and longitude. The geolocation field comprises three separate fields: latitude, longitude, and a field used for internal purposes. The Geolocation field comes bundled with special formulas, such as `DISTANCE` that calculates the distance between two geolocation fields:

Geolocation	Allows users to define locations. Includes latitude and longitude components, and can be used to calculate distance.

The geolocation field is broken down into separate latitude and longitude components demarked by `__s`; for example, if the field is called `Location`, then the latitude is stored as `myObject__c.Location__latitude__s` and Longitude is stored as `myObject__c.Location__Longitude__s`.

Currency field

The **Currency** field captures the currency values, such as `Price` and `Amount`. If your organization has multi-currency enabled, another field called `CurrencyIsoCode` is visible that allows you to select the type of currency. When multi-currency is enabled, the currency field converts the value into corporate currency and displays it on the field:

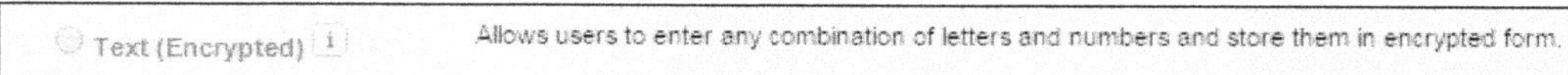

Currency
Allows users to enter a dollar or other currency amount and automatically formats the field as a currency amount. This can be useful if you export data to Excel or another spreadsheet.

We can specify the exchange rate in the setup. We can also specify historic exchange rates for existing values.

Currency fields are easy to export into Excel as they are directly compatible with the Excel currency format.

Encrypted fields

Let's take a look at the encrypted fields:

Text (Encrypted) Allows users to enter any combination of letters and numbers and store them in encrypted form.

If the Salesforce org is storing some sensitive information, such as credit card numbers, social security numbers, bank account numbers, and so on, we can use the encrypted field access to the Salesforce org.

The encrypted fields mask the value of the information with an *. For example, ******-****-****-1234** for a credit card field, as shown in the following screenshot:

We can choose the mask type of the encrypted field, as shown in the following screenshot:

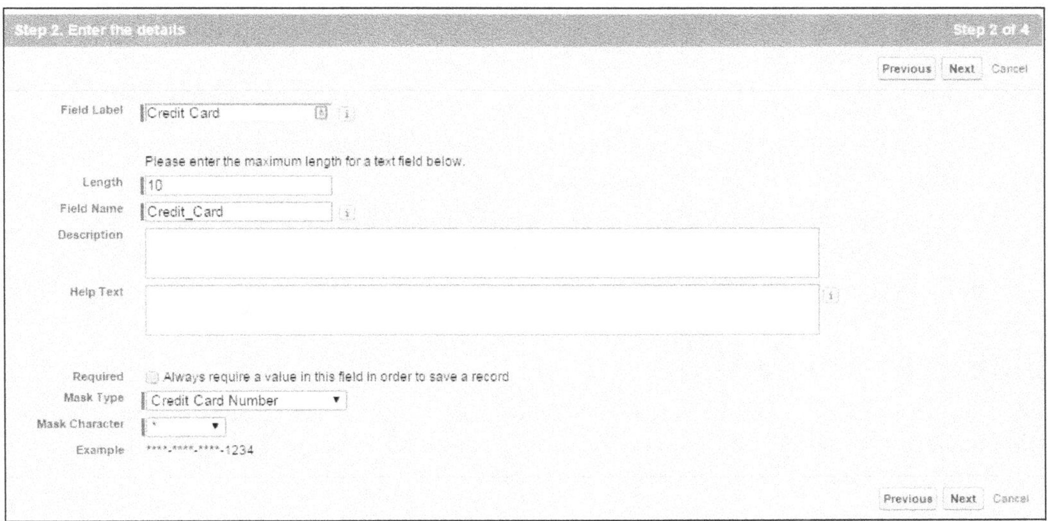

Encrypted fields are used to mask the value of the field from users. The only way to see the encrypted fields is by enabling the **View Encrypted Data** permission on the profile.

Encrypted fields cannot have default values and cannot be unique or external IDs.

The encrypted field can be edited irrespective of the **View Encrypted Data** permission. To prevent people from editing them, we need to use the field level security, validation rules, or mark them as read only on the page layout.

Encrypted fields are encrypted with 128-bit keys and use the **AES** (**Advanced Encryption Standard**) algorithm. They are 175 characters in length, unlike the normal text field, which is 255 characters.

Due to encryption, there are some limitations on the use of encrypted fields:

- Encrypted fields are not indexed and hence are not searchable
- They are not available in filters, such as reports, list views, and roll-up summary fields
- Encrypted fields cannot be used in the where condition in SOQL queries
- In an e-mail template, an encrypted value is always masked, irrespective of the **View All Data** permission
- If you clone a record that has encrypted custom fields, Salesforce will copy the data from the field only if the user has the **View Encrypted Data** permission

Platform encryption

Since Summer 2015, Salesforce has offered another level of encryption known as the platform encryption. When we enable the platform encryption, a few standard fields and some custom fields can be encrypted.

The following fields can be encrypted using the platform encryption:

- Standard Fields: Account object:

  Account Name

- Contact objects:

  E-mail

  Fax

  Home Phone

  Mailing Address (encrypts only Mailing Street and Mailing City)

  Mobile

  Name (encrypts First Name, Middle Name, and Last Name)

  Other Phone

  Phone

- Case object:

  Subject

  Description

- Case comments objects:

  Body
  Custom Fields:
  Email
  Phone
  Text
  Text Area
  Text Area (Long)
  URL

Only users with View Encrypted Field can see the data. For more information on the platform encryption, go to `https://help.salesforce.com/HTViewHelpDoc?id=security_pe_overview.htm`.

Formula fields

A formula field is a special type of field that uses a formula similar to an Excel formula. It is calculated at runtime and uses functions, operators, and other fields to calculate its value.

Here's an example of a formula field on a media object. It calculates the number of days after the due date has expired (assuming that we have all the fields in the media object):

```
If(TODAY()>BookIssueDate__c,TODAY() - BookIssueDate__c,0);
```

Exercise—calculating the return date

The members of the general library are allowed to borrow the media items for only 15 days. They want to reduce the typing work for the entry clerk and wish to auto-calculate the return date of the book.

The return date will be calculated on the CustomerMedia object that will record the transaction when the book is issued. To create the Return Date formula:

1. Create a **Date** field entitled **Issue Date**; this field will store the date of issue for the media item.

2. Create a new field entitled **Return date**, as shown in the following screenshot. It is of the **Formula** type and the return type is **Date**. Click on the **Next** button.

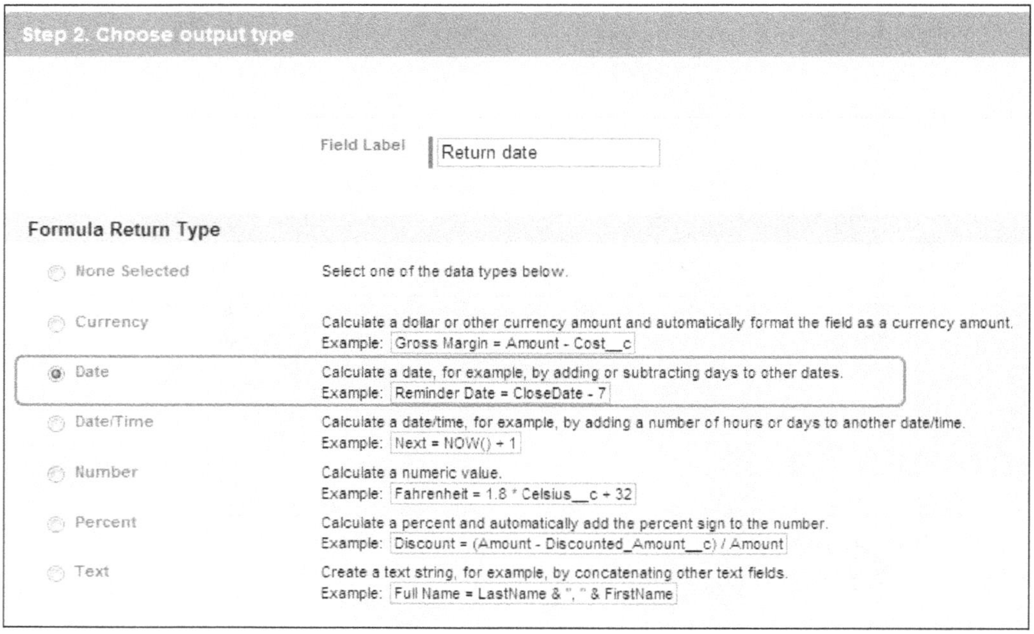

Step 2. Choose output type

Field Label: Return date

Formula Return Type

None Selected	Select one of the data types below.
Currency	Calculate a dollar or other currency amount and automatically format the field as a currency amount. Example: Gross Margin = Amount - Cost__c
Date	Calculate a date, for example, by adding or subtracting days to other dates. Example: Reminder Date = CloseDate - 7
Date/Time	Calculate a date/time, for example, by adding a number of hours or days to another date/time. Example: Next = NOW() + 1
Number	Calculate a numeric value. Example: Fahrenheit = 1.8 * Celsius__c + 32
Percent	Calculate a percent and automatically add the percent sign to the number. Example: Discount = (Amount - Discounted_Amount__c) / Amount
Text	Create a text string, for example, by concatenating other text fields. Example: Full Name = LastName & ", " & FirstName

3. The next page is the formula editor. We can create a **Simple Formula** or an **Advanced Formula**. A **Simple Formula** gives us a list of the fields of the existing object on which the formula is written along with some global variables. The **Advanced Formula** editor helps us write cross-object formulas. The other highlighted part is **Insert Operator**, which helps build the formula. Check Syntax checks for syntax errors before saving the formula. The **Advance Formula** editor also provides easy access to the list of functions that we can use in the formula:

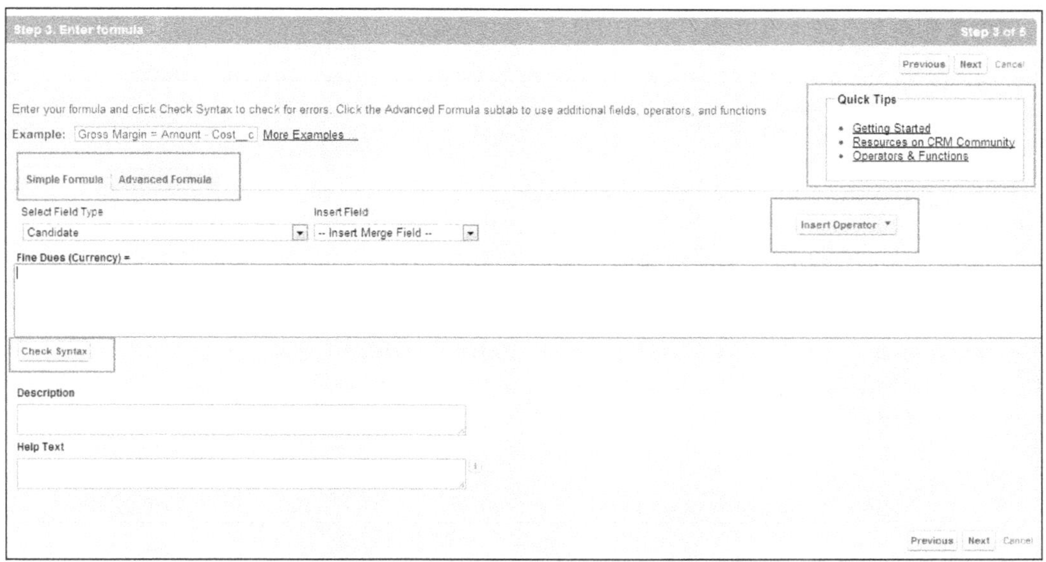

4. Add the `Issue_Date__c +15` formula to the formula editor, as shown in the following screenshot:

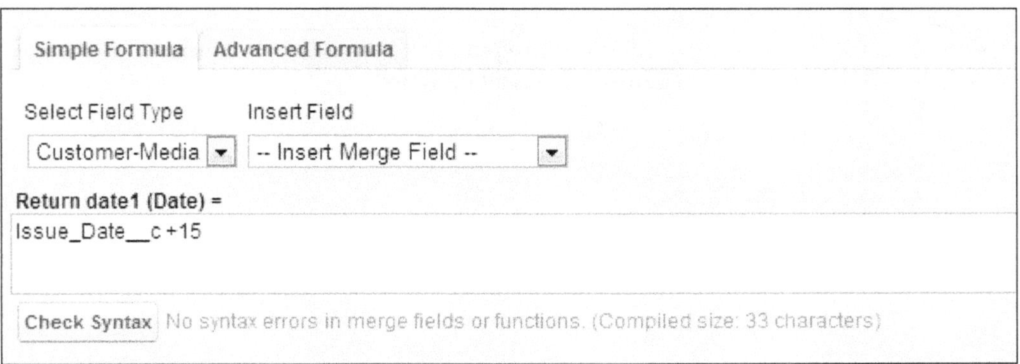

5. Here, `Issue_Date__c+15` is the date field used to store the issue date for the media. We can also use the `Insert` field's drop-down list to insert this field. Make sure that you click on the **Check Syntax** button to compile the formula and check for errors.

Every time a new record is created with the **Issue Date**, the **Return Date** field will automatically calculate and store the return date for it.

Cross-object formula fields

Using cross-object formula fields, we can calculate the value of a field based on fields in the parent record. We can traverse up to five levels upwards from the parent relationship.

The record owner and activity fields cannot be used in cross-object formula fields. Let's create the cross-object formula field for the Customer object.

Exercise—calculating the penalty

A general library wishes to calculate the **Penalty Amount** for a media resource when it is checked out late. Write a formula field that can calculate the amount for the **Customer–Media** object.

> Use the previous formula and assume that the penalty amount per day is stored in the media item to calculate the final amount.

The formula field is a read-only type of field that is auto-calculated. We define the formula on the basis of other fields and static values and the formulae are auto-calculated globally on the page.

Let's create a `formula` field to calculate the penalty. Select the **Formula** field in the list of fields. It will open the **Formula creation** wizard:

1. Choose the return type of the formula. For the purpose of the exercise, because we are calculating the fine amount on the book, the return type will be **Currency**, as shown in the following screenshot:

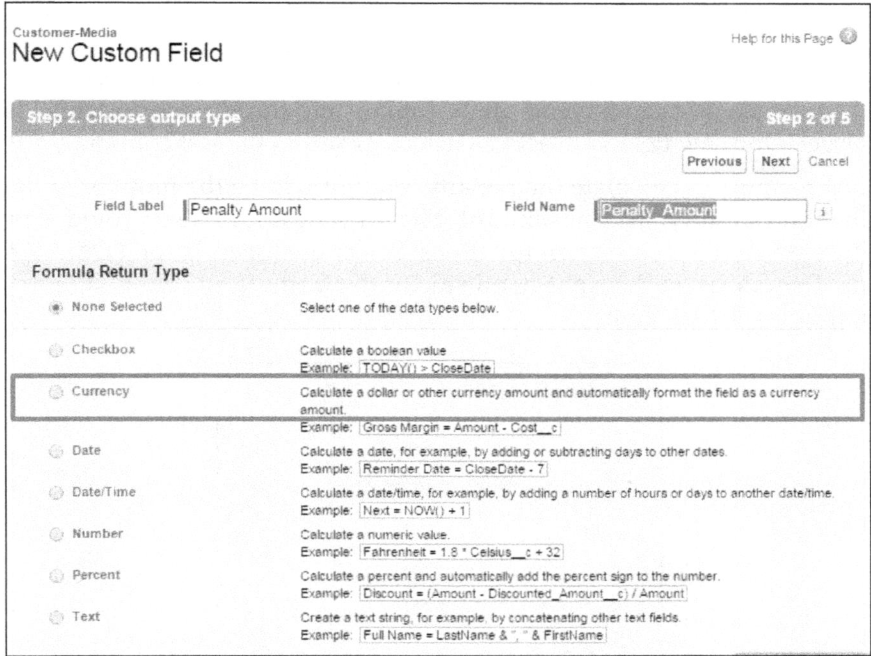

2. Click on **Advance Formula** to open the **Advance Formula** editor. In the **Advance Formula** editor, click on **Insert Field** to open a pop-up field, as shown in the following screenshot:

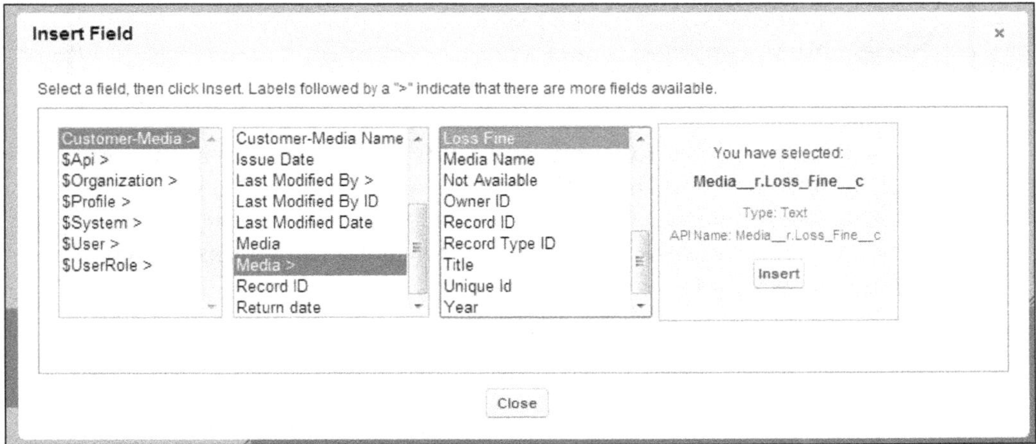

3. The **Insert Field** dialog box allows us to access fields of different objects that are related to the current object. In this case, we can access the field, **Loss Fine**, which is stored in the **Media** object, in the **Customer–Media** object to generate the formula. We can traverse all the lookup and the **Master-detail** fields on the object. Once the field is selected, click on **Insert** in the last column.
4. The formula to calculate the penalty amount will be the number of days after the return date × the fine amount. The formula editor also provides us with the system dates in system functions. Select the formula for **TODAY** from the **Functions** on the right-hand side of the formula editor, as shown in the following screenshot:

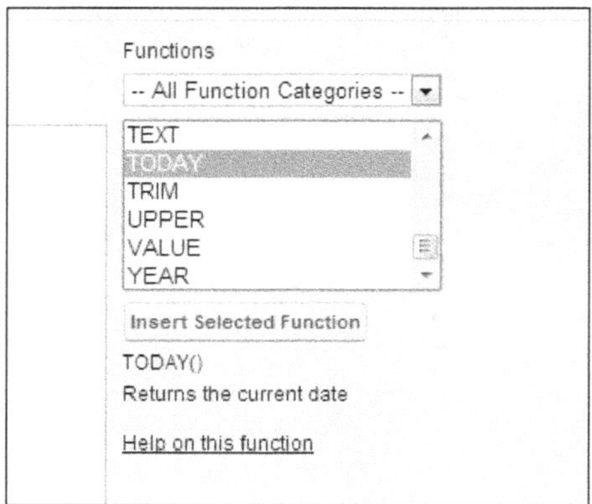

> The formula quick reference guide on Force.com provides an effective cheat sheet for the formulae. You can refer to it at `https://na3.salesforce.com/help/doc/en/salesforce_formulas_cheatsheet.pdf`.

5. Now, we have both the functions and fields that we require in the formula editor; we also need one more field called `Return_date__c`, which we created in the previous section. Create the `(TODAY() - Return_date__c )* Media__r.Loss_Fine__c` formula to calculate the fine, as shown in the following screenshot:

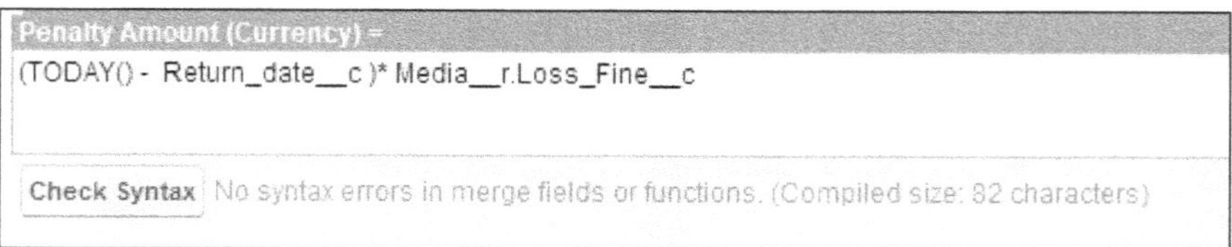

6. The next step determines the **Field Level Security**, as seen during the field creation; field level security determines who can see the field and who can edit it.
7. Select the appropriate page layout where the formula should appear. If no page layout is selected, it is not displayed on the screen.

Relationship fields

We have already discussed that Force.com is an object-oriented relational database management system. The backbone of the entire system based on Force.com is relationships.

Relationship fields determine how an object is related to another. For example, a library user will have a library card that can issue many books; an Account can have many opportunities. We can create these relationships using the relationship fields.

There are two main types of relationship fields, as shown in the following screenshot:

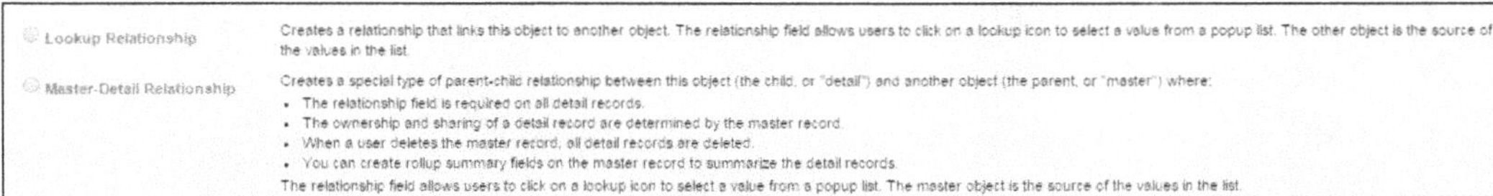

Let's take a look at each one of them.

Lookup relationship

The lookup relationship is the most basic form of a relationship. The lookup relationship is a foreign key on another object. While creating a lookup relationship, we can determine the behavior of the related record if the primary record is deleted.

If the primary record is deleted, then we need to choose from the following options:

- **Clear the value of this field**: This option allows us to loosely couple the two records. Deletion of the primary record has no effect on the secondary.
- **Don't allow the deletion of the lookup record that's part of a lookup relationship**: We can restrict the deletion of a primary record using this option.
- **Delete this record also**: This allows the cascading deletion of the secondary record.

The **Lookup** relationship can be visualized in the following figure:

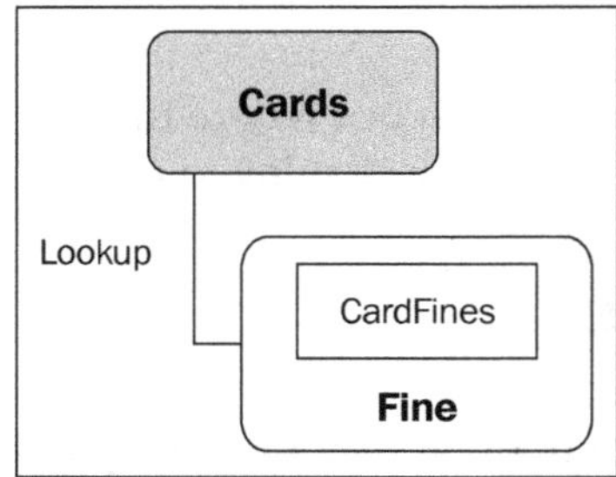

For example, a card of a member can have multiple penalties (fines) on it. The penalties on the card are shown at the bottom of the card in a list.

Lookup relationships have the following properties:

- The two object records have no relationship dependencies on each other
- The lookup field value is optional
- Updating and deleting the child record has no effect on the parent
- Both objects have their own owners and sharing rules
- A record can have 40 lookup fields with 40 different objects

Master-Detail relationship

The following figure illustrates the **Master-Detail** relationship:

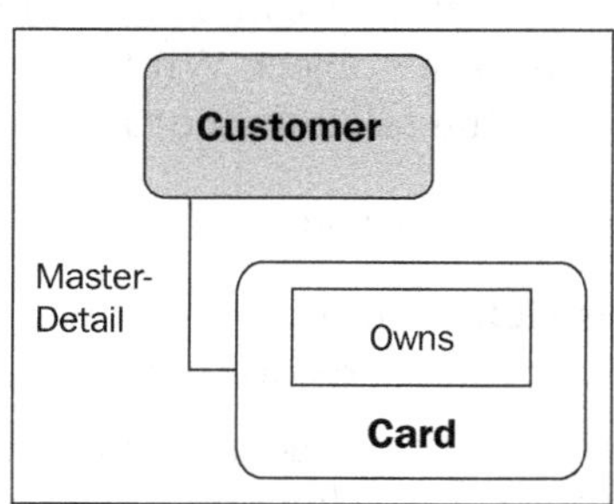

Master-Detail relationships are more tightly coupled relationships. One object is the Master or Primary object and the other is the Detail or Secondary object. The primary object controls the look and style of the tab as well as the security of both the objects. When the primary record is deleted, the secondary record is deleted as well.

For example, the relationship between the customer and the card in the library management will be Master-Detail where the customer is the master and the card is the child in the relationship.

Master-Detail relationships have the following properties:

- The ownership of the child record is given to the master object's owner. The child record does not have a separate owner.
- The detail record inherits the sharing and security settings as well as the look and feel of the master.
- A master record is always required to store the child record.
- If the master record is deleted, the child record is also deleted.
- We can define master-detail relationships between custom objects or between a custom object and a standard object. However, the custom object cannot be on the master side of a relationship with a standard object. In addition to this, we cannot create a master-detail relationship in which the User or Lead objects are the masters.
- An object can have a maximum of two master objects. In cases of multiple objects, both the masters are required. If one master is deleted, the child record gets deleted immediately.
- By default, records can't be reparented in master-detail relationships. However, we can allow child records on custom objects to be reparented to different parent records by selecting the **Allow re-parenting** option in the master-detail relationship definition.

We cannot create a Master-Detail relationship in an object that contains records in detailed objects. If there are records present in the detailed object, the trick is to create a lookup relationship first. Populate the lookup fields on the existing records and then change them to master-detail.

Roll-up summary fields

The roll-up summary field is a special type of field that can be used in a master-child relationship. Roll-up summary fields are used to aggregate the numeric fields from the Child object on the master object. The roll-up summary field uses aggregate functions, such as `SUM`, `MIN`, `MAX`, and `COUNT`. They are calculated periodically and their value is stored in the database.

Exercise—creating the roll-up summary

A general library wishes to keep track of all the media items issued to the customer. They want the total number of items issued in a single field called **Media Issued** against the member record.

The media items that are issued against the customer are stored in the **CustomerMedia** object; we will store their count in the **Customer** object:

1. Go to the Customer Object and click on new fields. When your object is the master object (in this case, Customer is the master for the CustomerMedia object), the data type for the roll-up summary field is visible, as shown in the following screenshot. Select the data type, and click on the **Next** button.

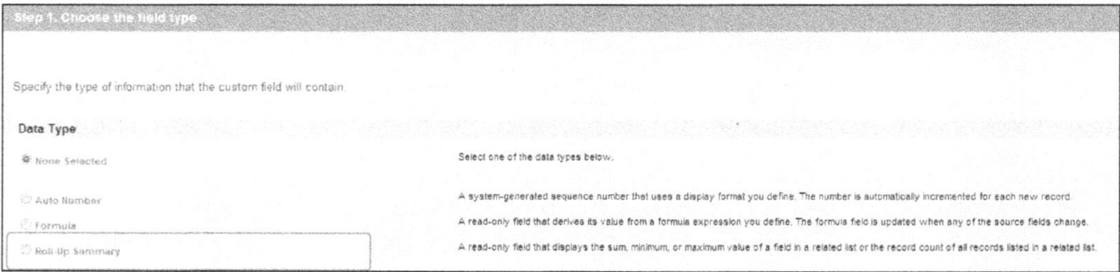

2. We will name this field **Media Issued**. Fill in the details, as shown in the following screenshot, and then click on **Next**.

3. On the next page, select the child object available for roll-up. In the example, select **Customer-Media**, as shown in the following screenshot:

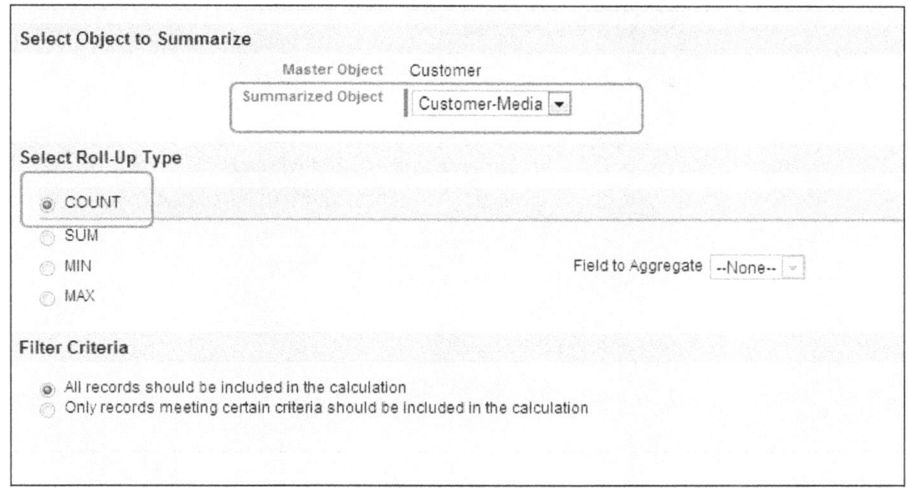

As we are counting the number of records, there won't be a need to select the aggregation field. When we calculate `Sum`, `Min`, and `Max` in the `Rollup summary`, we need to specify the field to summarize.

4. As mentioned previously, we will skip the field-level security for now and leave it for later chapters on security. On the final page, select the page layout to add the field and **Save** the field.

This covers the basic formulae and the logic that helps us simplify our work.

In the following section, we will discuss how to automate business processes using workflows and approval processes.

Special relationships

Using **Master-Detail** and **Lookup** relationships, we can create two more types of relationships:

- **Self-relationships**:
    - When an object has a lookup with itself, it is a self-relationship. A self-relationship creates a tree diagram of the objects. For example, the account has a lookup on itself, called **Parent Account**.

    - On the user object, a special self-relationship called a hierarchical relationship helps create superior roles, such as a supervisor and manager on the user object. The hierarchical relationship is a self-relationship of the user object.

- **Many-to-many relationships**:
    - A many-to-many relationship between two objects is a relationship in which an object A can have many child objects B, while object B can have multiple child objects A, as shown in the following figure:

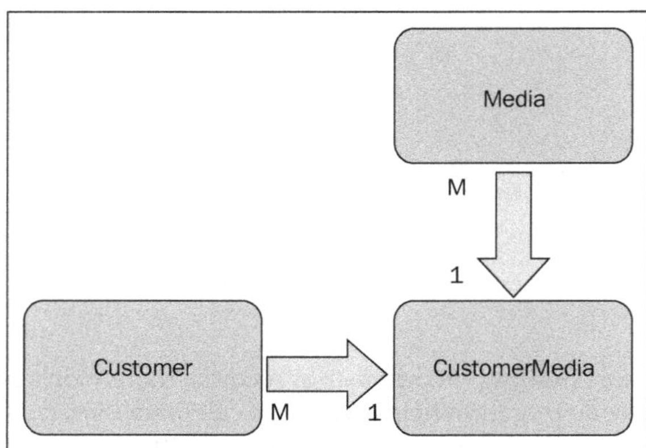

A real-world example is the relationship between a student and teacher. A student can be taught by multiple teachers while a teacher can teach multiple students. We can create a many-to-many relationship between two objects by creating a third object that has both the main objects as a primary relationship.

The third object thus created is called a **Junction** object. It is a junction between the two objects.

Some properties of the junction objects are as follows:

- The junction object identifies the first master as the primary master. It uses the look and feel of the primary master.
- If any master record is deleted, the junction record is automatically deleted.

Exercise – creating a junction object

Create a Customer object to collect information about the customer. Create a many-to-many relationship between the customer and media. This object will be used for checkout and checkin of the media item.

Entering the details

When we select the desired field types in the previous step, the second step allows us to customize the field and its properties. The following are the most common attributes in the text fields, as shown in the following screenshot:

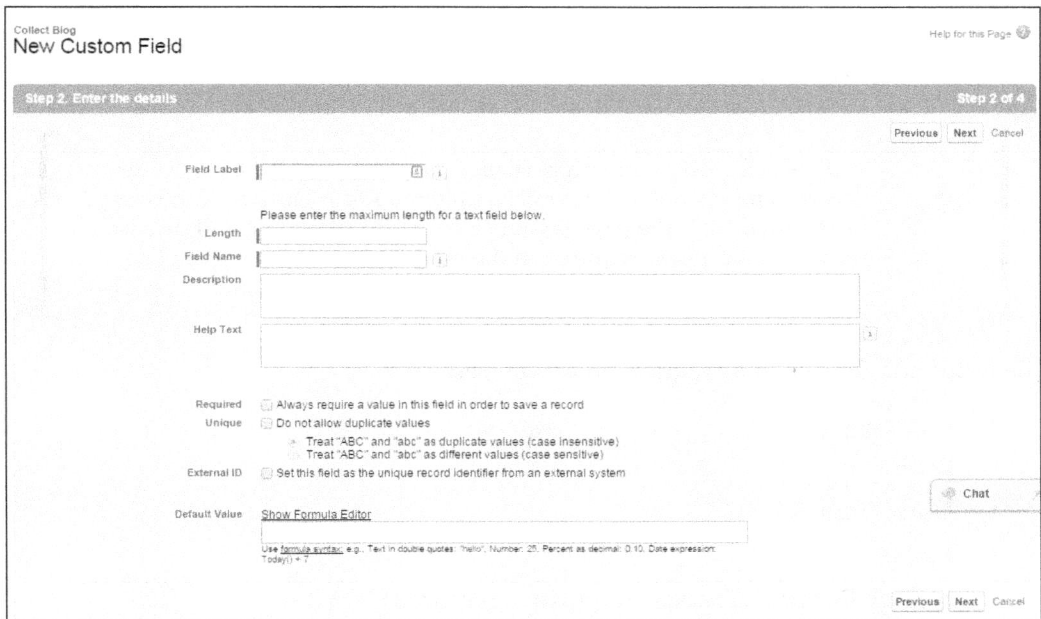

Field Label

The label used to display the field on the page.

Length

This is the number of characters that can be captured in the field.

Description

This gives the general description for audit purposes.

Help text

This is the text that will be displayed to the user when they hover over the help icon.

Required

A universally **Required** field is a custom field whose value is always required whenever a record is saved in Salesforce, the Force.com API, Connect Offline, Connect for Lotus Notes, Connect for Outlook, Salesforce for Outlook, the Self-Service portal, or processes such as Web-to-Lead and Web-to-Case.

To create a universally required custom field, check Always require a value in this field in order to save a record option.

If there is a need to make a particular field required for a particular record type, do not make it universally required. The field can be set as required from the page layout of the record type. We will discuss how to make a field required in the next chapter. Refer to the page layout section in *Chapter 3, User Interface* for more details.

The following fields can be made universally required:

- **Currency**
- **Date**
- **Date/Time**
- **Email**
- **Master-Detail Relationship** (always required)
- **Number**
- **Percent**
- **Phone**
- **Text**
- **Text Area**

Unique field

The custom field can be made unique and case-sensitive using this option. **Unique** fields will automatically get the duplicate check attach while inserting values in them.

To set a field as unique, select the **Set this field as the unique record identifier from an external system** checkbox, as shown in the previous screenshot.

External ID

External ID is a user-defined cross-application reference field. If the company is using some legacy system or any other computer system to store data, which is to be synced with Salesforce.com, the primary key in the external system is marked as an external ID in Salesforce.

The benefits of an external ID are as follows:

- The field is auto-indexed, which means that it has better search performance as compared to non-auto-indexed fields.
- It improves the API SOQL performance.
- Records can be upserted (Updated + Inserted) using the external ID to easily integrate with external systems. We will learn about this in detail in the Managing Data chapter.
- Only text, a number, or an e-mail ID can be marked as an **External ID** field.

Establishing field-level security

The third step to create the field is to set up the Field-level security. Whenever we create a new field, we need to determine who can edit it and who can only read it. This step is required for every new field as improper field-level security could prove hazardous for data-security.

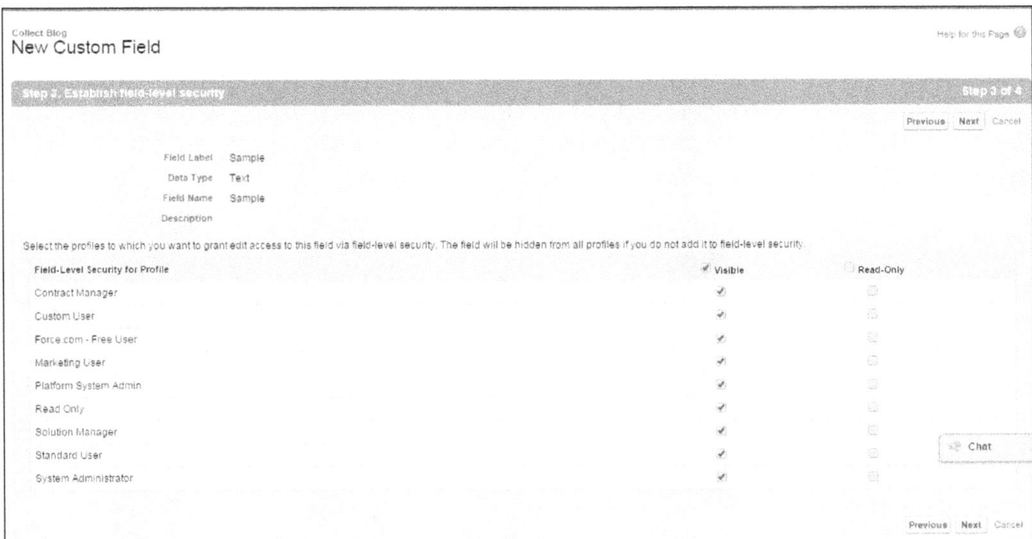

In the third step, we choose on which profile the field is **Visible** and on which profile the field is Read-only. We can customize the field-level security of each individual profile, and hence we will revisit this part again when we discuss the profile-based security.

Exercise – creating fields

The general library collects different information about books and videos. Create different fields (as required) to catalog the information.

We will add all the fields needed for books and videos in the media object only. In further chapters when we study record types, we will learn how to separate the two types.

To create a field on the object, perform the following steps:

1. Go to **Setup** | **Create** | **Objects**.
2. Click on the object you want to create the field on. In this case, click on **Media**.
3. On the **Custom Objects** details page, click on the **New custom** field and the **relationships** section.
4. It will open a **field creation wizard** will open.

Dependent picklist

A **dependent picklist** is a picklist whose values are filtered by another controlling picklist. The values in a dependent picklist are changed according to the values selected in the controlling picklist. Standard picklists are always controlling fields. Custom picklists can be dependent as well as controlling.

Exercise – creating a dependent picklist

The general library wishes to create categories and subcategories of books that are available. They first classify the books according to the fiction and nonfiction categories. Fiction books are further classified as children's fiction, fantasy, thriller, and comedy. Nonfiction books are then classified as self-help, management, spiritual, biographies, and inspirational.

We will create the picklist on the `Media__c` object that we created in our previous exercise.

To create a dependent picklist, we first need to create two normal picklists. First, create a general picklist of the fiction and nonfiction categories, as shown in the following screenshot:

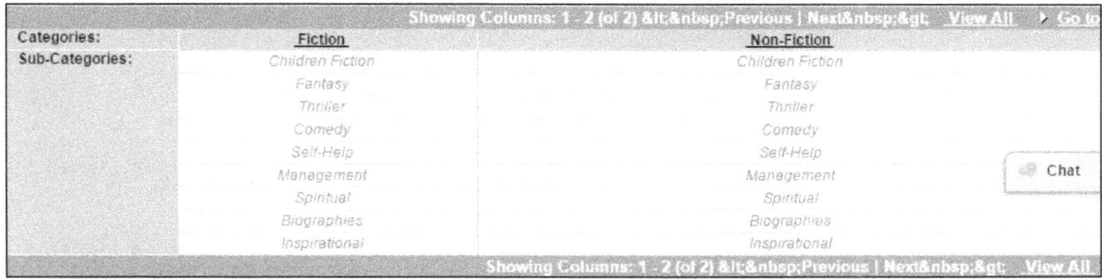

We create another picklist that has all the combined values of fiction and nonfiction, as shown in the following screenshot:

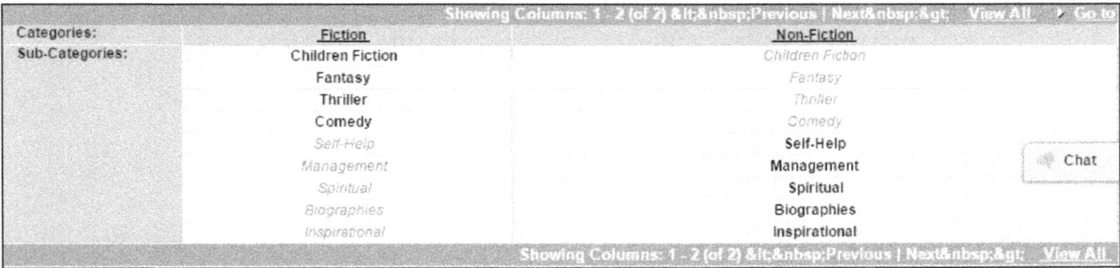

The steps to create a dependent picklist are as follows:

1. Navigate to **Setup** | **Create** | **Objects**, and click on the **Media object name**.
2. Go to **Custom Fields** and **Relationships** | **Field Dependencies** | **New**.
3. Most of the chapters in this book are based on custom objects. To customize standard objects, go to **Customize** | **Object Name** instead of **Create**.
4. In the **Controlling Field** drop-down menu, select **Categories**, and in the **Dependent Field**, select **Sub Categories**.

5. Click on **Continue**:

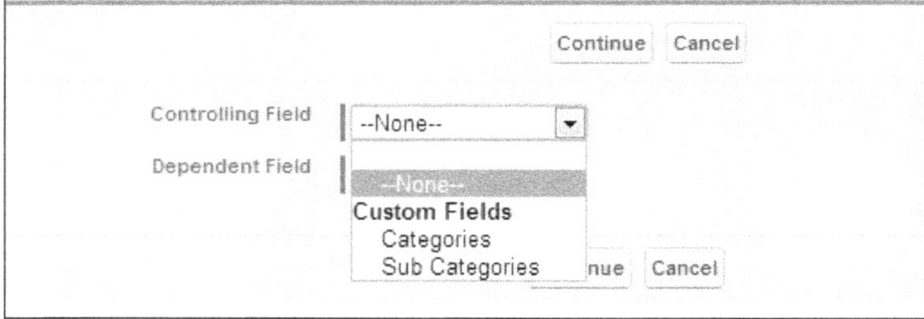

6. The preceding screenshot shows the interface for creating the dependent picklist. On the X-axis, we have the **Controlling Field** values and on the Y-axis the values of the **Dependent Field** are spread.
7. To select the values, press the *Ctrl* key and select the dependent values by selecting the corresponding controlling value:
    - **Fiction**: Children Fiction, Fantasy, Thriller, and Comedy
    - **Nonfiction**: Self-help, Management, Spiritual, Biographies, and Inspirational
8. Click on **Include values**.
9. Save the **record**.

If you directly click on **Save**, the values selected are not saved, so make sure that you click on **Include values** before **Save**.

Alternately, you can click on **Preview** to check whether the values you selected have been assigned. This is a good step if you have more values in the controlling picklist.

On the page layout, you will see that the **Sub Categories** checkbox is disabled until you select the categories.

Validation rules

Validation rules are used to preserve the data quality. We can use validation rules to prevent the data loss from the record. They are executed before the record is committed to the database. A validation rule is executed irrespective of whether the record is saved from the UI or from the API. If the evaluation of the error condition results in a true value, the record is not saved and an error message is generated.

Some standard fields have built-in validation. For example, an **E-mail** field checks for a valid e-mail, while the **Number** field checks for numbers entered in the string. For all other custom validations, we can use validation rules.

Let's take an example to check whether the discount given to a customer is not greater than 10%. For this example, we will use a percent field called **DISCOUNT** on the `Customer_Fine` object.

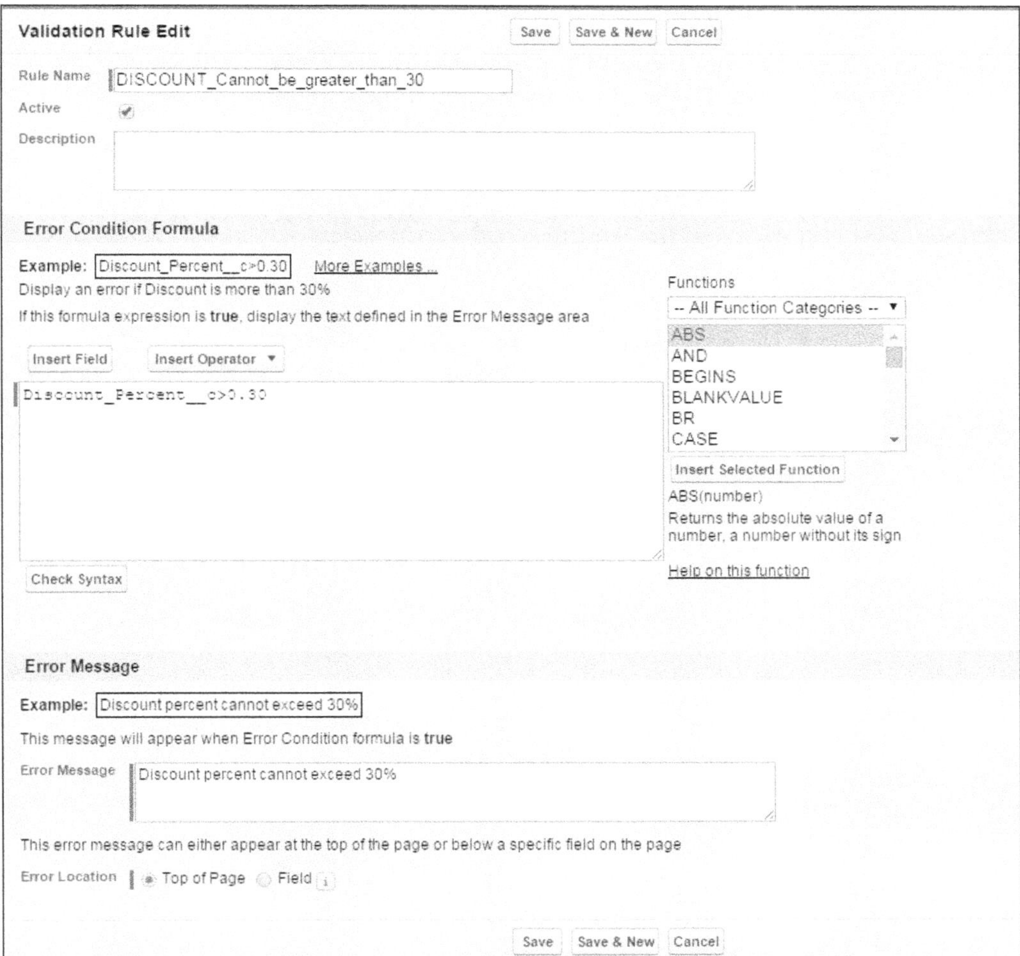

We can use the `isChange` formula to determine whether the value in a certain field is changed and the user profile.

Exercise—creating a validation rule

Our general library wishes to reinforce the rule on the number of books a user can check out. Every user will have a limited number of books they can issue, depending on their membership type. We will store `Total_media_allowed__c` in a **Number** field. `Total_Media_Issued__c` is a roll-up summary field that stores the number of Media issued to the customer.

To create a validation rule, perform the following steps:

1. Navigate to **Setup** | **Objects** | **Validation Rules** | **New**. This will bring you to a screen similar to the one shown in the following screenshot:

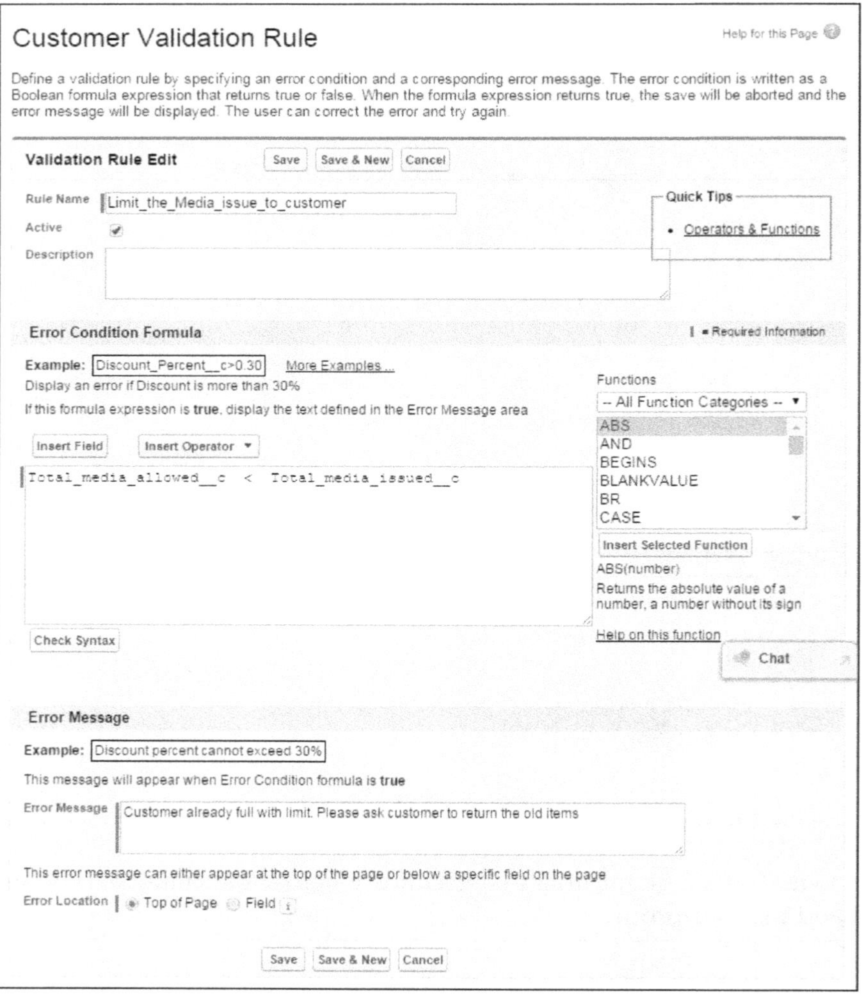

2. Add a user-friendly **Rule Name** to identify the rule in the first section.
3. In the second section, on the right-hand side of the screen, we see a list of all the **Functions** available to create the formula.

> The formula uses basic functions, which are provided by Salesforce.com. These functions are similar to the Excel-based functions. For a complete list of functions, visit the formula quick reference guide at `https://na3.salesforce.com/help/doc/en/salesforce_formulas_cheatsheet.pdf`.

4. We can also use **Insert Field** to insert fields in the formula to create a dynamic formula. The fields that can be selected while creating a formula are $ fields, which are globally available, such as login user fields. For example, `$User.City`.
5. The fields from related objects, such as a master object or a lookup object, are also available to be linked in the field name. We can include other custom object fields in the formula field using `ObjectType`.
6. In the **Error Message** section, we add the error message that will appear on the page if the validation rule evaluates to true.

> The error location determines where the error should appear. If there is a particular field in which the validation rule has failed, we can add it to the field level, helping users to quickly identify the wrong field.

An overview of Lightning Connect and external objects

Lightning Connect is one of the features that allows us to seamlessly integrate an external system with Salesforce in real time. We can import external data tables as external objects into Salesforce. For example, data stored on the enterprise resource planning (ERP) system can be connected as an external object via web service callouts.

The data is connected in real-time, so there is no scope for data being stale and out of sync. We can use external objects when:

- We want to connect Salesforce to a system with large amounts of data on an external system
- We want real-time access to the latest data

The following diagram illustrates the Lightning Connect process:

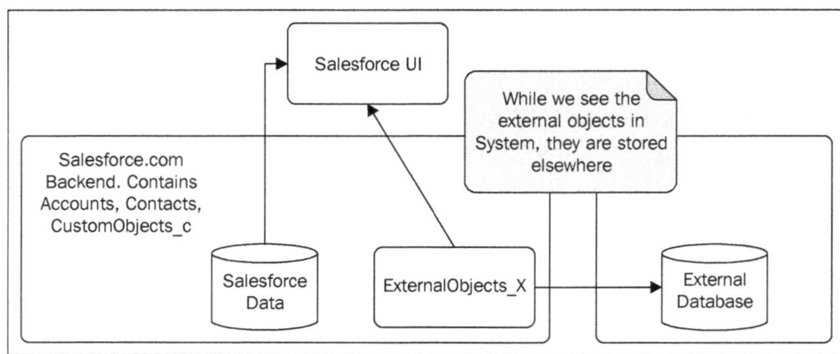

Let's start by connecting to a sample external web service. For this example, we are going to connect to a sample web service found at `http://Odata.org`.

We are going to connect to the web-service at `http://services.odata.org/V2/(S(l4iqzxoq5ftoav2fe5qcumtx))/OData/OData.svc/`.

1. Go to **Setup** | **Develop** | **External Data Sources** | **New**, as shown in the following screenshot:

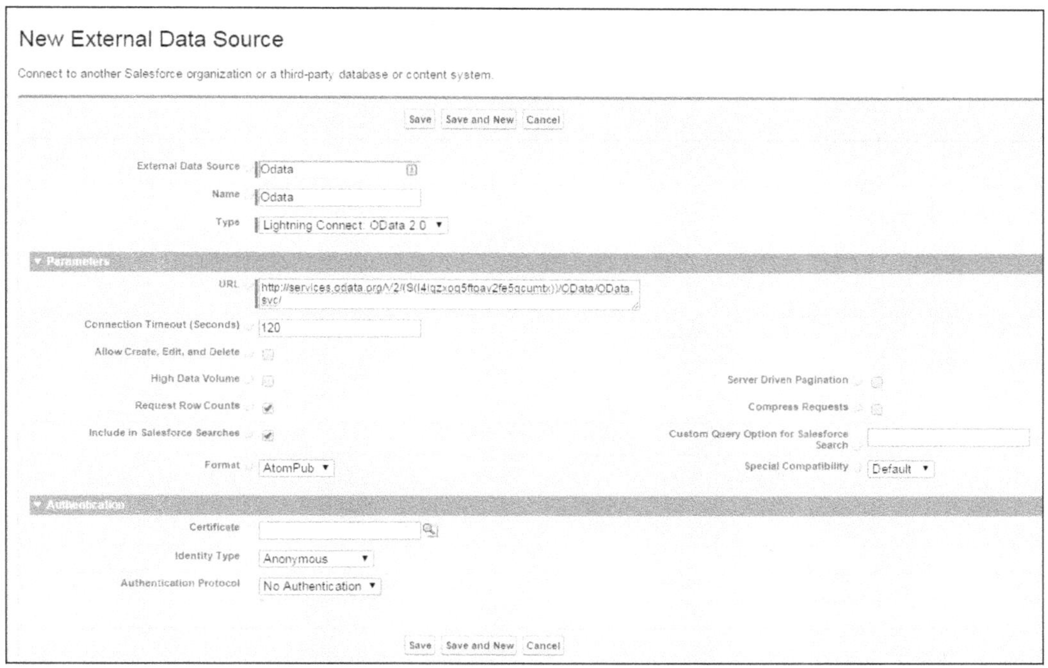

The **Type** should be **Lightning Connect: OData 2.0** and the server **URL** will be the one that we picked up for our example. Since this is an external open service, in the Authentication panel we will select **Identity Type** as **Anonymous** and **Authentication Protocol** as **No Authentication**.

2. On the detail page, we will click on the option to **Validate and Sync** our new service:

External Data Source: Odata

Help for this Page

Connect to another Salesforce organization or a third-party database or content system.

« Back to External Data Sources

| Edit | Validate and Sync | Delete |

External Data Source	Odata
Name	Odata
Type	Lightning Connect: OData 2.0

▼ Parameters

URL	http://services.odata.org/V2/(S(l4iqzxoq5ftoav2fe5qcumtx))/OData/OData.svc/
Connection Timeout (Seconds)	120
Allow Create, Edit, and Delete	
High Data Volume	
Server Driven Pagination	
Request Row Counts	✓
Compress Requests	
Include in Salesforce Searches	✓
Custom Query Option for Salesforce Search	
Format	AtomPub
Special Compatibility	Default

▼ Authentication

Certificate	
Identity Type	Anonymous
Authentication Protocol	No Authentication

| Edit | Validate and Sync | Delete |

🗨 Chat

External Objects

None

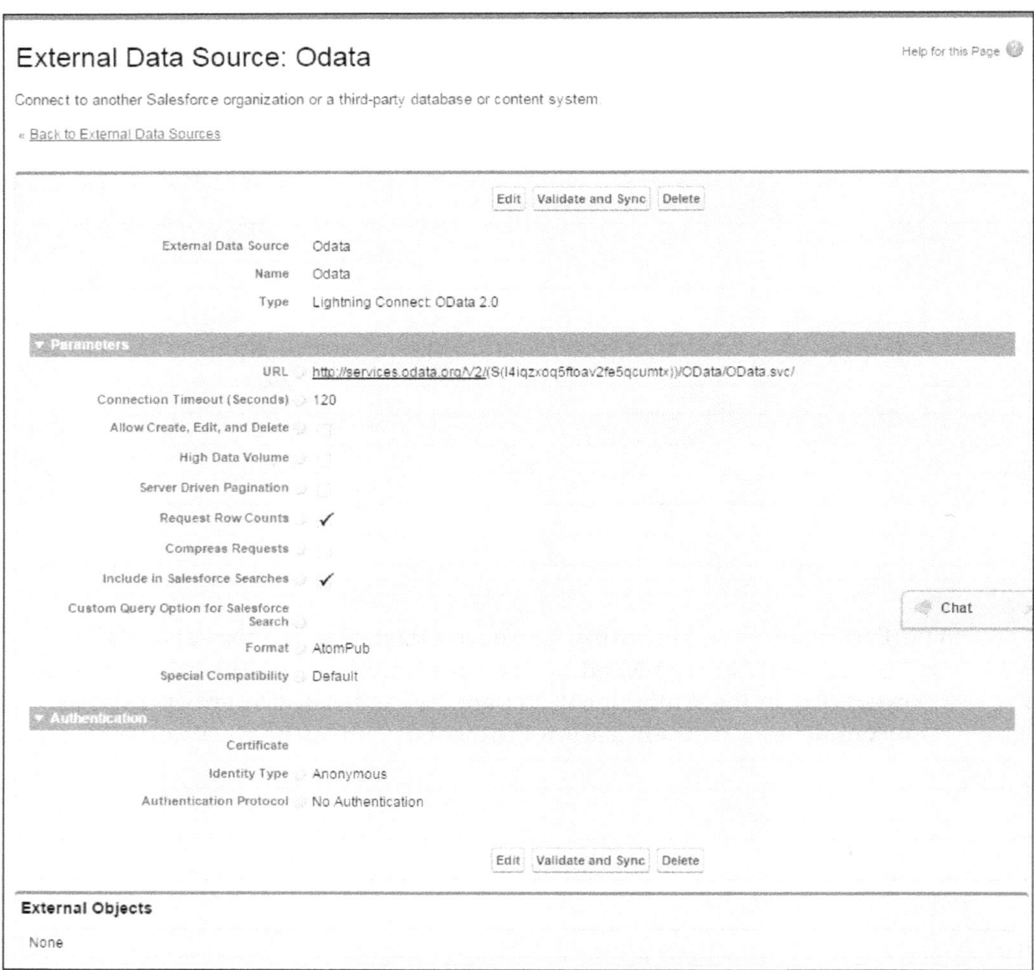

3. **Validate and Sync** will scan the URL and give you all the objects available to **Sync** with Salesforce. If it does not sync or you get an error, it will be shown in the **Status** field:

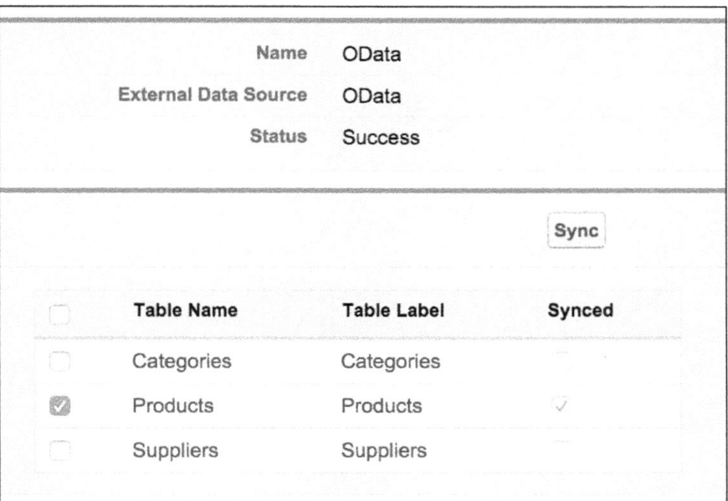

4. We are going to select a **Product Table** to Sync with Salesforce. We will select the products and click on the **Sync** button to import them as an external object. Under **Setup** | **External Object**, you can see the new object:

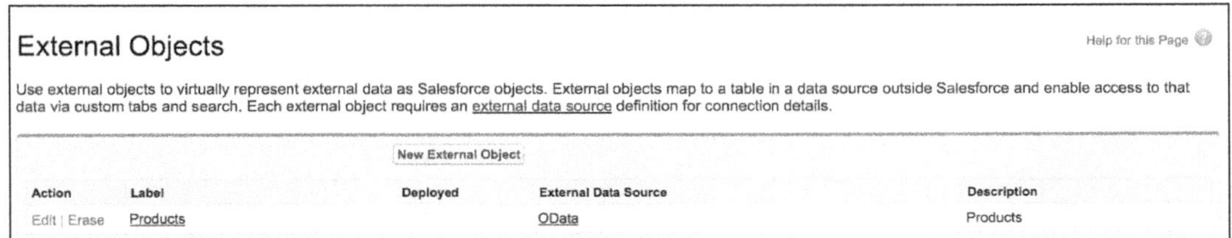

External Objects
Help for this Page
Use external objects to virtually represent external data as Salesforce objects. External objects map to a table in a data source outside Salesforce and enable access to that data via custom tabs and search. Each external object requires an external data source definition for connection details.
New External Object
Action
Label
Deployed
External Data Source
Description
Edit | Erase
Products
OData
Products

5. The external object thus created has its own object layout. We can create a lookup relationship with the existing object on the external object. Similarly, we can add a lookup to the external object from our standard object:

External Object
Products
Help for this Page
Standard Fields [2] | Custom Fields & Relationships [8] | Page Layouts [1] | Field Sets [0] | Compact Layouts [1] | Search Layouts [5] | Buttons, Links, and Actions [8]
External Object Definition Detail
Edit
Delete
Singular Label Products
Plural Label Products
Object Name Products
API Name Products__x
External Data Source Odata
Table Name Products
Display URL Reference Field
Created By Siddhesh Kabe, 11/01/2016 00:29
Description Products
Name Field External ID
Deployment Status In Development
Modified By Siddhesh Kabe, 11/01/2016 00:29
Standard Fields
Standard Fields Help
Action Field Label Field Name Data Type
Display URL DisplayUrl URL(1000)
External ID ExternalId External Lookup
Chat
Custom Fields & Relationships
New
Custom Fields & Relationships Help
Action Field Label API Name Data Type External Alias Modified By
Edit | Del Description Description__c Text(128) Description Siddhesh Kabe, 11/01/2016 00:29
Edit | Del DiscontinuedDate DiscontinuedDate__c Date/Time DiscontinuedDate Siddhesh Kabe, 11/01/2016 00:29
Edit | Del ID ID__c Number(18, 0) ID Siddhesh Kabe, 11/01/2016 00:29
Edit | Del Name Name__c Text(128) Name Siddhesh Kabe, 11/01/2016 00:29
Edit | Del Price Price__c Number(18, 0) Price Siddhesh Kabe, 11/01/2016 00:29
Edit | Del Rating Rating__c Number(18, 0) Rating Siddhesh Kabe, 11/01/2016 00:29
Edit | Del ReleaseDate ReleaseDate__c Date/Time ReleaseDate Siddhesh Kabe, 11/01/2016 00:29
Edit | Del Sample Sample__c Text(18) Sample Siddhesh Kabe, 11/01/2016 00:45

External object tabs

We can create a tab for our external object, just like how we can create a tab for a custom object. Go to **Setup** | **Create** | **Tab**, and select the external object from the list.

External lookups

We can create two special lookups on the external object along with the standard lookup relationship.

An external lookup creates a relationship that links an external object to another external object whose data is stored in an external data source.

An indirect lookup relationship creates a relationship that links an external object to a standard or custom object. We can only create an indirect lookup to an object that has a unique, external ID field on the parent object that is used to match the records in this relationship. For example, we can display a related list of sales orders from the SAP external record with matching external IDs on the Account record.

Summary

In this chapter, we learned about the creation of objects. We created different types of field to store different types of data, and finally we started building our first application data model on Force.com, a **Library Management System**. We discussed the data types, fields, and the relationship between objects.

In the next chapter, we will explore how to create a UI for the objects. We will also discuss tabs, page layouts, and Visualforce in brief.

We are just warming up, stay alert!

Test your knowledge

Q1 Which custom fields can be made universally required?

1. Formula
2. Lookup
3. E-mail
4. URL

Q2 Which of the following statements about encrypted fields are correct?

1. Encrypted text fields can be an external ID and can have default values
2. Encrypted fields are not searchable and cannot be used to define report criteria

3. Encrypted fields can be included in search results and report results
4. They are not available for use in filters, such as list views, reports, roll-up summary fields, and rule filters
5. Encrypted fields are not available in lead conversion, workflow rule criteria or formulas, formula fields, outbound messages, default values, and Web-to-Lead and Web-to-Case forms

Q3 A person, who does not have the **View Encrypted Data** permission, will see the field with masked characters. Assuming that the field is in the page layout, what happens if he/she clicks on the **Edit** button and tries to edit the value?

1. The field will not appear in the edit layout
2. The user will see only masked characters but can enter a new value and save it
3. It will throw an error when the field is changed and saved
4. He can see the original value and he can save it

Q4 Which is true about encrypted fields?

1. They are available in Validation Rules or Apex Scripts even if the user lacks the **View Encrypted Data** permission
2. Encrypted fields can be converted to other field types
3. A custom field can be converted to a encrypted field
4. In **Email Templates**, if an encrypted field needs to be displayed without the mask character, the user who receives the e-mail should have the *View Encrypted Data* permission

Q5 Which type of custom fields can be used as External IDs?

1. A text field that is unique
2. A text field that is required
3. A text field that is encrypted
4. Date
5. E-mail
6. Phone

Q6 The media object record needs to refer to a similar media object record. For this, a lookup field to `media` is created. What is this relationship type called?

1. Master-Detail
2. Lookup
3. Hierarchical
4. Many-to-many
5. Self

Q7 How many master relationships can be there for a detail object?

1. 1
2. 2
3. 3
4. 4
5. 5

Q8 How many lookup relationships can be there for a child?

1. 10
2. 20
3. 15
4. 40

Q9 A Standard object has more than one Master-Detail relationship?

1. True
2. False

Q10 How do we create many–to-many relationships?

1. Junction object (custom object) having a Master-Detail relationship to the other two objects.
2. Create a lookup on the first object for the other and a lookup on the second for the first.

3
User Interface

In the previous chapter, we created some objects for our fictional library. While a library is easy to relate with, in an enterprise-level data-centric solution, we need to deal with a lot more complex objects, such as Orders, Opportunities, and Accounts. Some of these objects are accessed by different people at different locations and different times. For example, a sales representative would like to know how much an Account is worth before going for a business meeting for a new product, but a customer service representative would like to know about the product or **Service Level Agreement** of the same account to service them better.

To access the object, the representatives will need tabs with a clear indication of what the object is. To determine who sees what part of the same object, we create separate page layouts for the object.

In the next chapter, we will see a much more granular way of controlling sensitive information. In this chapter, however, we will see one way of doing this using the user interface.

The objects that we created in the previous chapter need an equally rich UI for users to fill in data. They need placeholders and visual indicators to collect this data and the information.

Our primary focus in this chapter is on creating beautiful user interfaces. In this chapter, we will be using point-and-click controls to create some important page layouts and UI designs.

By the end of this chapter, you will be able to:

- Create tabs for easier navigation
- Create forms for data input
- Create page layouts to display the right data
- Bring them all together and build an application

So, let's start by creating some amazing user interfaces.

Customizing tabs

The Salesforce standard user interface is made up of different tabs that can be used to view, add, and edit data for an object. The tabs are further grouped together as an app.

When you select an app, the corresponding tabs are visible based on what is configured. However, we can customize the frequently used tabs and add them to any app.

To do this, perform the following steps:

1. Click on the **+** icon at the end of the tabs, as shown in the following screenshot:

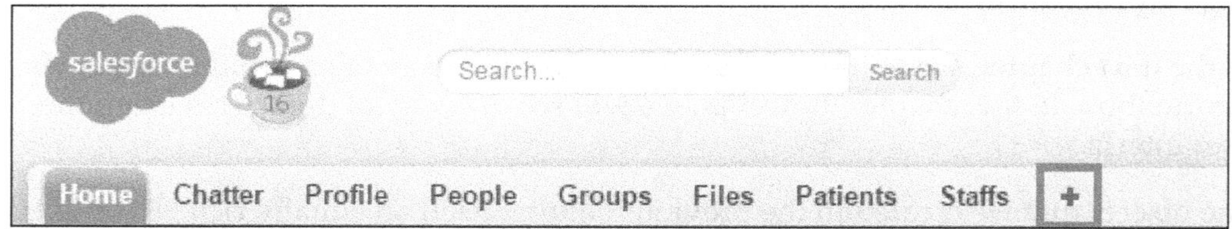

2. The **All Tabs** page will appear that displays all the tabs your user has access to.

3. Click on **Customize My Tabs** in the top-right corner of the page:

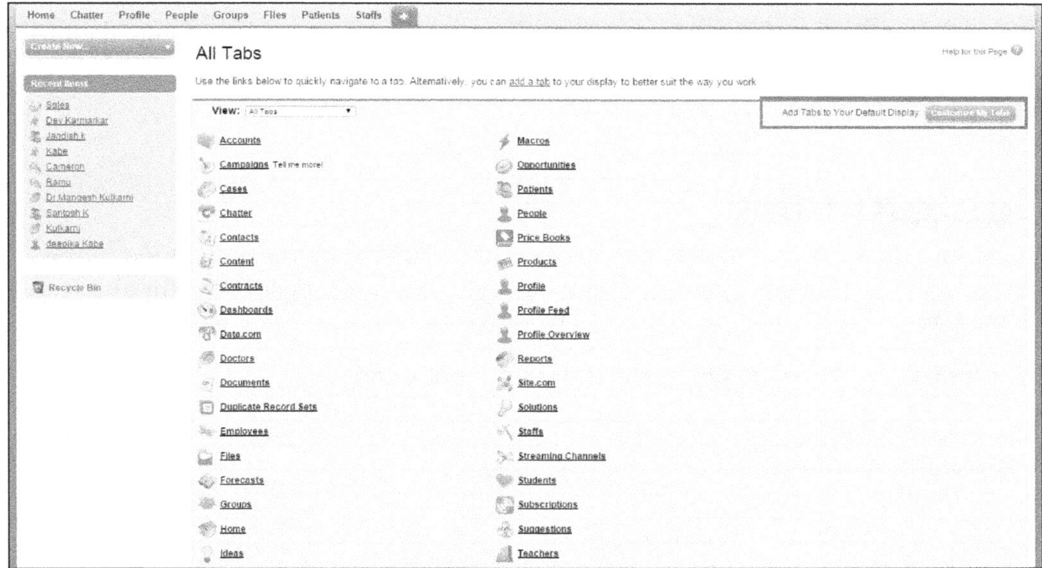

4. On the **Customize my Tabs** page, select the app that you will use frequently in the **Custom App** drop-down:

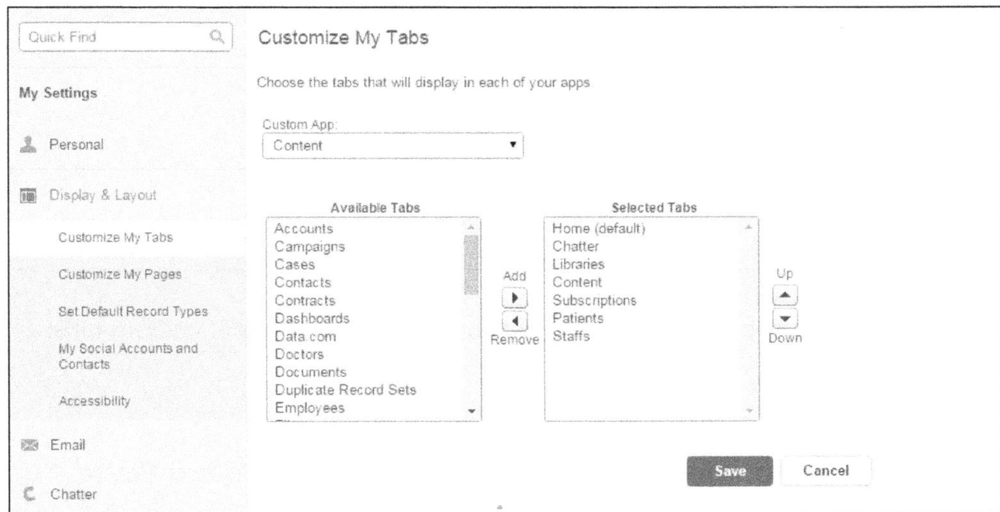

5. It will display a list of **Selected Tabs** on the right-hand side of the screen and all the **Available Tabs** on the left-hand side of the screen.
6. Select the tabs that you want to see frequently. You can also change the order in which they appear using the arrow buttons.
7. Click on **Save.**

Custom tabs

A **custom tab** is used to display the object data or other contents embedded in the application. Custom tabs have a unique tab style. We can choose the color and icon for the tab.

The following screenshot shows the different types of tabs:

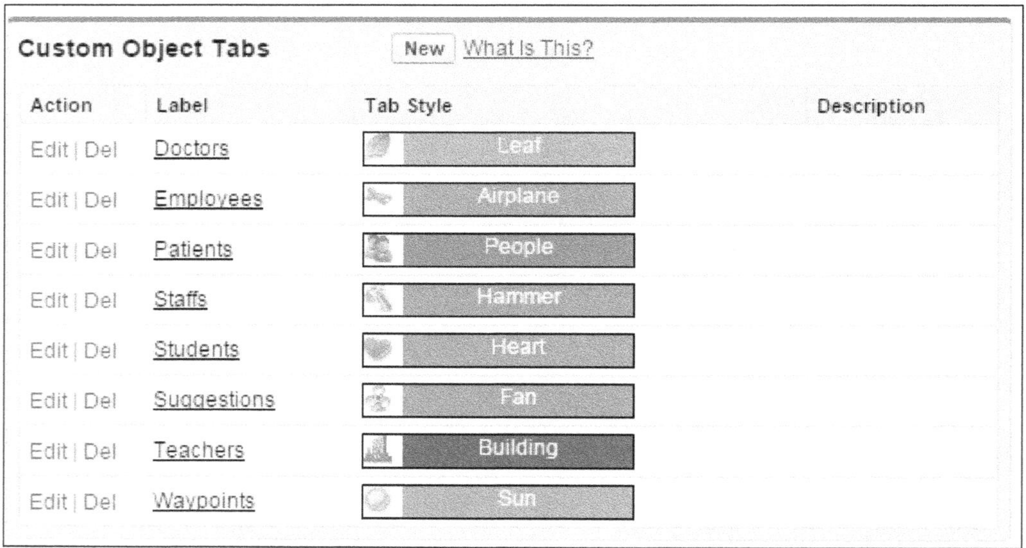

Custom Object Tabs
New
What Is This?
Action
Label
Tab Style
Description
Edit | Del
Doctors
Leaf
Edit | Del
Employees
Airplane
Edit | Del
Patients
People
Edit | Del
Staffs
Hammer
Edit | Del
Students
Heart
Edit | Del
Suggestions
Fan
Edit | Del
Teachers
Building
Edit | Del
Waypoints
Sun

We cannot create tabs for standard objects. There are three types of custom tabs:

- **Custom Object tabs**:
  - These tabs display the custom object data.
  - They provide the options to Create, Read, Update, and Delete (also called CRUD rights) an object.

- The plural name of the object is given to the tab by default.
- Users can see the buttons to `EDIT`, `DELETE`, or add `NEW` records on the page layouts, depending on their permissions to the object. We will learn how to control the user settings in *Chapter 7, Application Administration*.

- **Web tabs**:
    - We can display any external website using web tabs
    - Web tabs are useful if we want to show external web-based applications (for example, Google and Evernote) inside Salesforce
    - Web tabs are read-only websites that are loaded in iFrames inside Salesforce; they are not connected to Salesforce in any way

- **Visualforce tabs**:

  Visualforce is a component-based user interface framework of the Force.com platform. It is a tag-based markup language used to create visual interfaces that are completely flexible. We can also embed client-side JavaScript, such as Angular JS and AJAX components, and create custom UIs. Using Visualforce tabs, we can make these custom user interfaces accessible to the users.

- **Lightning Page tabs**:

  The lighting page tabs are used to display single-page lighting apps for smartphones. These tabs are auto-created from the lighting process builder. These apps are not available in the full Salesforce site and do not show up in the **All tabs** page when we click on the (+) icon. Lighting page tabs are only available in the navigation menu of the Salesforce1 mobile app.

Exercise – creating custom tabs

In the library management system, we have so far created different objects to collect data on media and customers. In this exercise, we will continue working on the same application and create tabs for the objects.

Create object tabs for all the objects created in *Chapter 2, Creating a Database on Force.com*. To create a **Custom Object** tab, perform the following steps:

1. Go to **Setup** | **Create** | **Tabs**.
2. Click on **New** in the **Custom Object Tab** section to open the **New Custom Object Tab** wizard, as shown in the following screenshot:

New Custom Object Tab
Help for this Page
Step 1. Enter the Details
Step 1 of 3
Choose the custom object for this new custom tab. Fill in other details.
Select an existing custom object or create a new custom object now.
Object
--None--
Tab Style
(Optional) Choose a Home Page Custom Link to show as a splash page the first time your users click on this tab.
Splash Page Custom Link
--None--
Enter a short description.
Description
Next
Cancel

3. Select the **Object** in the **Object** dropdown. Note that if there are no objects in the Org, the dropdown will have no values.
4. We can choose the color combination and icon for the tab in the **Tab Style field**. Click on **Next**.

5. On the next page, we can select who the tab should be visible to. Every user will have a profile associated with their account. On this screen, we can specify the visibility of the tab on each profile:

6. There are three types of **Visibility** that we can set on the tab:
   - **Default on**: If the tab is set to **Default On**, it is visible on the UI on the **App** of the user.
   - **Default off**: This tab is not shown in the UI; however, the user can see the tab in the **All Tabs** layout and, therefore, can customize it on their app.
   - **Tab Hidden**: When you hide this tab for a profile, the user does not have access to that tab at all. Note that this is by no means a way to prevent the user from accessing the object. It merely prevents the user from seeing the UI of that object. They can still access the object from the API and data loader. We will discuss the security considerations in *Chapter 7, Application Administration*.

7. In the last step, we select the app to include the tab. As a word of caution note that you should never include the tab in the other applications as it may affect multiple users. Even if we do not include the tab in an application, if the tab isn't hidden for the profile, the users can still customize their tabs by going to the **All Tabs** layout.

Layouts

The tabs will be the starting point for the user in the journey of that object. When the user logs in to Salesforce, they will navigate to the object tab and come across the **List View** of their recently viewed records.

The following screenshot shows the list view layout of the **Opportunity** object:

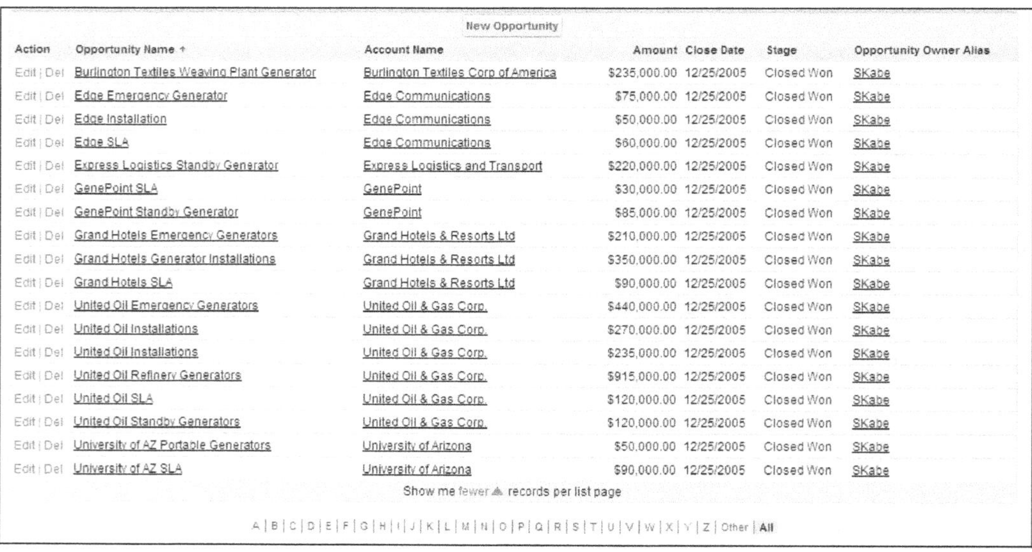

New Opportunity

Action	Opportunity Name ↑	Account Name	Amount	Close Date	Stage	Opportunity Owner Alias
Edit | Del	Burlington Textiles Weaving Plant Generator	Burlington Textiles Corp of America	$235,000.00	12/25/2005	Closed Won	SKabe
Edit | Del	Edge Emergency Generator	Edge Communications	$75,000.00	12/25/2005	Closed Won	SKabe
Edit | Del	Edge Installation	Edge Communications	$50,000.00	12/25/2005	Closed Won	SKabe
Edit | Del	Edge SLA	Edge Communications	$60,000.00	12/25/2005	Closed Won	SKabe
Edit | Del	Express Logistics Standby Generator	Express Logistics and Transport	$220,000.00	12/25/2005	Closed Won	SKabe
Edit | Del	GenePoint SLA	GenePoint	$30,000.00	12/25/2005	Closed Won	SKabe
Edit | Del	GenePoint Standby Generator	GenePoint	$85,000.00	12/25/2005	Closed Won	SKabe
Edit | Del	Grand Hotels Emergency Generators	Grand Hotels & Resorts Ltd	$210,000.00	12/25/2005	Closed Won	SKabe
Edit | Del	Grand Hotels Generator Installations	Grand Hotels & Resorts Ltd	$350,000.00	12/25/2005	Closed Won	SKabe
Edit | Del	Grand Hotels SLA	Grand Hotels & Resorts Ltd	$90,000.00	12/25/2005	Closed Won	SKabe
Edit | Del	United Oil Emergency Generators	United Oil & Gas Corp.	$440,000.00	12/25/2005	Closed Won	SKabe
Edit | Del	United Oil Installations	United Oil & Gas Corp.	$270,000.00	12/25/2005	Closed Won	SKabe
Edit | Del	United Oil Installations	United Oil & Gas Corp.	$235,000.00	12/25/2005	Closed Won	SKabe
Edit | Del	United Oil Refinery Generators	United Oil & Gas Corp.	$915,000.00	12/25/2005	Closed Won	SKabe
Edit | Del	United Oil SLA	United Oil & Gas Corp.	$120,000.00	12/25/2005	Closed Won	SKabe
Edit | Del	United Oil Standby Generators	United Oil & Gas Corp.	$120,000.00	12/25/2005	Closed Won	SKabe
Edit | Del	University of AZ Portable Generators	University of Arizona	$50,000.00	12/25/2005	Closed Won	SKabe
Edit | Del	University of AZ SLA	University of Arizona	$90,000.00	12/25/2005	Closed Won	SKabe

Show me fewer ▲ records per list page

A | B | C | D | E | F | G | H | I | J | K | L | M | N | O | P | Q | R | S | T | U | V | W | X | Y | Z | Other | All

We can choose the fields that are displayed on the list view and remove the unnecessary ones. The list view gives a glimpse of multiple records at a time; it is important to show valid and relevant data, which the users can further drill down after they click on the name.

When the users click on the name of the record, they are shown the **Detail View** of the record. The following screenshot shows the **detail** page for sample records:

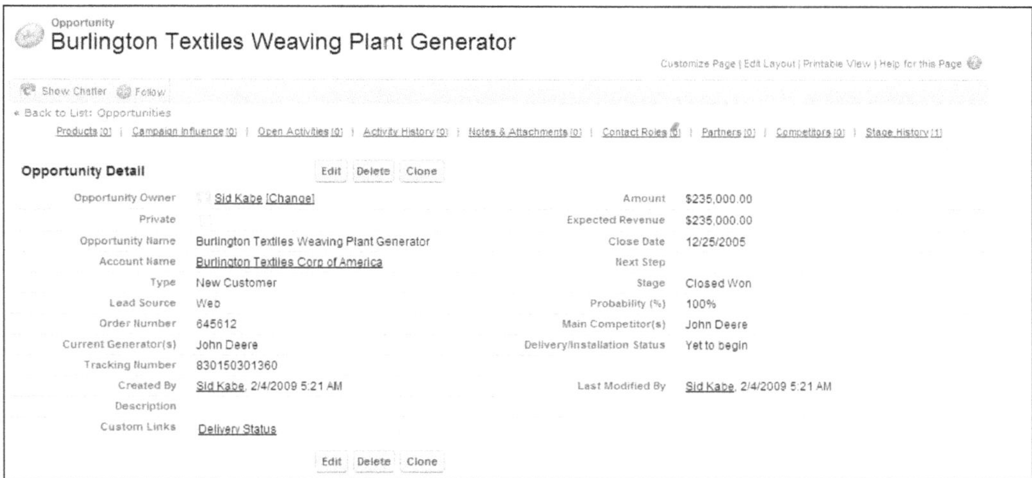

We will take a look at the layout editor in detail in the next section.

When the user clicks on the **Edit** button on the detail view, they are taken to the edit view of the record. The edit view provides an input form for different types of fields. The edit view follows the pattern of the detail view and only editable fields are shown in this view. The edit view cannot be customized separately from the detail view.

The following screenshot shows the edit view for the same opportunity:

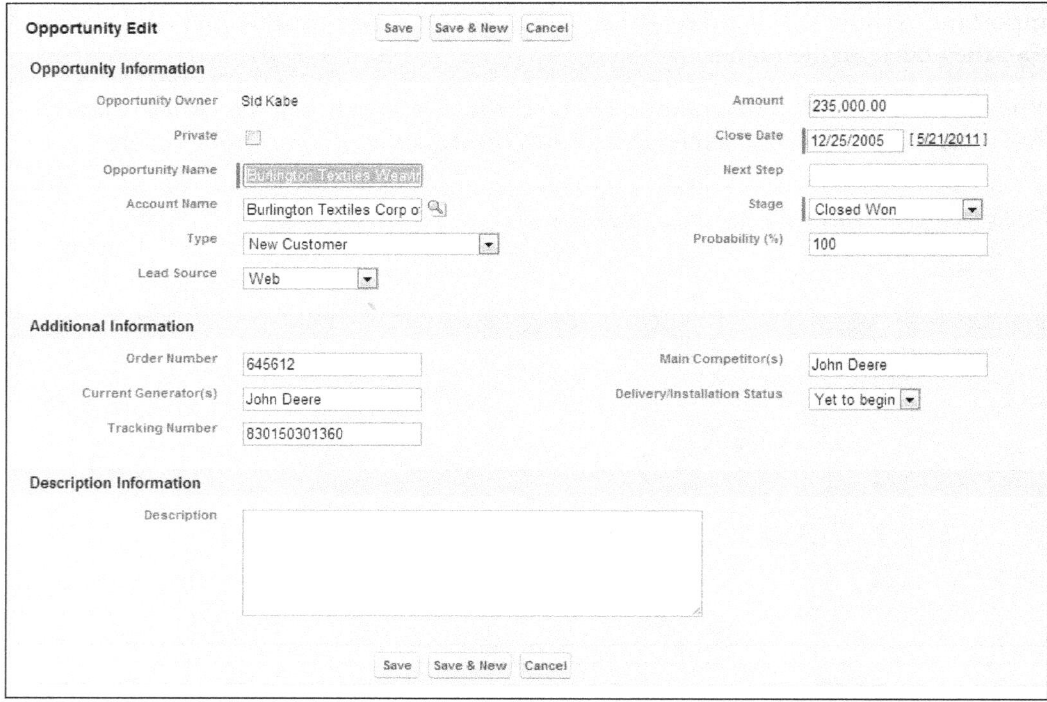

The page layout editor

Using the page layout editor, we can customize the data they can see on the **Detail View**. We can highlight the important data at the top of the page for easy access. We can logically group different fields in sections so that it all looks aesthetically pleasing. Using the page layout editor, we can also mark a few fields as read-only for users. However, we need to keep in mind that the page layout editor can only hide or show fields on the UI. The user can still access the field from the API and data loader if they have access to it.

Using the page layout editor

To open the page layout editor, go to **Setup** | **Create** | **Objects** | **Custom Object name** | **Page Layouts**.

As mentioned in the previous chapter, alternatively, for a standard object, go to **Setup** | **Customize** | **Object Name** | **Page Layouts**.

Normally, every object will be assigned a single default page layout that is accessible to all the people. Some standard objects have multiple page layouts, for example, the case object has a separate **Close Case Layout**. The account object has separate page layouts for marketing, sales, and service. To modify a page layout, make sure that you identify which profile the page layout is accessible from to prevent data visibility problems. The following screenshot shows the enhanced page layout editor:

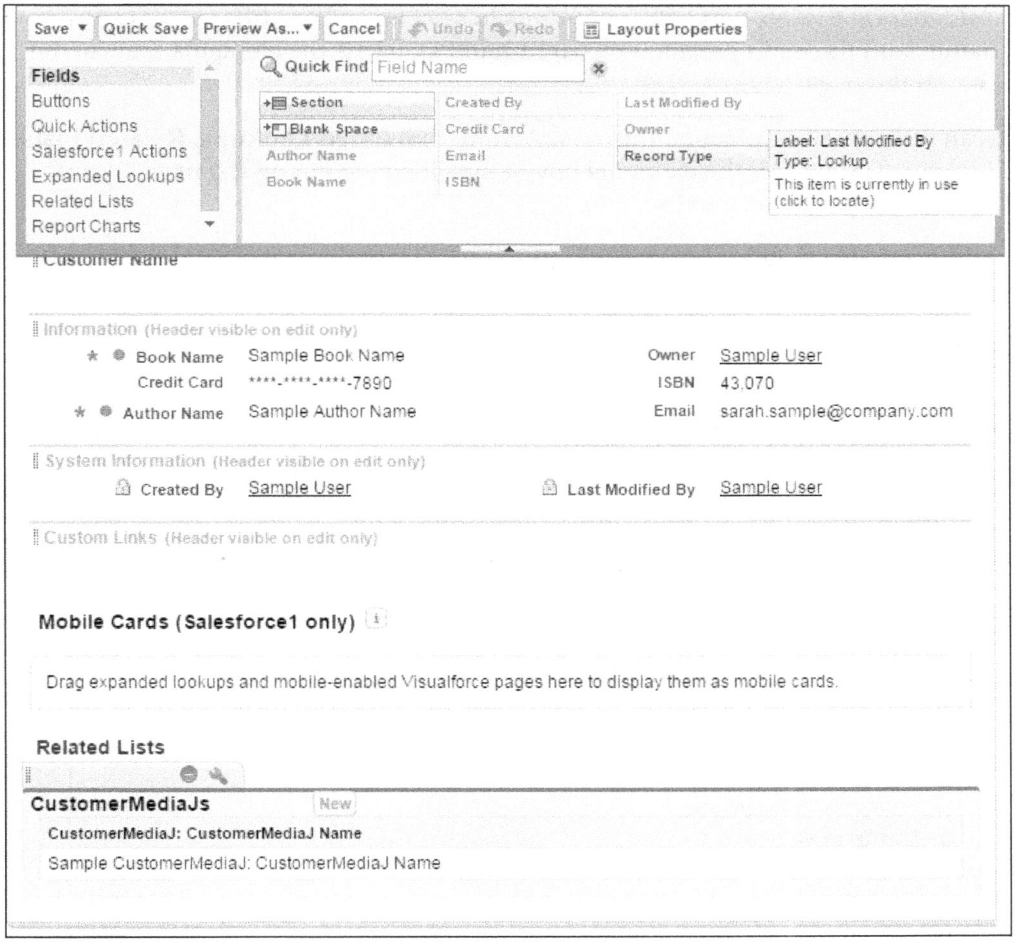

Save ▾ | Quick Save | Preview As... ▾ | Cancel | Undo | Redo | Layout Properties

Fields
Buttons
Quick Actions
Salesforce1 Actions
Expanded Lookups
Related Lists
Report Charts

Quick Find Field Name

Section | Created By | Last Modified By
Blank Space | Credit Card | Owner
Author Name | Email | Record Type
Book Name | ISBN

Label: Last Modified By
Type: Lookup
This item is currently in use (click to locate)

Customer Name

Information (Header visible on edit only)

Book Name Sample Book Name | Owner Sample User
Credit Card ****-****-****-7890 | ISBN 43,070
Author Name Sample Author Name | Email sarah.sample@company.com

System Information (Header visible on edit only)

Created By Sample User | Last Modified By Sample User

Custom Links (Header visible on edit only)

Mobile Cards (Salesforce1 only)

Drag expanded lookups and mobile-enabled Visualforce pages here to display them as mobile cards.

Related Lists

CustomerMediaJs New

CustomerMediaJ: CustomerMediaJ Name

Sample CustomerMediaJ: CustomerMediaJ Name

At the top of the page, we will see the panel that contains the elements that can be added to the page:

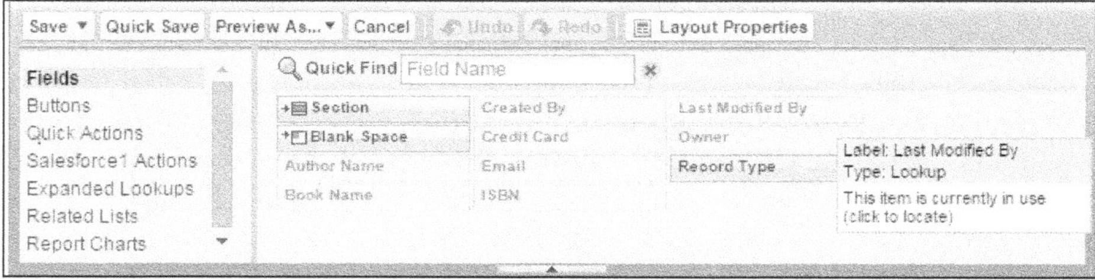

The sidebar on the left-hand side allows us to select from the different categories of elements, and the main panel on the right-hand side lists the elements that can be added on the page.

We can select between **Fields**, **Buttons**, **Action**, **Expanded Lookups**, **Related Lists**, and **Report Charts**. All the elements have a specific position on the page layout, which we will see in the next section.

To add a new element to the page, simply drag it from this panel onto the layout; the relevant section is highlighted in green.

We will take a look at each of them in detail in the upcoming sections.

The highlights panel

The next part of the page layout editor is the highlight panel. We can drag the quick actions onto the highlight panel. These actions are visible on the Salesforce1 Mobile view:

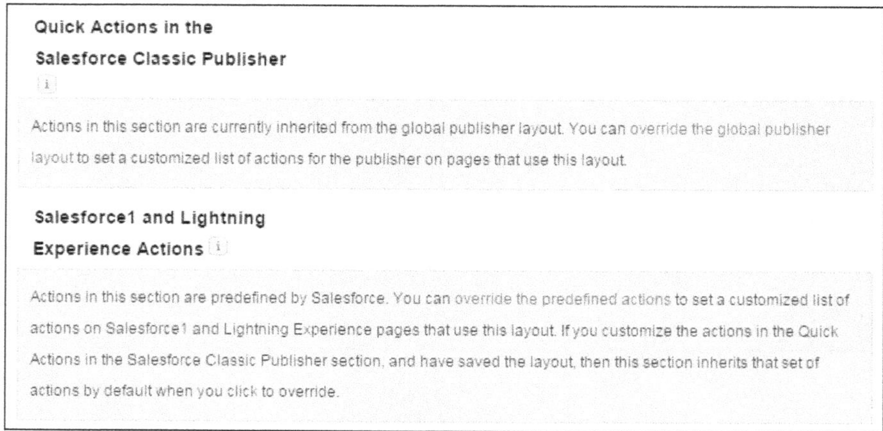

The quick actions are available in the Salesforce classic view, and the Salesforce1 actions will be visible in the new *Lightning Experience*, as shown in the following screenshot:

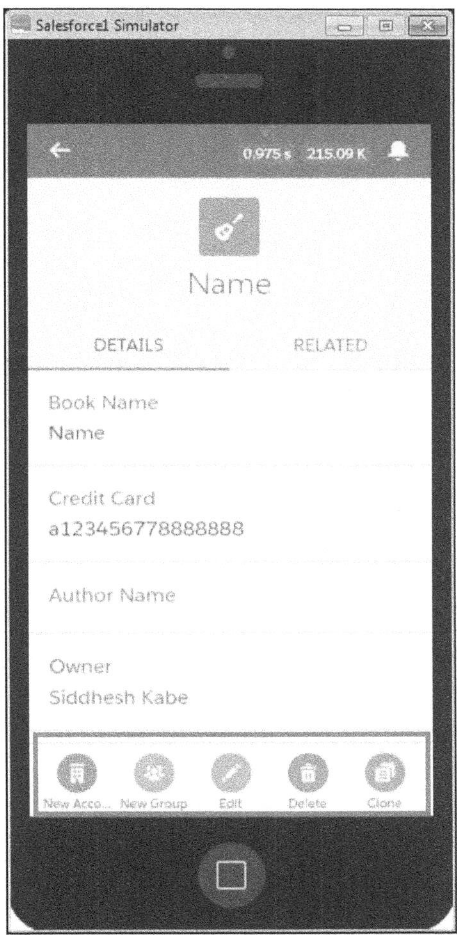

Adding fields

The main panel displays the fields in two columns and is grouped together by sections. We can add multiple sections that can logically group the fields for convenience and better user experience. The blue dot on the field indicates that the fields are required to save the record. A red star against the field indicates that the fields are required on the page layout.

We can create the field as required on the page layout that was not previously marked as required during field creation. However, doing so will make the fields required only on this particular page layout and the user will be able to insert the record without any data in the field. The lock item indicates that the field is uneditable on the page; this field will not be displayed on the **Edit** layout:

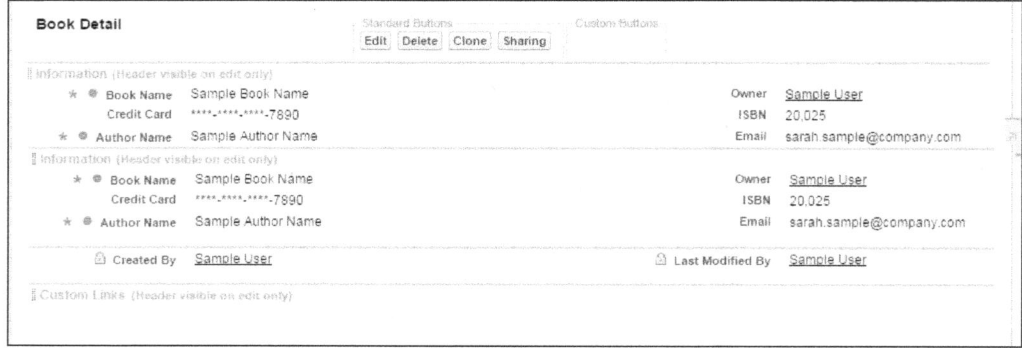

Sections and blank spaces

Apart from adding **Fields** and **Buttons**, the advance page layout editor also helps us group different fields in sections and add blank spaces for the alignment. The following screenshot shows **Section** and **Blank Space** in the editor:

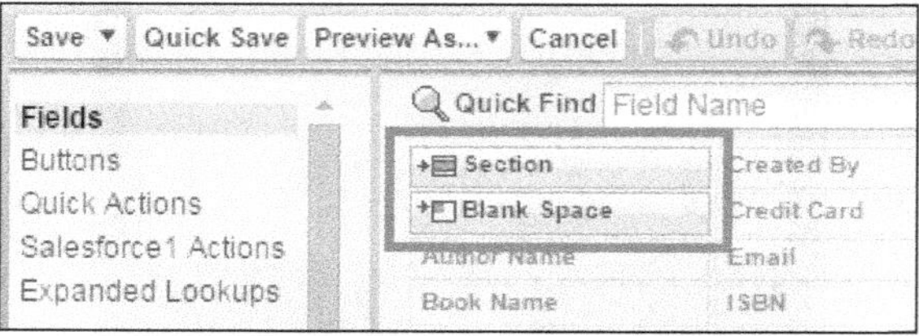

Section and **Blank space** are explained as follows:

- **Section**: We can create a logical or functional grouping of fields for the ease of the user. For example, we can group the contact information, such as the address field, phone number, and e-mail address under one section.

The following screenshot shows **Section Properties**:

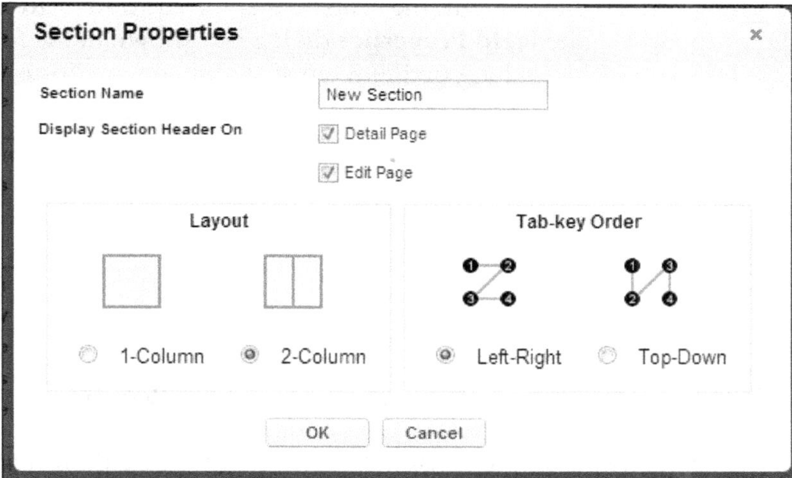

A section can have a **1-Column** or a **2-Column** layout. In a two column layout, fields are arranged in two separate columns. We can control the **Tab-key** order and set it to **Left-Right** or **Top-Down**.

- **Blank Space**: A blank space can be added to align the fields properly in the section. This is used if we need to add a blank space intentionally on the page layout:

Field options

When we add fields on the page layout, they can be made **Required** or **Read-Only** by setting their properties. The **Field Properties** dialog box shown in the following screenshot can be accessed by clicking on the wrench symbol on the desired field:

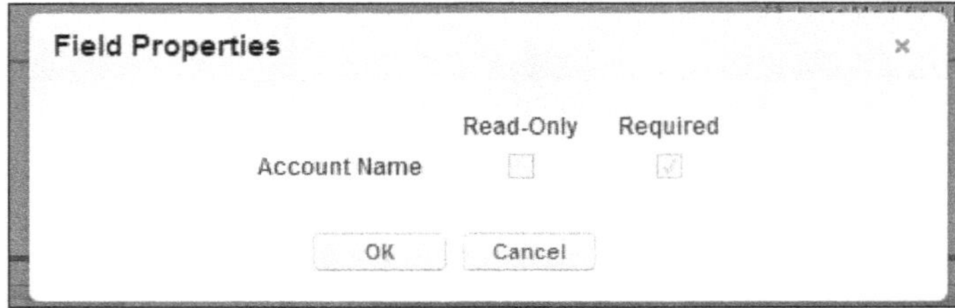

As shown in the preceding screenshot, we can set the field to **Required** or **Read-Only** on the page layout. As mentioned in the previous chapter, if the field is not universally required (set as required during the creation of the field), it can be made required on the page layout.

> It should, however, be noted here that a field marked as required will be required only on this page layout; it will not be required if the data is filled from the backend or through the API or any other page layout. This option is useful if we have a single page layout that requires this field.

We can also set the field as read-only in the same option. The field appears uneditable on the page only and the user can still fill the value from the other page layouts or the backend.

Custom buttons and links

We can add the custom buttons and links to the record. Buttons and links have actions attached to them referring to the functionality they are achieving. For example, a **Save** button saves the data filled in the application to the server. The buttons are also differentiated based on their placement on the application.

We can create three types of custom button or link:

- **Detail Page Link**:
    - We can create a detail page link that can be added in the **Custom Links Section**, as shown in the following screenshot:

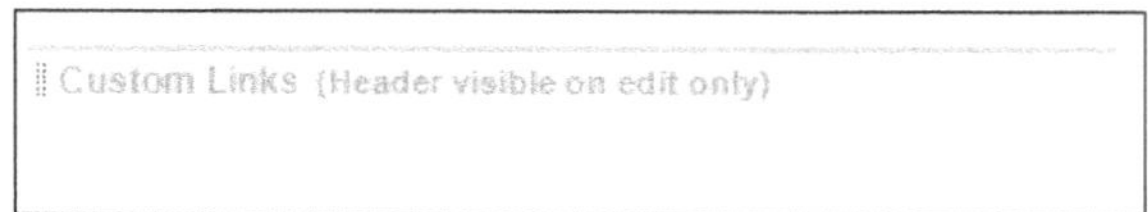

    - The **Custom Links Section** is a special type of section on the page layout that organizes all the custom links in one place. As with any other section, it can be dragged around and placed before and after any other section. By default, it is placed at the bottom of the page layout.
- **Detail Page buttons**:
    - **Detail Page Buttons** are added at the top and bottom of the page in the center, as shown in the following screenshot:

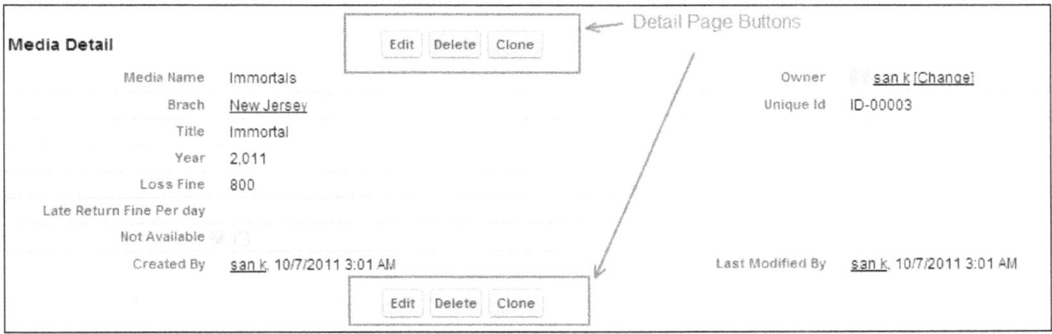

    - The button can open a JavaScript, which points to Visualforce or opens a URL.

- We can add **Custom Detail** page buttons in the **Custom Buttons** section on the detailed page layout, as shown in the following screenshot:

- **List View Button**:
  - The **List View button** can be added to the tab page or the related list of the object. The following screenshot shows the List View button on the related list for Opportunity. The **List View** button is the only type that can be added to the related list of the object and not on the detail page layout:

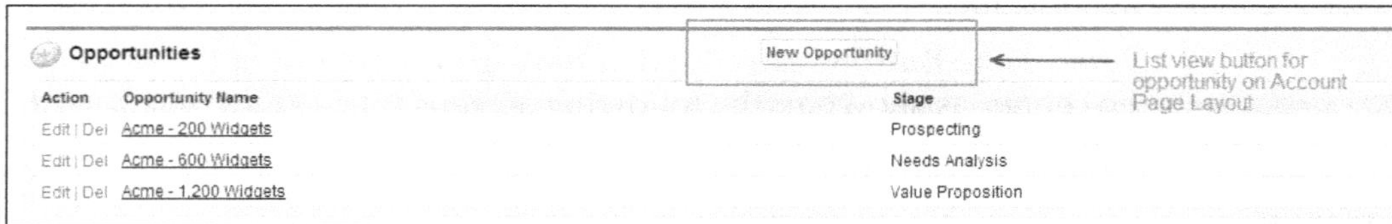

  - We cannot add any buttons or links to the **Edit** page of the record.

Page layouts for the user object only include the **Custom Fields**, **Custom Links**, and **Visualforce** pages. **Tagging**, **Related Lists**, **Custom Buttons**, and **Standard Field** customizations are not available.

Creating a custom button or link

Let's create a custom button in **Contact layout** that will automatically Google the person when you click on it:

To create a new button, perform the following steps:

1. Go to **Setup** | **Custom Object Name** | **Custom Buttons and Links** | **New**, as shown in the following screenshot:

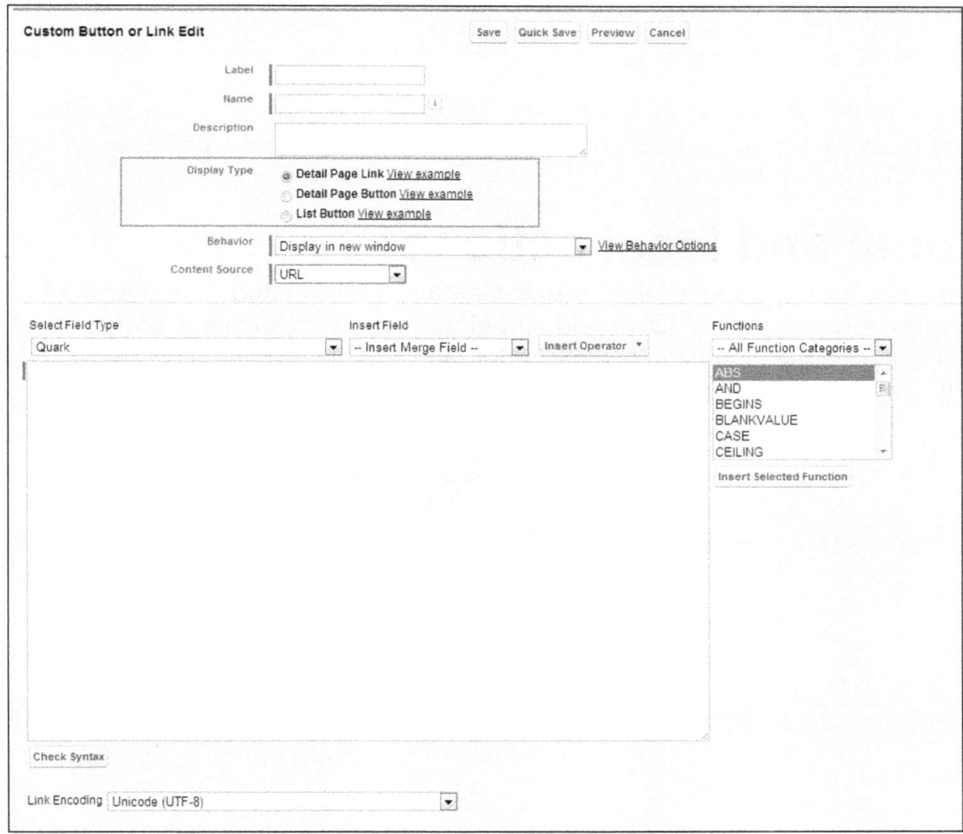

2. Choose the Detail Type as **Detail Page Button**.
3. We can choose one of the following display behaviors:
    - Display in new window
    - Display in the existing window with a sidebar
    - Display in the existing window without a sidebar
    - Display in the existing window without a sidebar and header
    - Excecute JavaScript

4. For the purpose of the exercise, choose **Display in new window**.
5. Choose the content source as the URL.
6. In the formula field, enter the following formula:

```
http://www.google.com/search?q={!Contact.Name}
```

7. **Save** the custom button.

After the button is created, go back to the advanced page layout editor and drag the button from the top panel to the page layout, as explained in the previous section.

Global and local actions

Actions allows a user to perform tasks in Chatter publisher and the Salesforce1 smartphone apps. We can define and add global actions to any page that supports actions, such as the Home page, the Chatter tab, and Object page. The global actions are shown in the following screenshot:

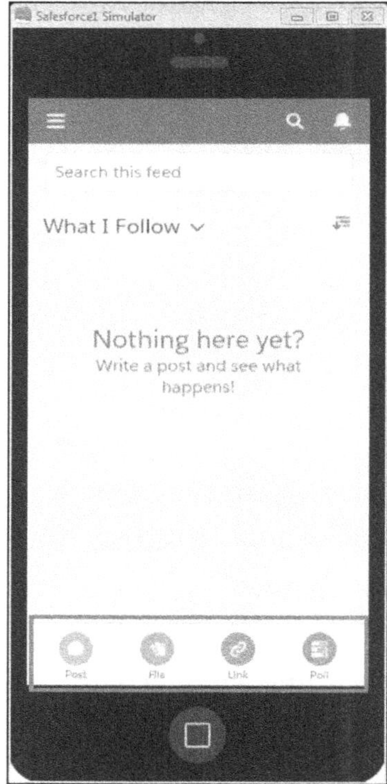

Local actions perform tasks on the record that are in focus. They are only visible on the record detail page:

Actions are supported in the new lighting experience web and mobile application.

Creating an action

Let's see how to create a new action:

1. Now, let's click on **New Action** on the **Button, Links,** and **Action** of the Media Object page, as shown in the following screenshot. Alternatively, to create a global action, go to **Setup** | **Create** | **Global Actions**:

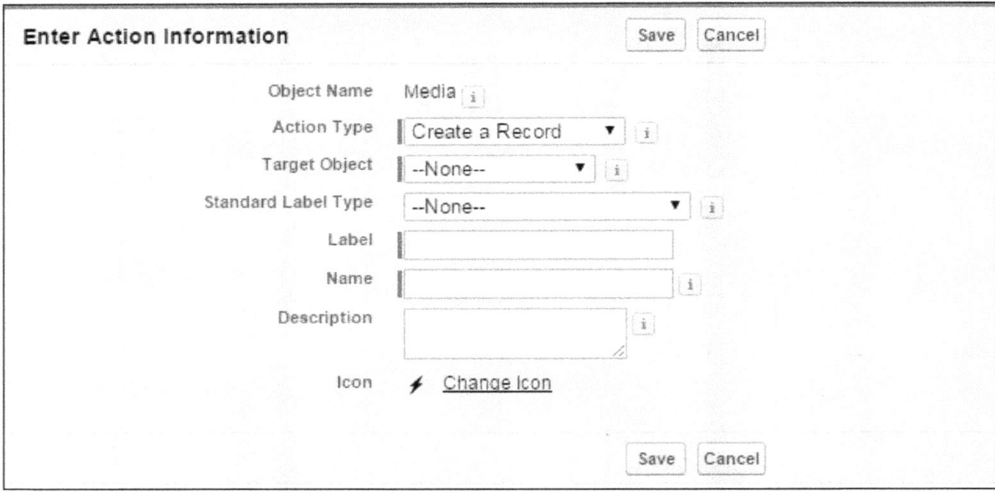

2. We can create four different types of action:
    - **Create a record**: This creates the target object record. We can specify the object to be created in the next dropdown.
    - **Update a record**: This allows users to update the fields of the record that are opened; the Update a record action is not available on the **Global Action**.
    - **Log a call**: This allows the user to record details of the call.
    - **Custom Visualforce**: We can specify a custom action using the Visualforce page.

    Specify a custom label or a Standard label for this action. We can also provide an icon for the action.

3. On selection of a type of action, it will take us to the page layout editor where we can specify the fields the user can enter while performing the action:

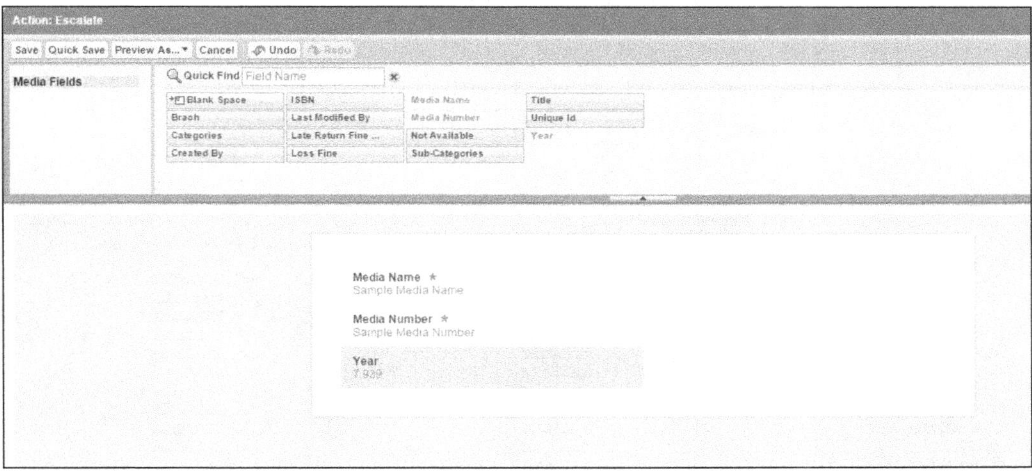

4. Once the action is created, we will have to go back to the page layout for the object and drag the action onto the **Quick Actions** panel on the page layout. To add a global action, go to **Publisher Layout,** which is nested, by going to **Setup** | **Create** | **Global Actions** | **Publisher Actions**.

Page layout assignment

Once we finish making the page layouts, we can assign different page layouts for different profiles and **RecordTypes**. To assign a page layout for a profile, click on the **Page Layout Assignment** button in the **Page Layouts** section, as shown in the following screenshot:

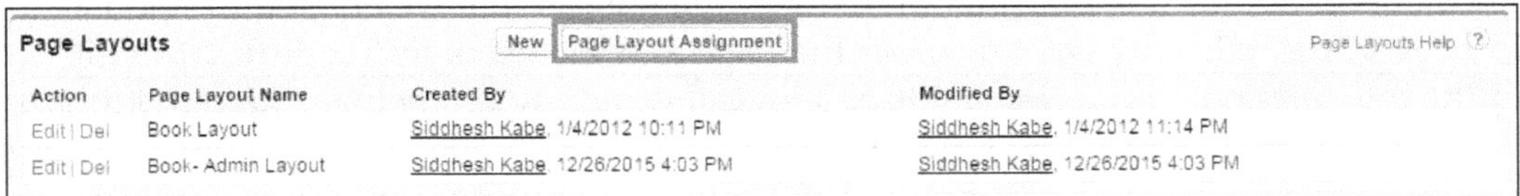

On the **Page Layout Assignment** page, the record types that are created in the object are displayed on the top header of the table, while the profiles are displayed as the columns, as shown in the following screenshot:

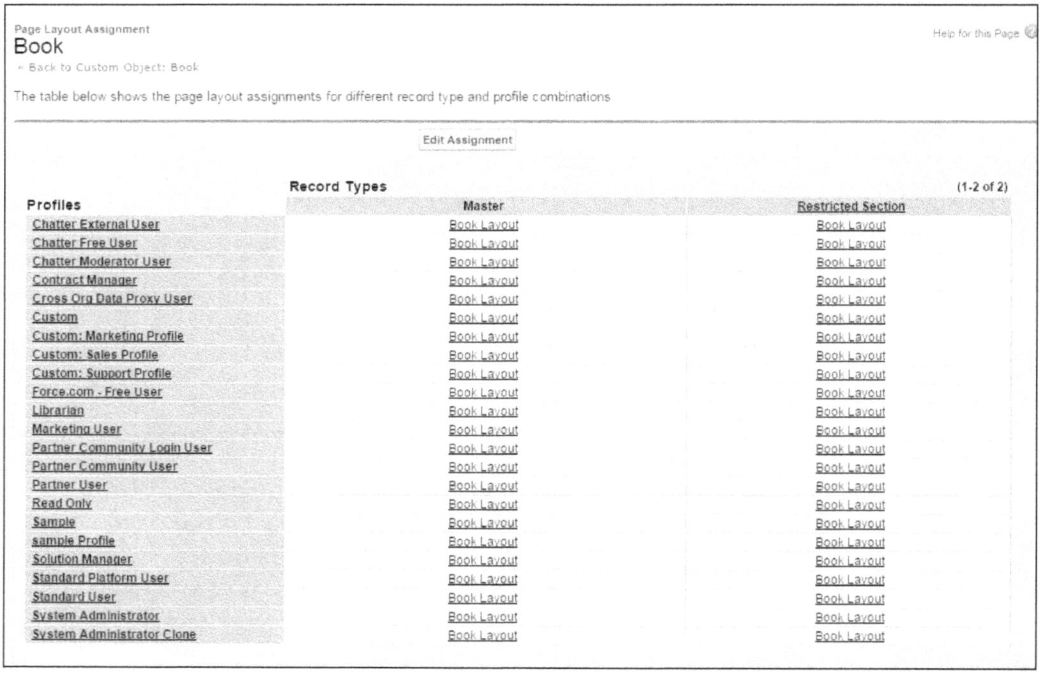

Page Layout Assignment

Book

« Back to Custom Object: Book

Help for this Page

The table below shows the page layout assignments for different record type and profile combinations

Edit Assignment

Record Types (1-2 of 2)

Profiles	Master	Restricted Section
Chatter External User	Book Layout	Book Layout
Chatter Free User	Book Layout	Book Layout
Chatter Moderator User	Book Layout	Book Layout
Contract Manager	Book Layout	Book Layout
Cross Org Data Proxy User	Book Layout	Book Layout
Custom	Book Layout	Book Layout
Custom: Marketing Profile	Book Layout	Book Layout
Custom: Sales Profile	Book Layout	Book Layout
Custom: Support Profile	Book Layout	Book Layout
Force.com - Free User	Book Layout	Book Layout
Librarian	Book Layout	Book Layout
Marketing User	Book Layout	Book Layout
Partner Community Login User	Book Layout	Book Layout
Partner Community User	Book Layout	Book Layout
Partner User	Book Layout	Book Layout
Read Only	Book Layout	Book Layout
Sample	Book Layout	Book Layout
sample Profile	Book Layout	Book Layout
Solution Manager	Book Layout	Book Layout
Standard Platform User	Book Layout	Book Layout
Standard User	Book Layout	Book Layout
System Administrator	Book Layout	Book Layout
System Administrator Clone	Book Layout	Book Layout

Click on the **Edit Assignment** button at the top of the table and change the page layout required for each profile. We can also set the default `RecordType` and `Page Layout` on the profile page, which we will be revisiting in *Chapter 7, Application Administration*.

The general library fills information in the Media object that we created previously. However, the fields are spread across the page and the users find it difficult to fill in the information. Group the fields in a logical grouping on the page layout editor. Some fields are different for books and videos.

Create two separate layouts: one for books (with the ISBN number) and the other one for videos (with the title and year).

Search layouts

Apart from the page layout editor, we can customize the search and lookup layouts for the object. We can select the fields that are displayed in columns on these layouts. Let's edit the Media Lookup layout as an example:

1. Go to **Setup** | **Create** | **Media** | **Search Layouts**, as shown in the following screenshot:

Search Layouts
Action
Layout
Columns Displayed
Edit
Search Results
Media Name
Edit
Lookup Dialogs
Media Name
Edit
Lookup Phone Dialogs
Media Name
Edit
Media Tab
Media Name
Edit
Media List View
N/A
Edit
Search Filter Fields

2. After you click on **Edit** for the **Lookup Dialogs** option, a dialog box similar to the one shown in the following screenshot will appear:

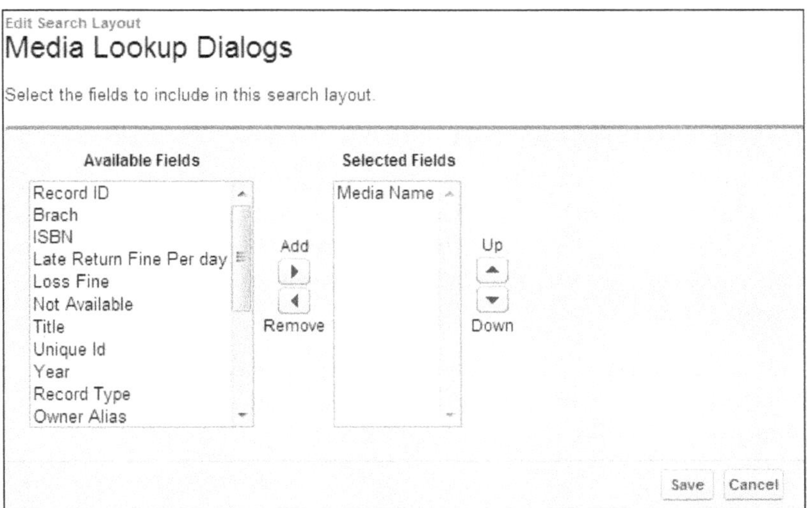

3. Select the fields that will appear on **Lookup Dialogs**. For example, select the **Not Available** field and click on **Add**.
4. Click on **Save** to save the record.
5. Now every time there is a lookup on the media object, it will show the **Not Available** field in it, as shown in the following screenshot:

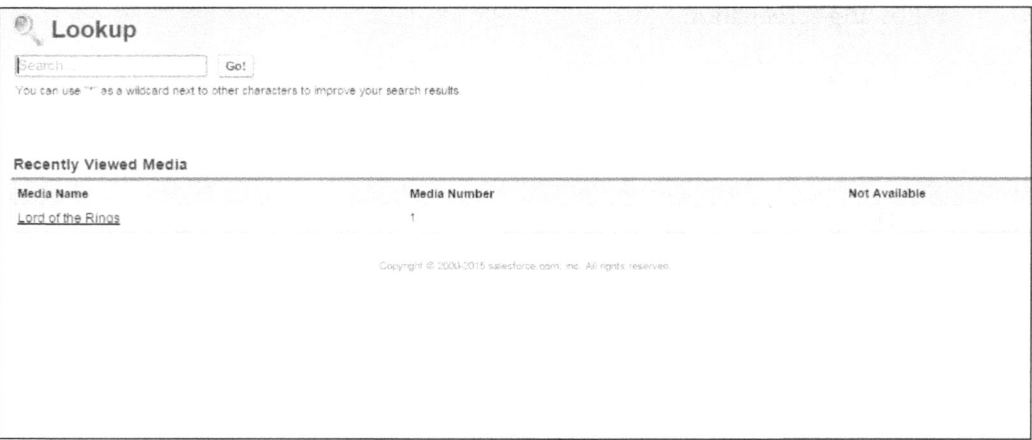

We can add a custom list button to the search results and media list view. On the other layout, we can only select the fields that are to be displayed on the screen.

Similarly, we can customize the other layouts for the object as well.

Mini page layouts

We can define mini page layouts for the records that appear in the **Console** tab, hover details, and event overlays. A **Mini Page Layout** contains a subset of the items in an existing page layout. Mini page layouts inherit record types and profile associations, related lists, fields, and field access settings from their associated page layouts.

The visible fields and related lists of the **Mini Page Layout** can be further customized, but the other items inherited from the associated page layout cannot be changed on the **Mini Page Layout** itself.

To create a **Mini Page Layout**, navigate to **Setup** | **Create** | **Object Name** | **Page Layout**. Click on **Mini Page Layout** on the bar at the top of the page layout:

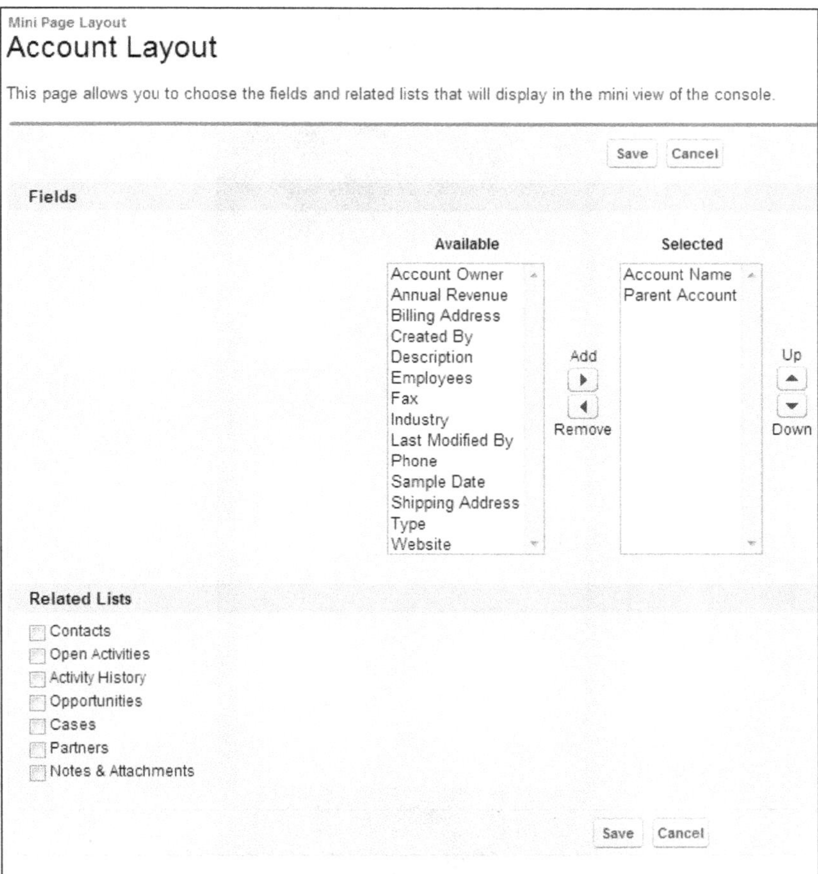

Just like **Search Layout, Mini Page Layout** and Mini Console Layout give us the option of the field names that can be added to the layout.

Compact layouts

Compact layouts are used to display important information in the Salesforce1 mobile application at a quick glance on touchscreen devices with a limited screen size.

However, compact layouts are not available for the Salesforce classic, Chatter mobile for BlackBerry, Salesforce Touch, or Dashboards for iPad mobile apps.

Compact layouts display important data in the highlights area of the record on the mobile app, as shown in the following screenshot:

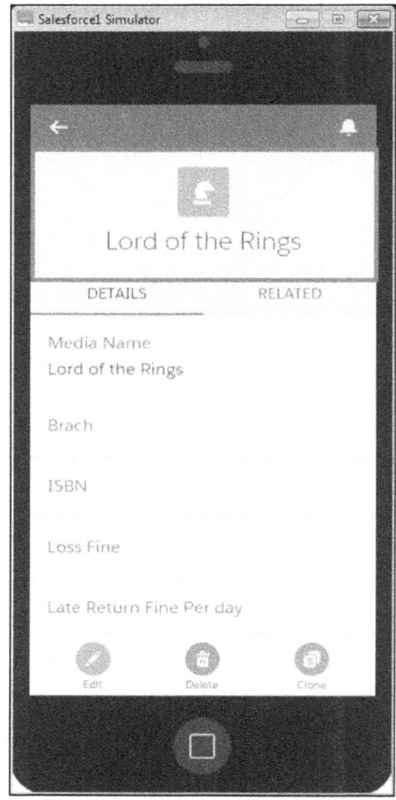

The compact layout does not support all the text area (`Long`, `Rich`, and `Text Area`) as well as a multi-select picklist.

Let's create a compact layout for our media object that will display its category and sub-category on the highlighted panel:

1. Go to the **Compact Layouts** section on the **Object** page of the **Media** object, as shown in the following screenshot, and click on **New**:

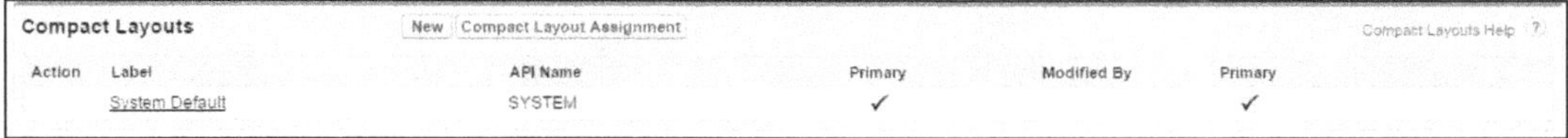

2. Select **Title**, **Categories,** and **Sub-categories** as the fields in the **Compact Layout Edit,** as shown in the following screenshot, and click on **Save**:

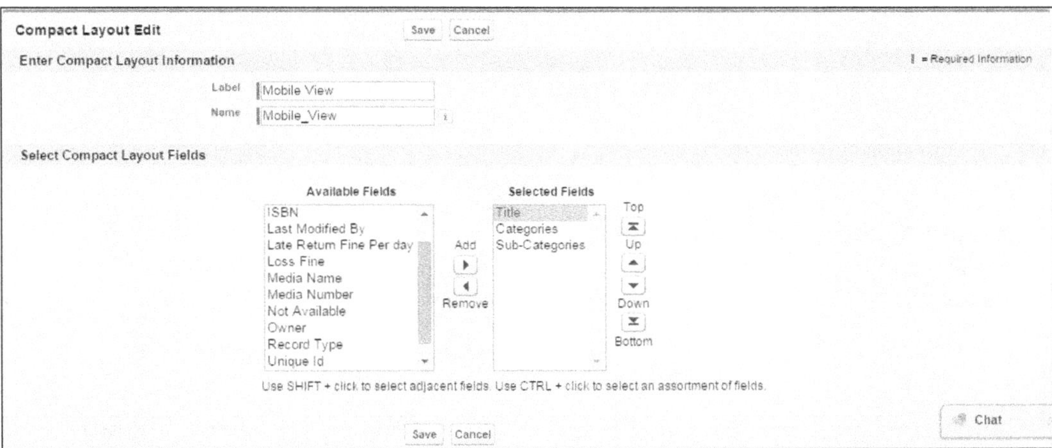

3. When we create a **Compact Layout**, it is not automatically assigned to the user. We first need to assign the layout for it to be visible. Click on **Compact Layout Assignment,** and subsequently, click on **Edit Assignment** on the next page:

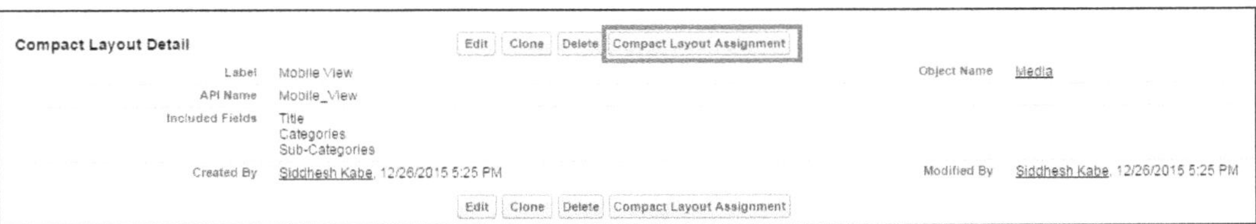

4. Select the **Primary Compact Layout** as the newly created **Mobile View** and click on **Save**:

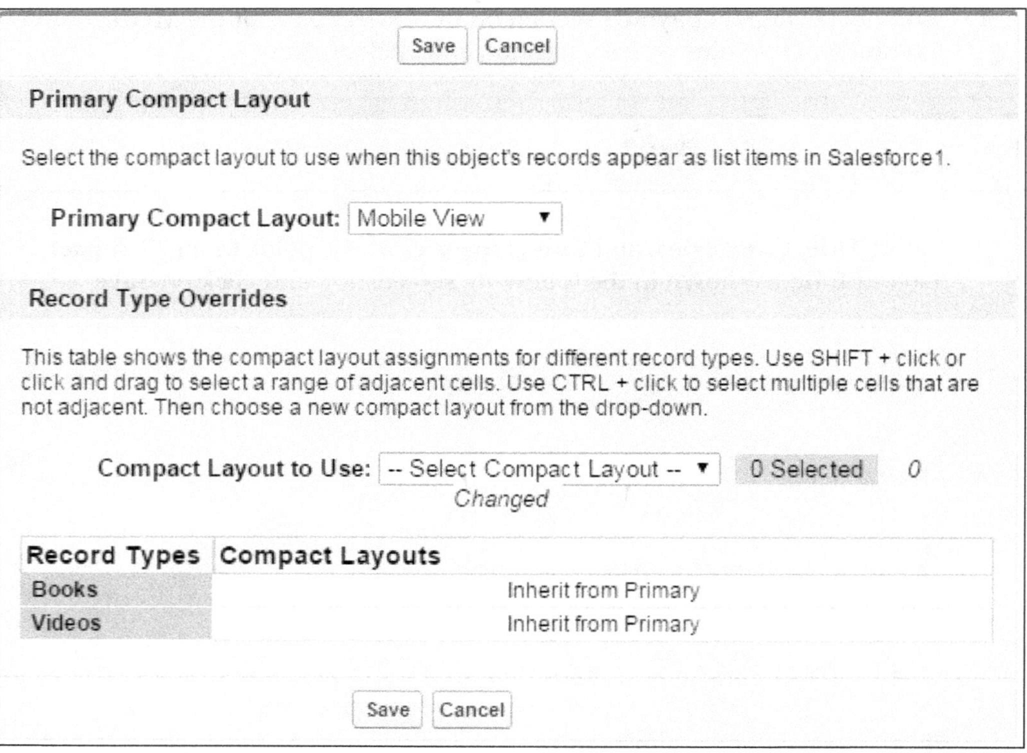
Save Cancel
Primary Compact Layout
Select the compact layout to use when this object's records appear as list items in Salesforce1.
Primary Compact Layout: Mobile View
Record Type Overrides
This table shows the compact layout assignments for different record types. Use SHIFT + click or click and drag to select a range of adjacent cells. Use CTRL + click to select multiple cells that are not adjacent. Then choose a new compact layout from the drop-down.
Compact Layout to Use: -- Select Compact Layout -- 0 Selected 0 Changed
Record Types Compact Layouts
Books Inherit from Primary
Videos Inherit from Primary
Save Cancel

5. In the Mobile View, you can see the Categories and Sub Categories in the top panel of the Media record:

6. This completes the different types of layouts on Force.com

Building an application

An application or an app is a logical grouping of tabs used for a common business process. Different tabs are grouped together to form a single business unit for user convenience; however, users can further customize it for themselves, as discussed at the beginning of this chapter.

The following screenshot shows the standard applications provided by the platform by default:

Salesforce provides standard applications, such as **Sales**, **Call Center**, **Marketing**, **Community**, and **Force.com**.

Understanding custom applications

We can customize an application by giving it a custom logo, a custom name, a custom description, and a custom landing page. We can give the instructions to use the objects on the custom landing page.

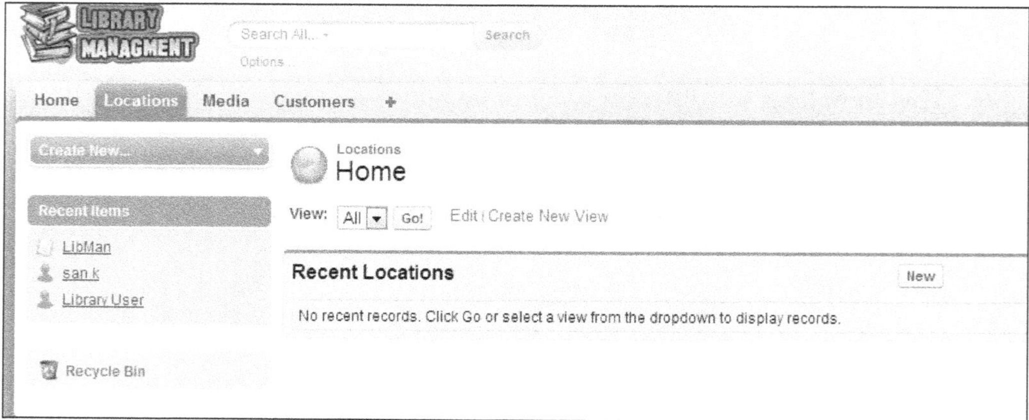

Exercise – building your own application

Let's continue building the **Library Management System**. Build an application for the **Library Management System**. Design a simple custom logo for it as well.

To build your own application, perform the following steps:

1. Go to **Setup** | **Create** | **Apps**.
2. Click on the **New** button to open the tab creation wizard. In the following few sections, we will take a look at multiple steps involved in creating an app.

Selecting your type

In the first step, select **Custom app** and click on **Next** to create it, as shown in the following screenshot:

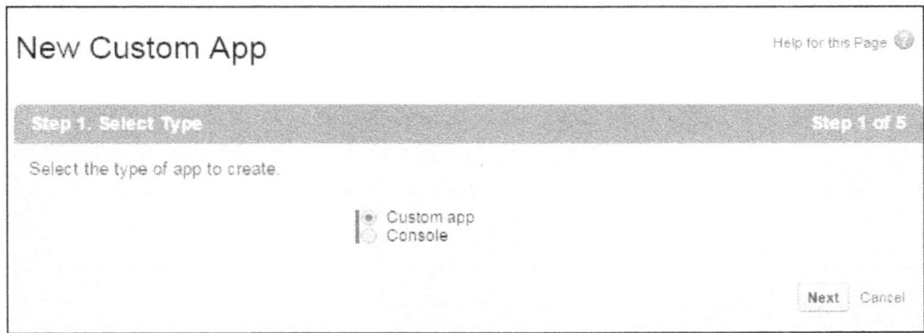

Entering the details

In the second step, give an appropriate name for the application you are building. In our case, we will name it **Library Management**.

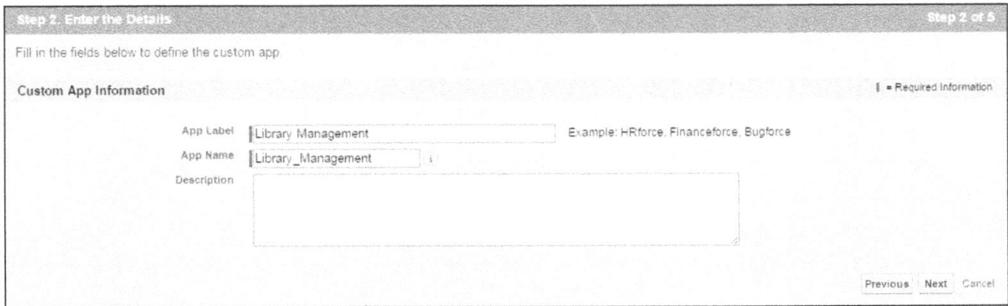

Choosing the image source for the Custom App Logo

All custom applications display the standard Salesforce logo. The logo can be replaced with a custom logo.

The custom logo can be any GIF and JPG file from the **Documents** tab.

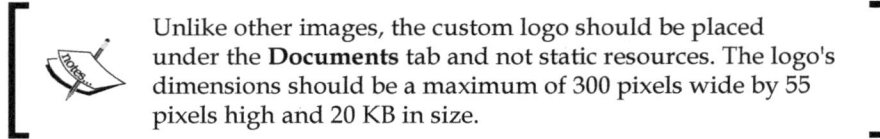

> Unlike other images, the custom logo should be placed under the **Documents** tab and not static resources. The logo's dimensions should be a maximum of 300 pixels wide by 55 pixels high and 20 KB in size.

Select an appropriate logo for the application:

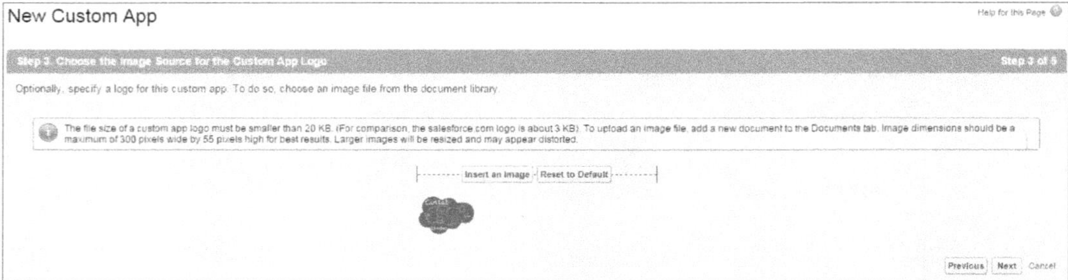

New Custom App
Help for this Page
Step 3. Choose the Image Source for the Custom App Logo
Step 3 of 5
Optionally, specify a logo for this custom app. To do so, choose an image file from the document library.
The file size of a custom app logo must be smaller than 20 KB. (For comparison, the salesforce.com logo is about 3 KB). To upload an image file, add a new document to the Documents tab. Image dimensions should be a maximum of 300 pixels wide by 55 pixels high for best results. Larger images will be resized and may appear distorted.
Insert an Image
Reset to Default
Previous
Next
Cancel

Choosing the tabs

Once we are satisfied that the application name and the logo are correct, we can choose to add tabs to the new application.

On the next page, it will ask for the tabs to be included in this application. Choose the tabs that are created for library management and include them in this application.

Assigning it to profile

On the next page, the platform will ask you to assign a profile the application to the profile. Whenever we create a new app, we can choose a **Profile** that can see the application. If we choose to hide the application from the profile, the user won't be able to see the application in the selector's drop-down menu.

However, note that this is not a security measure but a way to prevent the user from accessing the application. If, however, the tab is default on or default off, the user can still access the tab without the app.

Profile	☐ Visible	☐ Default
Contract Manager	☐	☐
Custom User	☐	☐
Marketing User	☐	☐
Platform System Admin	☐	☐
Read Only	☐	☐
Solution Manager	☐	☐
Standard User	☐	☐
System Administrator	☐	☐

Declaractive lighting components and actions

With Winter 16, Salesforce introduced the new Lighting Experience that lets us create apps for all types of devices. Using the Lighting Components, we will build applications that work seamlessly on smartphones, tablets, and the Web.

Using the Lighting App Builder

The Lighting App Builder is a point-and-click tool that makes it easy to create a single-page app for Salesforce1. With the Lighting App Builder, we can use various predefined components to drag and drop on the app.

With the Lightning App Builder, we can build single-page apps, such as a dashboard, to track sales or enter expenses with the ability to drill down into the details.

Note

At the time of writing this book, the Lighting App Builder is in pilot mode and the final version can change.

The Lightning App Builder is used to build **Lightning** pages with a custom layout. A lightning page is made up of regions that contain components. The structure of the page changes based on the device it is opened on.

The following screenshot is a sample of an app built using the Lightning App Builder:

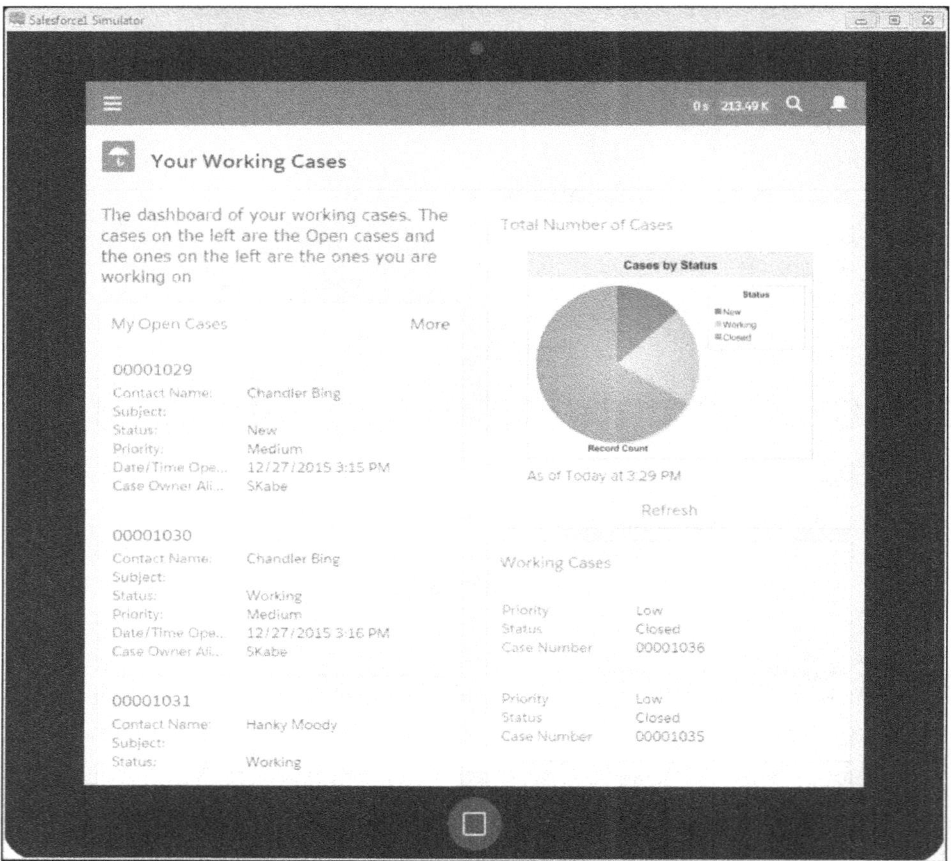

In the next section, we will build a sample Lighting app that will display **Recent Cases** and **Working Cases** in two lists along with the chart of **Cases by Status**. We will explore the components that are provided by the Lightning App Builder.

Building an app using the Lightning App Builder

The Lightning App Builder is located under the **App Setup** menu item under **Setup**. Just type in Lightning App Builder in the Quick Find/Search box in Setup.

Click on the **New** button on the **Lightning Pages** Setup, and click on **Next** on the first introduction page:

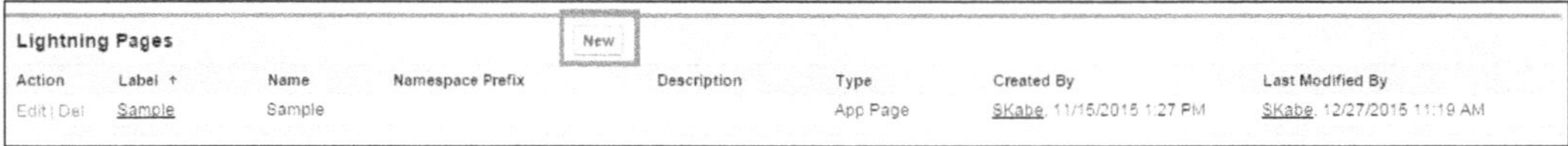

Lightning Pages
New
Action
Label
Name
Namespace Prefix
Description
Type
Created By
Last Modified By
Edit | Del
Sample
Sample
App Page
SKabe, 11/15/2015 1:27 PM
SKabe, 12/27/2015 11:19 AM

The Lightning page template

On the next page, we can choose an appropriate template for our app. The template divides the page into different regions. The template that we choose at this stage determines how the **Lightning Page** displays on a given device. Choose a **Two Columns - 2 Regions** template for this exercise:

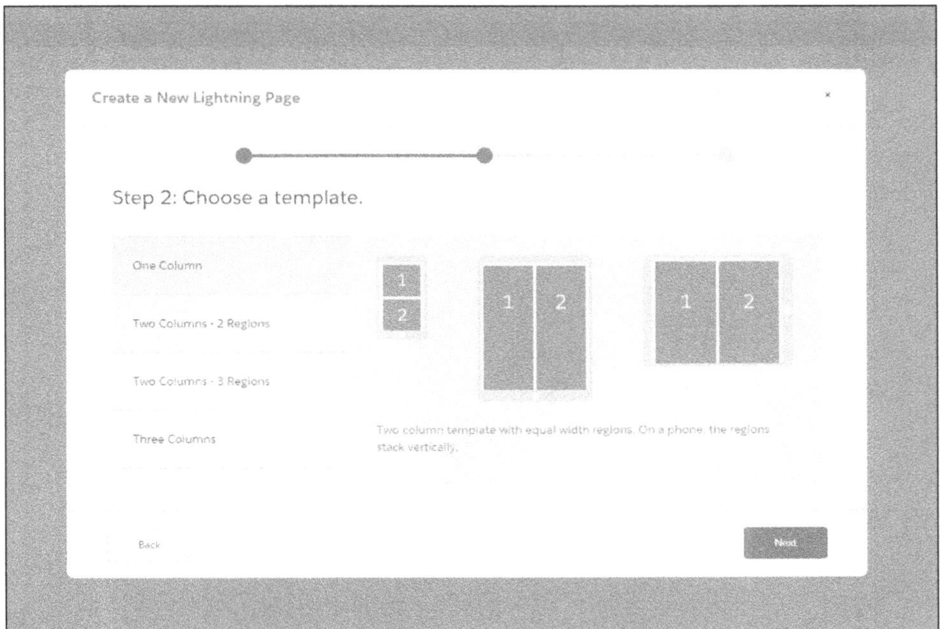

On the next page, give a relevant name to our new App, and we will name it **Working Cases** right now:

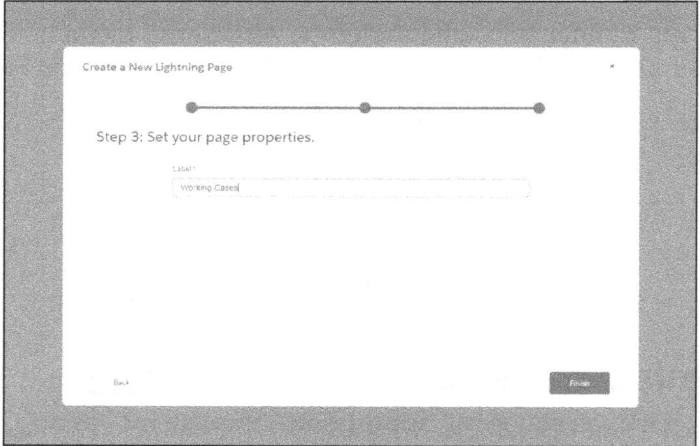

The Lightning App Builder is divided into different sections. This is a screenshot of an app that is filled with components:

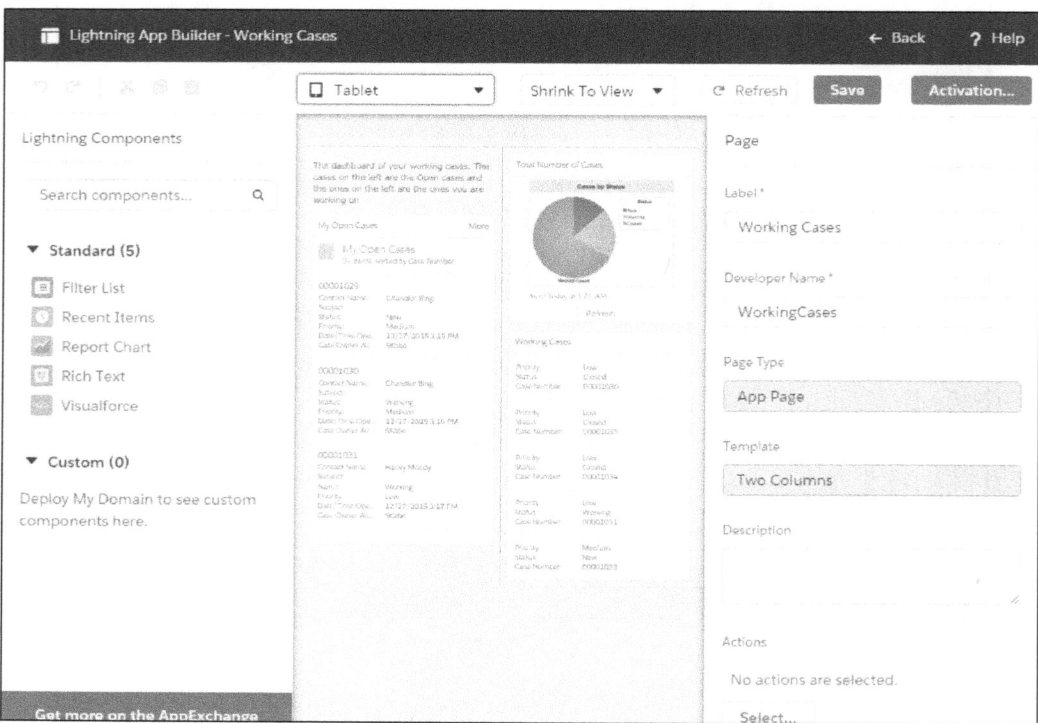

Lightning components

A Lightning component is a configurable and reusable element that we can drag and drop in the Lightning App Builder to build our Lightning page. We can use standard, custom, and third-party components from AppExchange in the Lightning App Builder.

Standard components

Salesforce provides us with five standard components (till date). They are as follows:

- **Filter List (List View)**: This displays the **List View** of an object
- **Recent Items**: This displays the recent items of an object
- **Report Chart**: This displays the chart that was created on a report
- **Rich Text**: This displays a message for the user on the **Lightning Page**
- **Visualforce Page**: This displays a Visualforce page on the **Lightning Page**

Custom components

Developers can build their own custom components using the Lightning Framework that can be reused.

Third-party components

We can download third-party components from AppExchange that are preconfigured and ready to use:

- For example, on the left-hand side panel, the first component is Rich Text and contains a message for the user: *The dashboard of your working cases. The cases on the left-hand side are Open cases and the ones on the left are the ones you are going to work on.*
- The next component is *Filter List of My Open Cases* for the Case object.
- The first panel on the right-hand side is a Report Chart that was created for cases and statuses. We will learn how to create reports in *Chapter 6, Analytics and Reporting*.
- The next component on the right-hand side panel is a Recent Items Component for cases that display the recently working cases.

Using Global Actions

On the bottom-left side of the sidebar, we can add Global Actions to our Lightning Page. Actions allow a user to record call details, create or update records, send e-mails, or create tasks directly from the Lightning page. When a user visits a Lightning Page in Salesforce1, the page's actions appear in its action bar.

Summary

In this chapter, we explored the view capability of Salesforce.com. We learned how to create tabs and page layouts. We saw the advance page layout editor and learned how to create pages. We explored the new Lightning App Builder and learned about the components that can be used in the app builder.

In up coming chapters, we will explore how to show a different page layout for different login names or data types. We will be revisiting these lessons after we see the roles and profiles part.

Now, we can create applications with complete page layouts and the tabs for users to enter data; in further chapters, we will explore the logic as a service provided by Salesforce.

Test your knowledge

Q1 Which of the following statements are true about page layouts?

1. They can have one or two columns per section
2. We can add a list button using a page layout editor
3. We can hide a section header detail view, edit view, or both views
4. We can add blank spaces instead of fields
5. We can preview the layout for different profiles

Q2 In a Model View Controller architecture, which of the following are appropriate to Views? (Select two)

1. Page layouts
2. Validation rules
3. Tabs
4. Workflows

Q3 What is possible through page layouts for custom objects? (Select two)

1. Adding custom fields and buttons
2. Setting a mandatory field based on a certain value on another field
3. Adding inline Visualforce pages
4. Setting a three-column display

Q4 Which of the following cannot be included in the user page layout (Select two)

1. Tagging
2. Custom links
3. Inline Visualforce pages
4. Custom buttons
5. Custom fields

Q5 Which editions support Apex and Visualforce? (Select two)

1. Unlimited Edition
2. Enterprise Edition
3. Apex Edition
4. Professional Edition
5. Group Edition

Q6 Position is a custom object containing details of each position. A **candidate** contains the details of each candidate such as skills. When a user is viewing position records, they should also be able to see all those candidates who match the skills required for the post. However, a position can have no candidate, and a candidate record can also be kept blank. A position can be applied by multiple candidates, while a candidate can also apply to multiple positions. What can be done to achieve this?

1. Creating a master-child relationship between them
2. Creating a junction object to store both the values
3. Creating a lookup relationship of a candidate on a position
4. Creating a Visualforce page

Q7 What are the different custom tabs that you can create? (Select three)

1. Web tabs
2. Apex tabs
3. Visualforce tabs
4. Custom object tabs
5. Standard object tabs

4
Implementing Business Logic

We studied the basics of App Development on Force.com. We created database objects, page layouts, and tabs. Now that we have created our model and view, it is time to add some business logic. Business logic is the brain of the application; it makes sense of the data and responds to the button clicks in the UI.

A controller in the Model-View-Controller architecture forms the bridge between a Model (Data) and View (Display). We can write the business logic in the Apex code as well as in a declarative syntax. In this chapter, we will focus on the declarative syntax to write business logic.

In this chapter, we will cover the following topics:

- Choosing between different automation tools
- Automating the business process using workflows
- Setting up a workflow rule that fires after a particular time
- Routing records using an approval process
- Automating using the Lightning Process Builder
- Creating wizards with Visual workflows

Automating business processes

There are different ways to automate repetitive business processes on the platform. We can use any of the following tools to do this:

- The Lightning Process Builder
- The Visual workflow
- Workflows
- Approvals

The automation tool that we need depends on the type of business process that we are automating.

For example:

- If a user does not return the book in seven days, the librarian sends an e-mail reminder to him to return the book
- If a user updates his address in the system, an automated update should happen in an external inventory management system or an address book
- If a user misses out on a payment of a fine or returns a book after the due date, the user is marked as black-listed
- Managers approve the discount requests for the amount of the fine
- Customer Support uses a wizard to capture new cases and so on

Doing something when a record has values

- The most common repetitive business process is to perform actions based on the value of the record. This type of process automation can be created in workflows, the Process Builder, and visual workflows.
- If the process boils down to a single if/then statement, it is recommended that you use the Process Flow.
- If there is a time-dependent action (a delayed trigger) or the action is an outbound message, we should use workflows.
- If the process is far too complex with multiple if/then statements and follow-up if/then statements, we must use visual workflows.

Getting information from customers

One of the biggest drawbacks for all the process automation tools on Salesforce has been the inability to perform actions on the data, while it was being entered. This limitation is solved using Visual Workflow.

For example, creating an Opportunity capture wizard that lets the customer representative fill out a form to create opportunities.

Getting a record approved

If the process requires an approval from a manager in the hierarchy, we can use an approval process.

Features

The following table explains the features used in the various tools:

	Workflow	Process Builder	Visual Workflow	Approvals
Single if/then Statement	YES	YES	YES	YES
Complex if/then- if/then statements	No	No	YES	No
Drag and Drop designer	No	Yes	Yes	No
Is triggered when	The record is changed	The record is changed	A user clicks on a button or link A user accesses the custom tab The process starts The Apex method triggers	A user clicks on a button or link A process or flow calls the **Submit for Approval** action The Apex method triggers
Supports time-based actions	Yes	Yes	Yes	No
Supports user interaction	No	No	Yes	Yes (Only for approvals)
Call Apex methods	No	Yes	Yes	No
Create and Delete Object records	Only Tasks	Only Create	Create and Delete	No
Post to Chatter	Yes (Pilot)	Yes	Yes	
Send email	E-mail alerts	E-mail alerts	Yes	E-mail alerts
Send outbound messages without code	Yes	No	No	No
Submit for approval	No	Yes	Yes	No
Update fields	The record or its parent	Any related record	Any record	The record or its parent

Automating business processes using Process Builder

Process Builder is a tool that helps us automate business processes in an easy-to-use visual editor. We can set the criteria for which the process will run, and if triggered, which actions will be performed immediately. We can also add a time-trigger for the actions.

In this section, we will create a process for the following requirements.

Library Management wants to send an e-mail to a member who has borrowed a book or CD. They would like to highlight the name of the borrowed item and the date of return.

To open the Process Builder, perform the following steps:

1. Go to **Setup**, enter **Process Builder** in the **Quick Find** box, click on **Process Builder**, and then click on **New**.
2. Name the process **Book_Return_reminder**, as shown in the following screenshot:

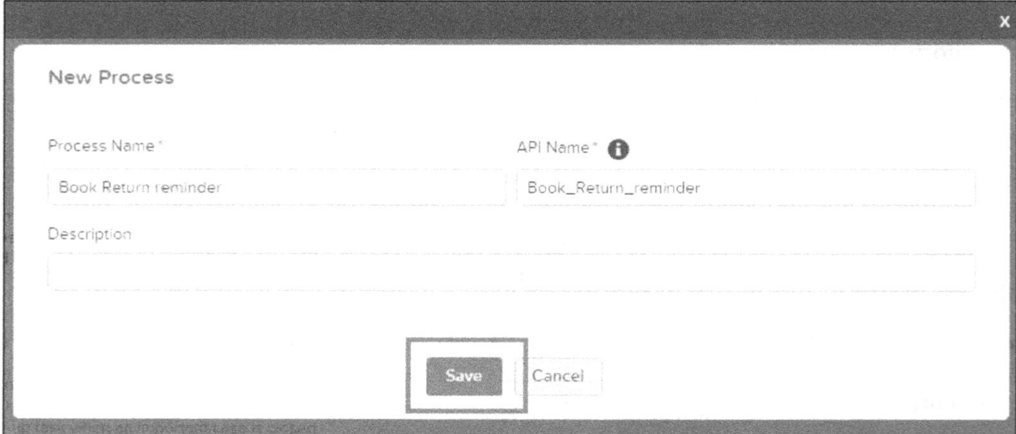

3. Click on **Save**. Once we save the new process, it opens the process builder, as shown in the following screenshot. Let's take a look at each element of the builder:

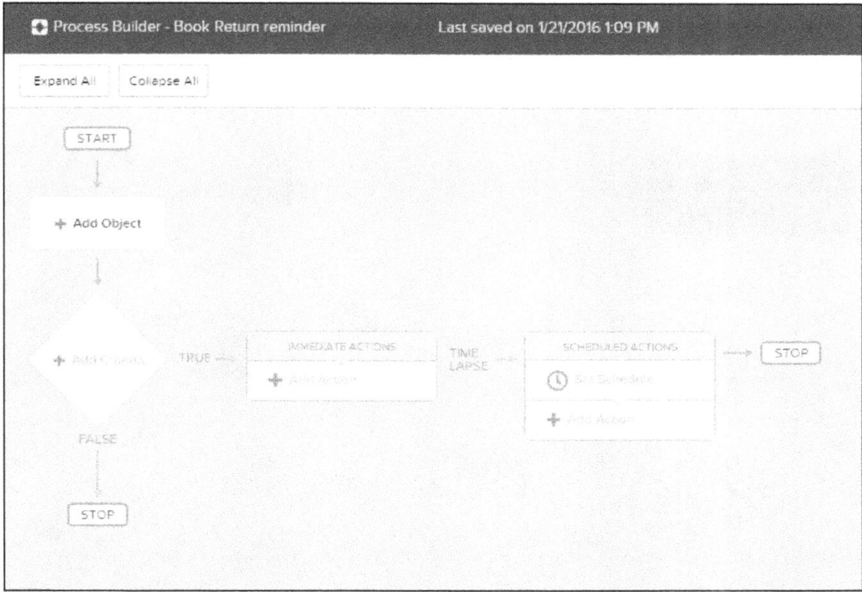

Now, let's add an Object:

1. Click on **Add Object**, as shown in the preceding screenshot, and it will open a dialog box where we will select the object as **Customer-Media** and **when a record is created or edited** as the entry criterion.
2. Click on **Save** at the bottom of the dialog box:

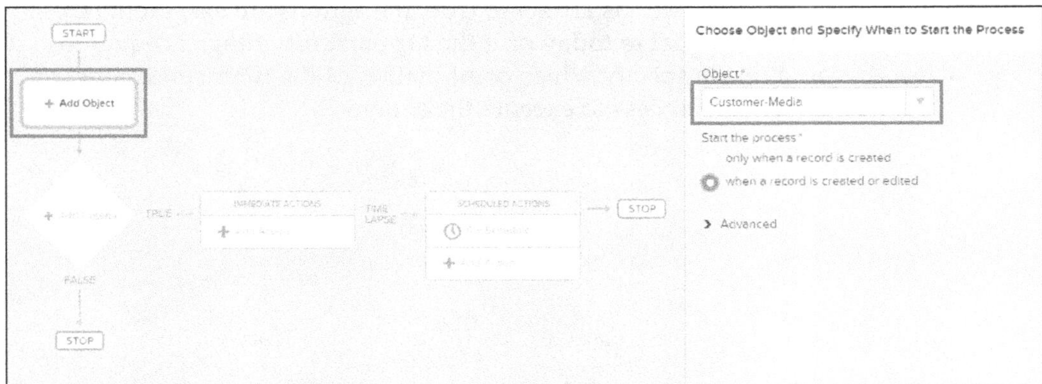

Now, let's add criteria:

1. After selecting the object, we select **Add Criteria** to filter the records that will enter the process once it is fired:

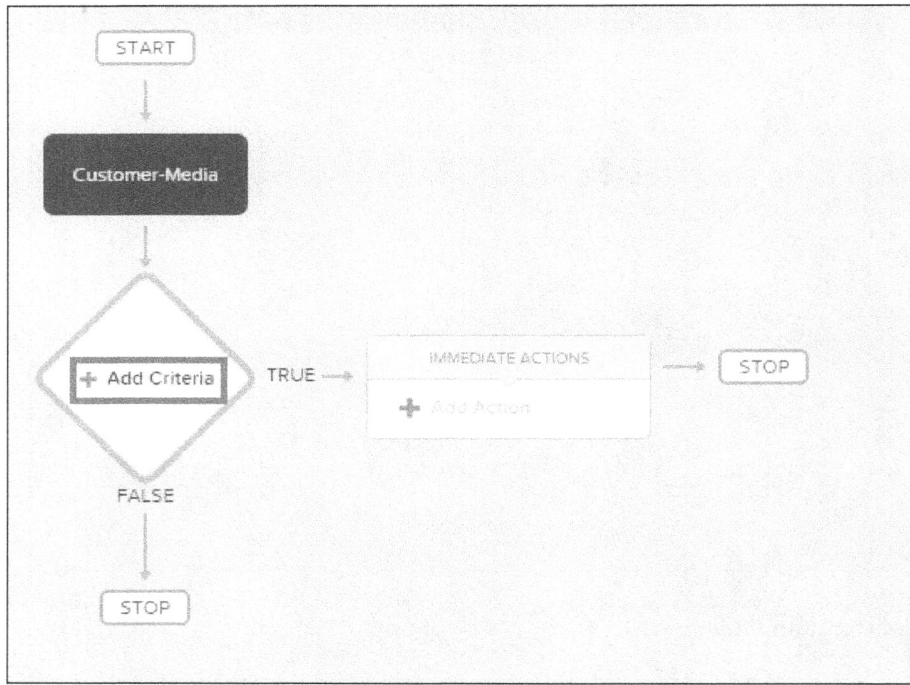

2. We can set three criteria types to execute the actions:

   Conditions are met:

   When these set of conditions are set to **true**, the actions are executed. For example, if **Date** is equal to **today** or if the **Opportunity Stage** is equal to **Closed Won**. We can specify which combination of the filter conditions must be **true** for the process to execute the actions.

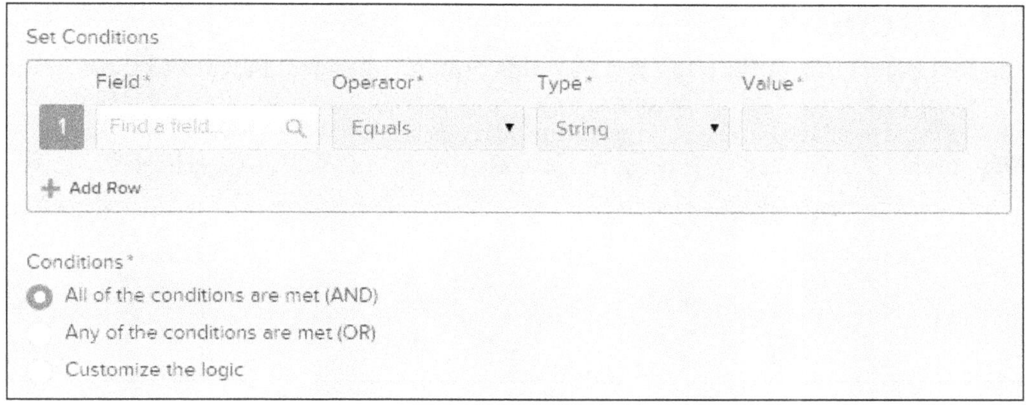

Formula Evaluates to `true`.

When conditions are good enough for simple logical statements, we can use the formula editor to create complex rules, using Excel, such as formulas and field data. If the formula evaluates to **true**, the actions are executed.

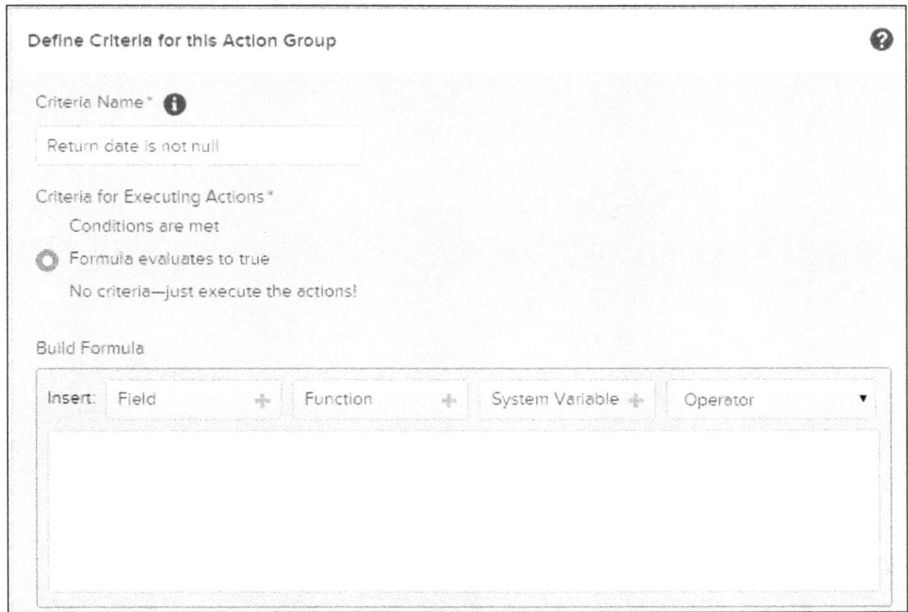

Advanced

When we select this option, the process runs only on changes relevant to the criteria. For example, if a user edits the record and no conditions are met, the process won't execute the associated actions. This setting isn't available if the process starts only when a record is created or if the criteria node doesn't evaluate any criteria.

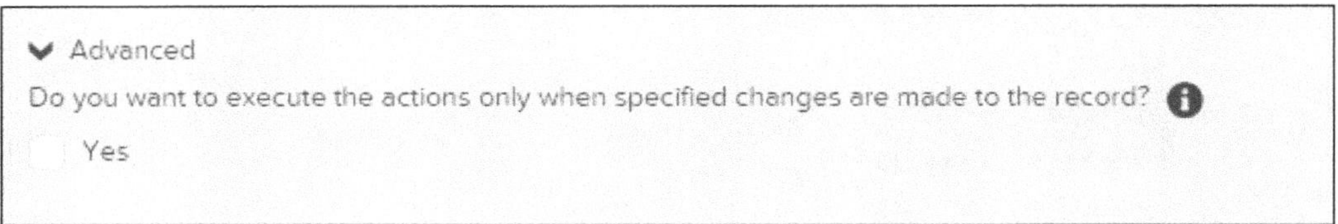

No Criteria

For our example, we will not be using any criteria.

Let's add the actions:

After setting up the criteria and conditions, the next step in the Process is to set Actions that will be executed if the formula is `true`:

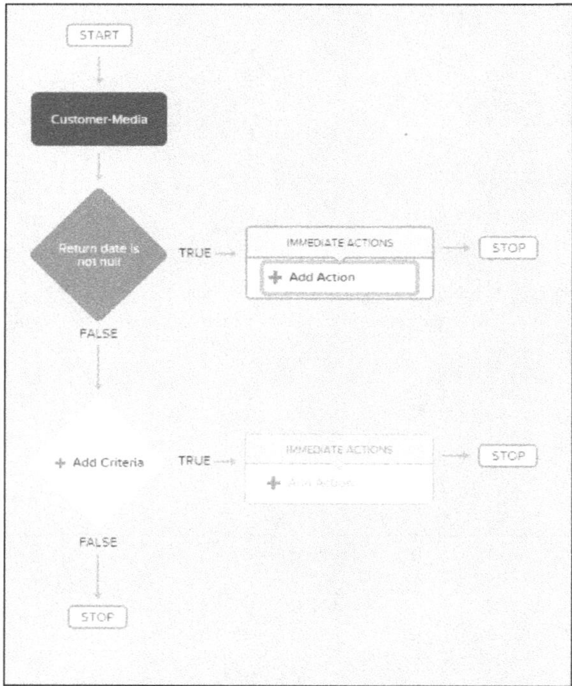

We can add the following actions to our process. These actions are shown in the following screenshot:

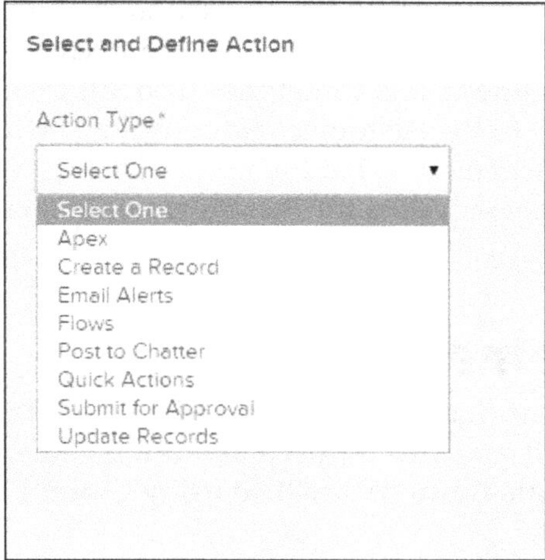

Process Builder limitations

Before we create a Process, we have to be cognizant of the following:

- After we activate the process, we can no longer edit that process; we can clone the process and work on a separate version
- Processes can invalidate the previous valid fields because updates made to records based on processes don't trigger validation rules
- Processes are invisible to the user and can start automatically
- Saving or creating records can trigger more than one process

Salesforce processes rules in the following order:

- Validation rules
- Assignment rules
- Auto response rules
- Workflow rules and processes (and their immediate actions)
- Escalation rules

Designing wizards with the Visual Workflows

Using the process builder, we can automate the business processes; however, they do not contain any UI components or data entry points. The platform stores data in different business objects that are logically linked to each other. However, in the daily business environment, it is sometimes difficult to maintain this level of segregation. During a call to the customer, the consultant will not always be able to open multiple tabs to collect data. What the users expect is a single consistent page that can collect all the necessary data for them to enter and create objects that they can update after the call.

What's in a name?

If you are like me, you must have heard the words, Visual Workflows and Flows, thrown around a lot. So, if you are confused about the name, Visual Workflows is the product that helps us create flows. We will be using Cloud Flow Designer to do this.

Cloud Flow Designer

The following screenshot shows the new Cloud Flow Designer:

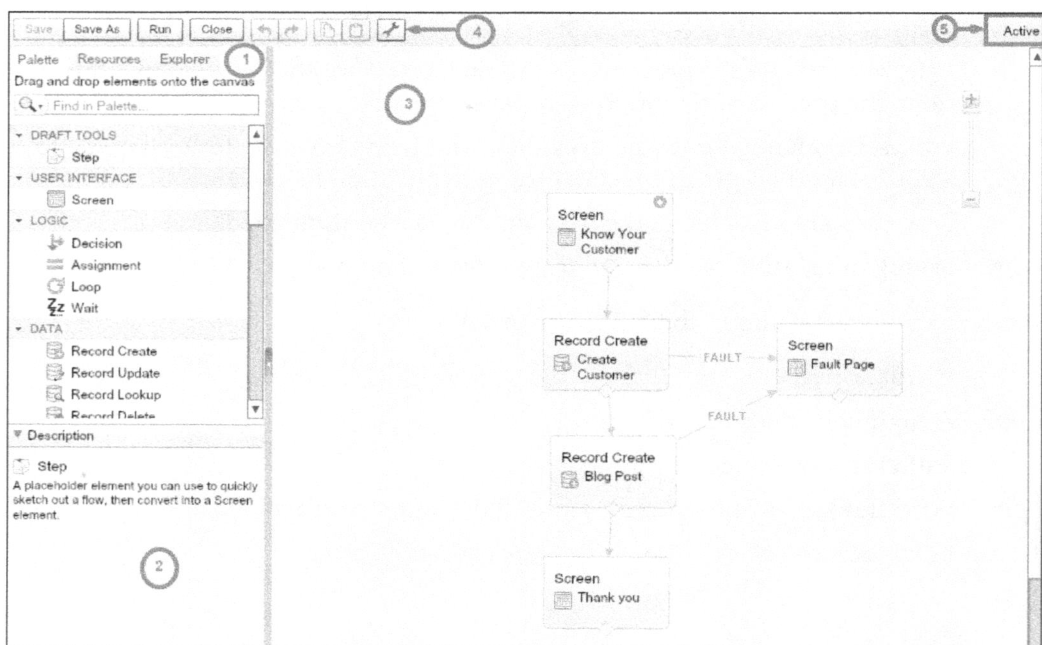

- The left-hand side panel marked by (**1**) contains three tabs.
- **Palette**: This contains all the elements that we can add to the flow.
- **Resources**: These are resources that can be added to the flow.
- **Explorer**: The Explorer contains all the elements and resources that are already added to the flow in one single view.
- The description panel on the left-hand side that is marked by (**2**) gives details about the elements and resources that are selected.
- The Canvas (**3**) is the place where the flow is visualized.
- Finally, we can use the button bar (**4**) on the top to manage the flow.
- The **Run** button runs the last saved version of the flow. It does not run unsaved changes.
- The **Close** button takes us back to the setup menu.
- We can **Edit** properties, such as `name`, `description`, and `interview` labels.
- We can monitor the flow version's status, as well as check whether it has any errors or warnings, with the indicator in the top-right corner.
- We can monitor the flow version's status, as well as check whether it has any errors or warnings, with the indicator in the top-right corner (**5**).

The Model-View-Container values of the flow

The elements that are dragged from the **Palette** onto the canvas contain actions that flows can execute:

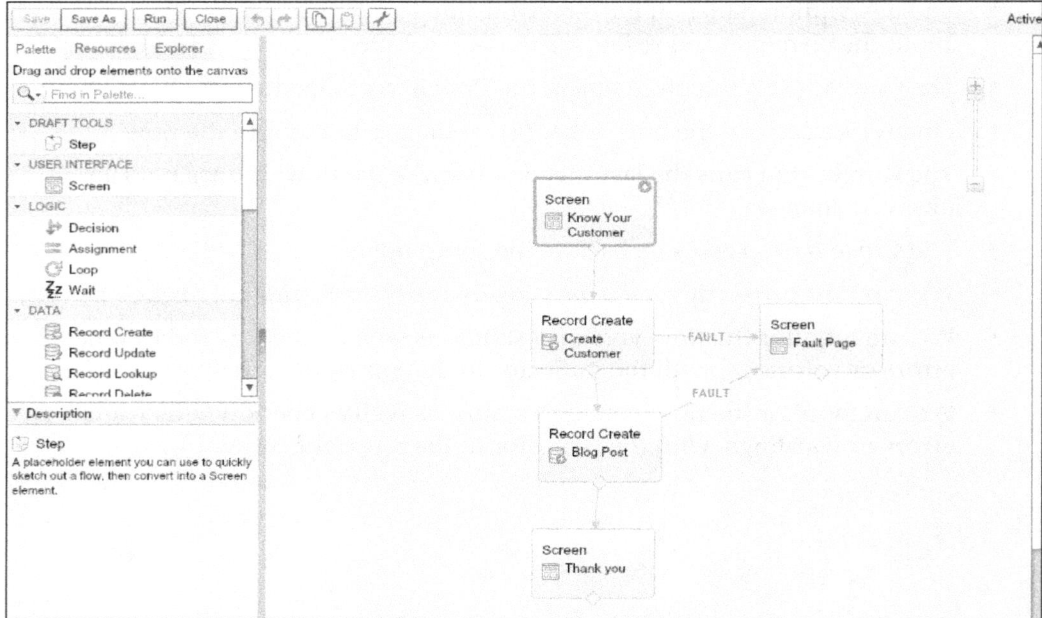

Each element is connected to each other by a connector. If the element contains a decision path, we can connect it to two elements. And finally, there are resources that bind the data to the different elements. We can declare variables and constants that can be used throughout, or we can use screens such as the following one to collect user inputs and map them to the variables.

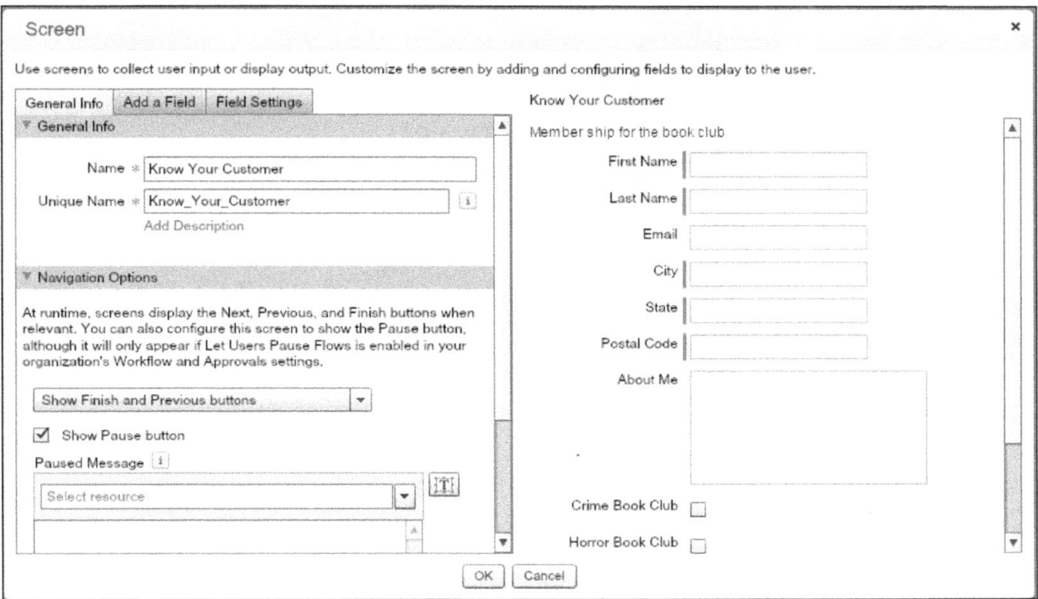

Exercise—creating a quick customer

We are going to create a simple flow for the customer to donate a book to the library. The input form is going to collect the customer data and check whether the customer is present in the system. If not, we will create the customer and the book they want to donate. If the customer is present, we are simply going to add the book to our media object.

So, let's begin:

1. Go to **Setup** and enter **Flows** in the **Quick Find** box. Then select **Flows** and click on the new **Flow**.
2. We will add a screen where we can collect information from the user who runs the flow:

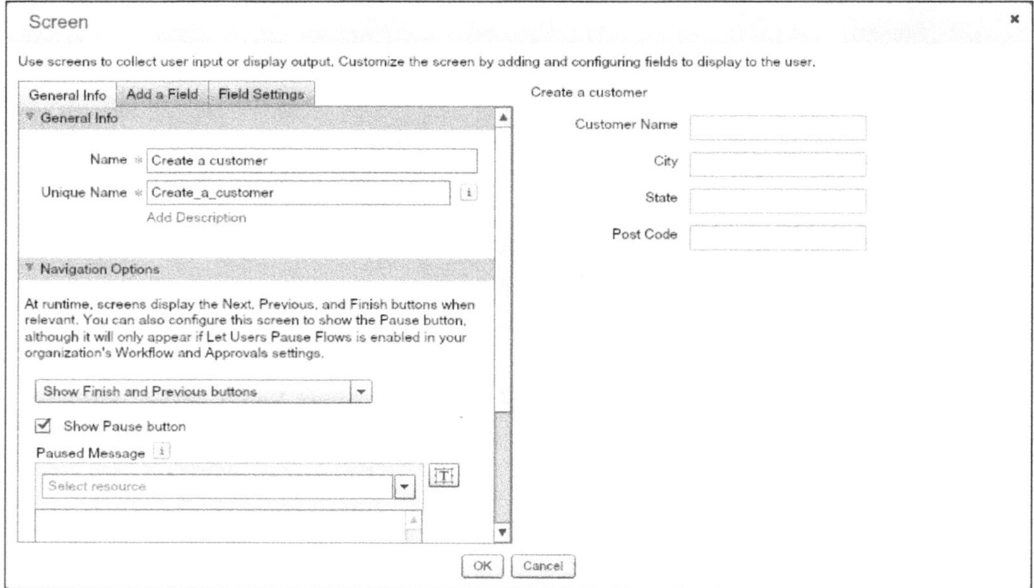

   - From the Palette, drag a **Screen** element onto the canvas
   - In the **General Info** tab, name it `Create a customer`
   - In the **Add a Field** tab, double-click on **Textbox** to add the field on the screen
   - Repeat the same for six other text fields
   - Select each field in the preview pane and enter the field label, as shown in the preceding screenshot, and click on **OK**

3. Select the **Record Create** element from the **Palette** on the screen:

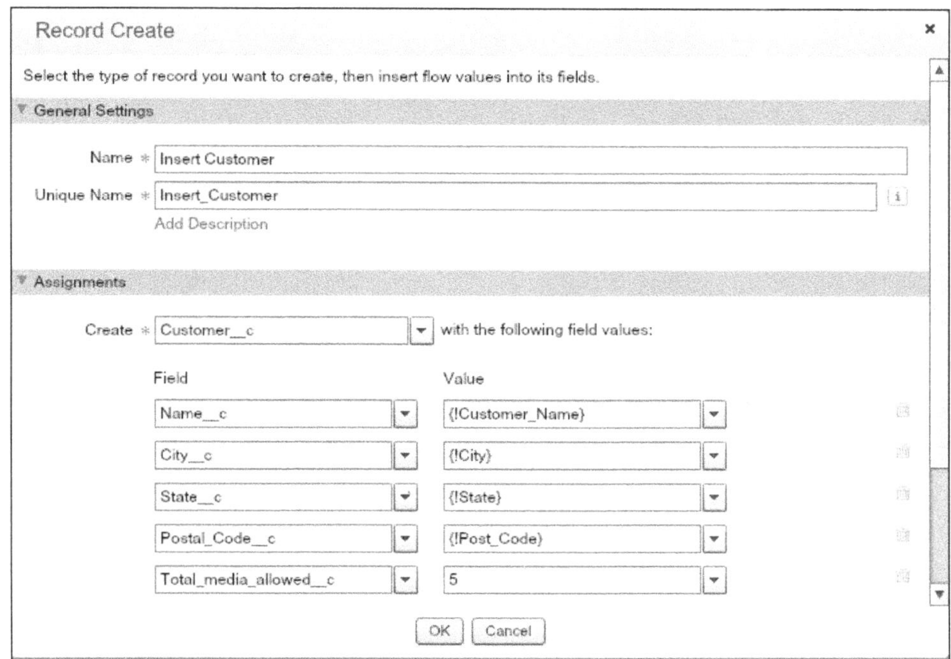

- From the **Palette**, drag the **Record Create** element onto the canvas
- Enter **Insert Customer** as the name of the element
- Select **Create**, and then go to **Custom** | **Customer__c**
- Now we map the input fields to **Customer__c**
- Go from **Custom** | **Name__c** to **Screen Input Field** | **Customer Name**
- Go from **Custom** | **City to Screen Input Field** | **City**
- And so on
- Click on **OK**

4. Connect the two elements together by clicking on the node at the bottom of the Screen element and dragging the connector onto the **Record Create** element.

5. Finally, add one more screen by dragging the Screen element onto the canvas:

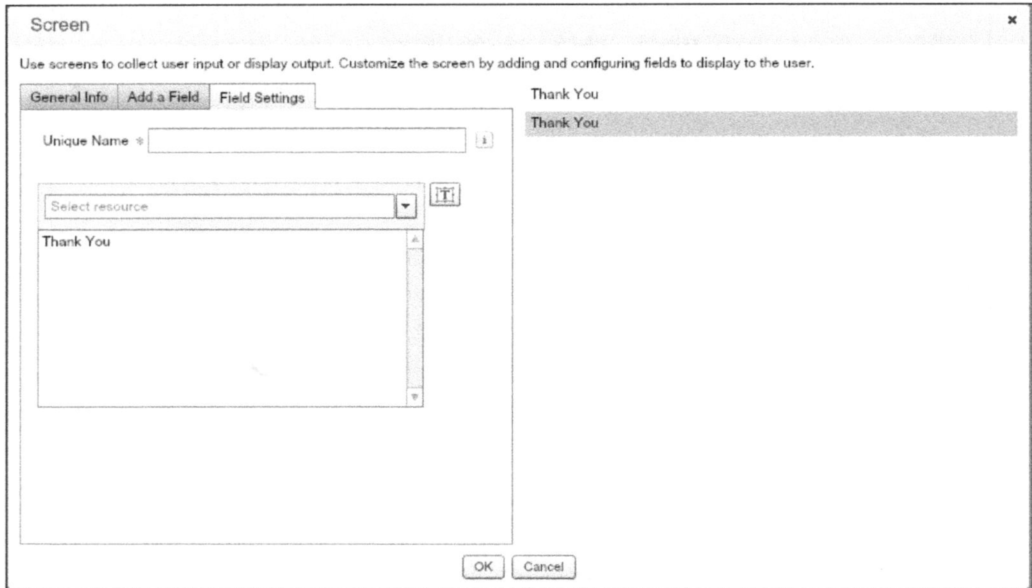

    - Drag the screen element from the palette onto the canvas
    - In the **General Info** tab, name it **Thank You**
    - Go to the **Add a Field** tab, and double-click on **Display Text** to add the field on the screen
    - In the field setting, give a user-friendly message: *Thank you for your input*

6. Now, we have three elements on the canvas. We will connect them together by dragging connectors. Click on the node at the bottom of the **Create Customer** screen and drag it onto the **Insert Customer** element. Similarly, from the Insert **Customer Element**, drag the same to the `Thank You` screen.

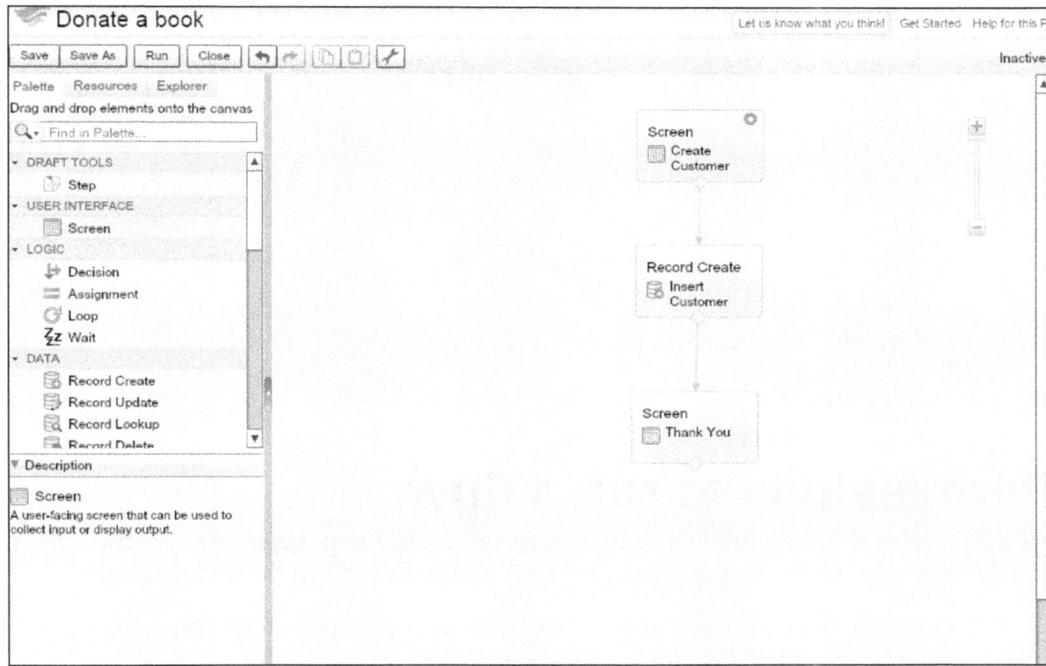

7. Finally, we have to indicate which element is the first element in this process.

   Select the **Create Customer** screen element, and click on the green arrow in the top-right corner of the screen:

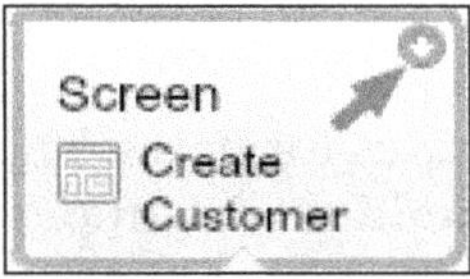

8. Save the flow and name it **Quick Customer**.
9. Now, click on the **Run** button on the button bar to test your flow.

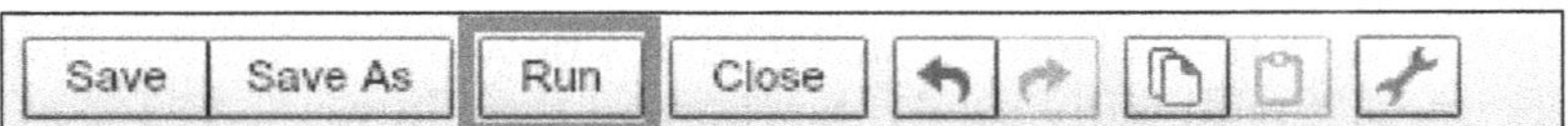

10. The final flow should look like the following screenshot:

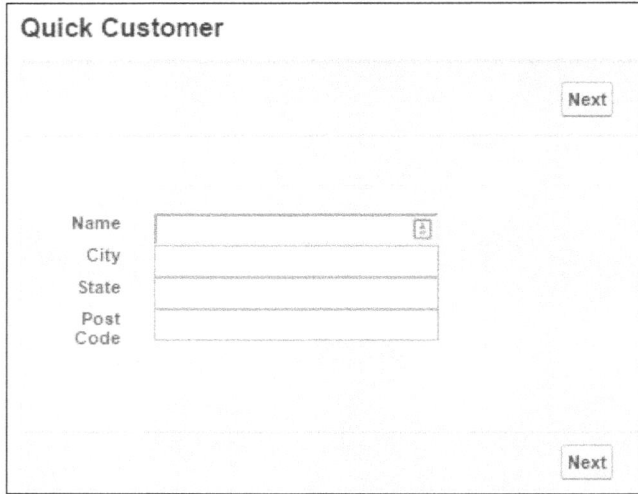

Permissions to run a flow

We can embed the flow in a Visualforce page and add the page as a tab on the app. For the user to actually run the flow, we require the following three conditions:

- The user must have either the *Run Flows* user permission or Force.com Flow User selected on their user record
- The user must have access to the Visualforce page in which the flow is embedded
- The flow must be active. Only flow creators can run inactive flows

More flows

We have seen the most basic use cases for flows. The flow designer can help us design very complex flows with multiple conditions. A few things need to be considered when designing a flow:

- It does not run a validation rule unless specified in the field's settings. If a field is marked as required while created, it won't be highlighted until the record is saved and throws an error.
- A flow interview is a running instance of a flow. When we distribute a flow, users interact with individual interviews of that flow.

- A flow can consist of multiple flow versions. Once we activate a flow, we can't make changes to it. We can, however, make the necessary changes to a new version of that flow and later activate the new version.
- We cannot delete an active flow; to delete a flow, we must first deactivate it. If the flow has an active interview (or is running), it cannot be deleted.

Automating time-based actions using workflows

A workflow is a simplified version of Process Builder. They work on a simple statement: if the condition is satisfied, do something. A typical workflow is shown in the following diagram:

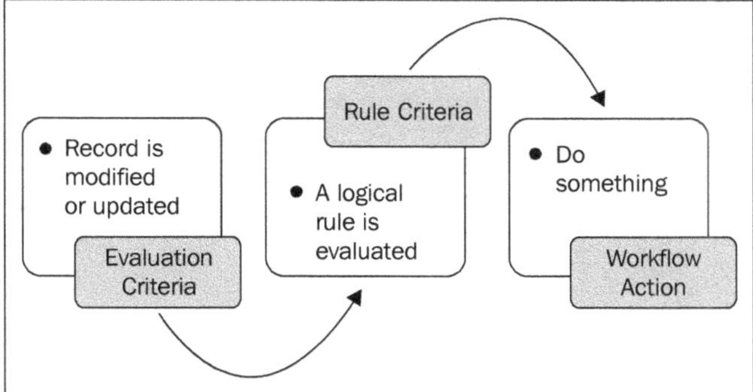

Exercise—sending e-mail to members

Library Management wants to send an e-mail reminder to any member who, seven days after taking out a book, has still not returned it. They have an e-mail template ready to send the reminder.

The following steps will illustrate how to create a workflow:

1. Navigate to **App Setup** | **Create** | **Workflow & Approvals** | **Workflow Rules**.
2. Click on **New Rule** to begin.

3. Select the object on which the workflow will be triggered and click on **Next**. In this example, we will select the **Customer–Media** object:

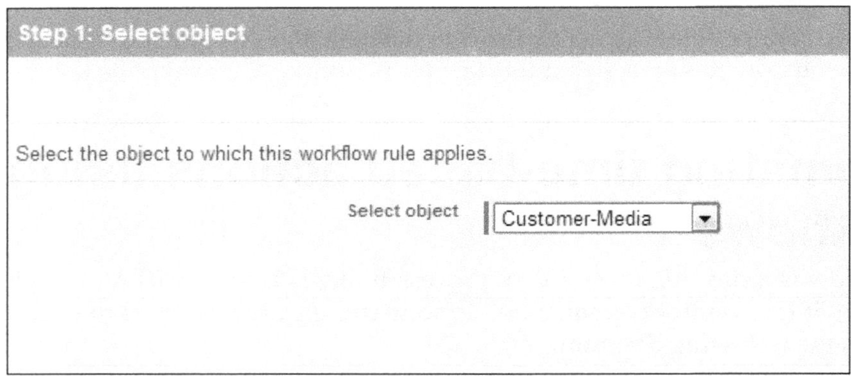

4. Give the rule a name: **Send an email**:

5. Select the **Evaluation Criteria**. The evaluation criteria for a workflow can be any of the following:
   - **When a record is created or when a record is edited and did not previously meet the rule criteria**: This rule triggers during creating and updating the object until the criteria are met. It is not retriggered once the criteria are satisfied.
   - **Only when a record is created**: This ignores updates to existing records.
   - **Every time a record is created or edited**: This option triggers during creating and updating records irrespective of whether it still meets the criteria. The workflow is repeated every time there is change in the value. We cannot add time-dependent actions to the rule if we choose Every time a record is created or edited.

6. For the purpose of the example, the evaluation criteria will be when a record is created or when a record is edited and did not previously meet the rule criteria:

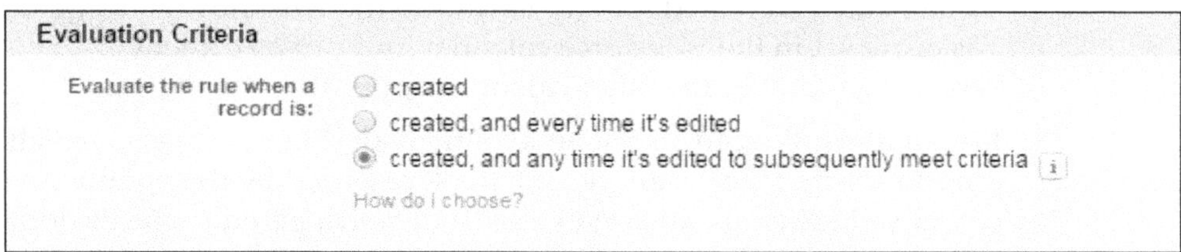

Rule Criteria: We can create a formula as the rule criteria or select a rule. Select formula evaluates to true as the Rule criteria and select `AND(NOT( ISBLANK( Issue_Date__c ) ),ISBLANK( Return_date__c ))` as the rule criteria. The formula checks for the Issue Date and confirms that the book is not returned yet:

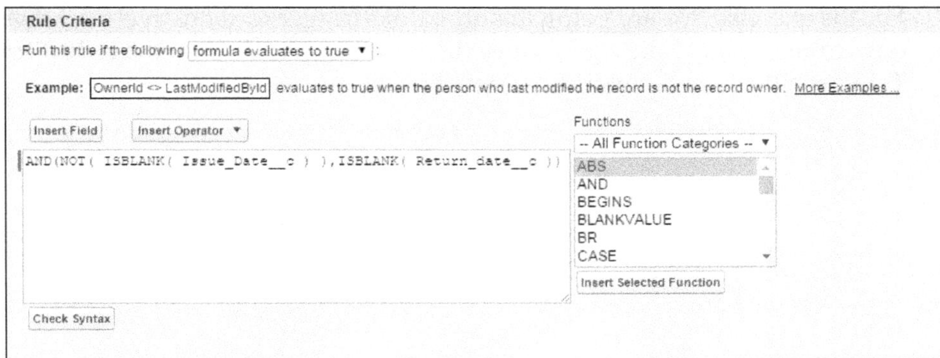

7. Click on **Save** and then **Next**.
8. We can add immediate actions, as shown in the following screenshot:

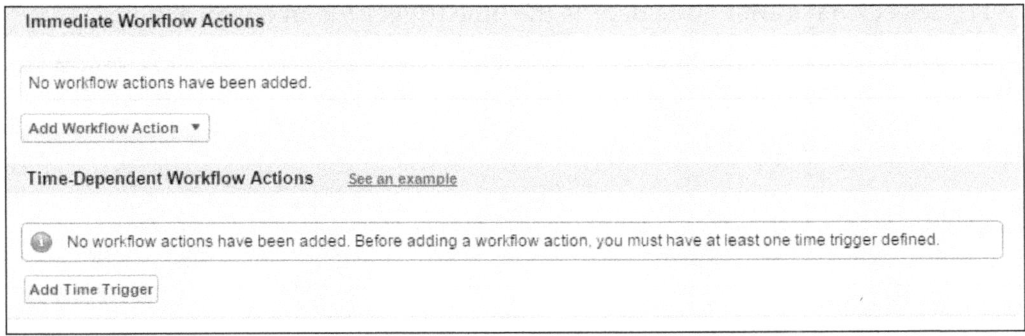

9. **Workflow Actions:** We can add different actions for the workflow to perform once the workflow rule criteria and the entry criteria are evaluated. We can add the following actions to the workflow:
    - **Task**: A task is created for any user once the workflow is triggered. Tasks are set in the Salesforce calendar and can be directly synchronized with the other calendar application by the user.
    - **E-mail alert**: We can also send an e-mail alert to reach recipients if the criteria are met. For example, if a book reserved by the member has recently checked in, an e-mail alert will be triggered to the customer to collect the book.
    - **Field update**: We can make an automatic field update after a certain criterion is met. For example, if we automatically change the status of the book once it is returned, we can update the field using this action.
    - **Outbound message**: An outbound message is sent to the external server or web service.
10. For the exercise, we are going to add a time-trigger to send an e-mail seven days after `Issue_date__c`. To add the time-trigger, click on the **Add Time Trigger** button on the workflow detail page:

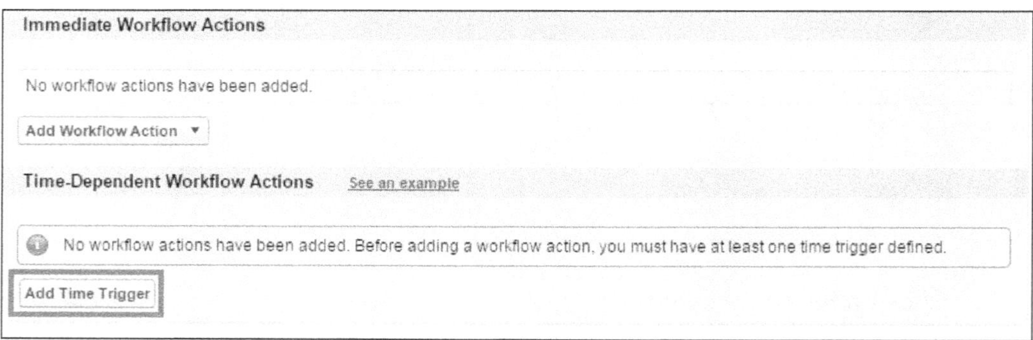

11. Select 7 days after Issue date as the time trigger for an e-mail action:

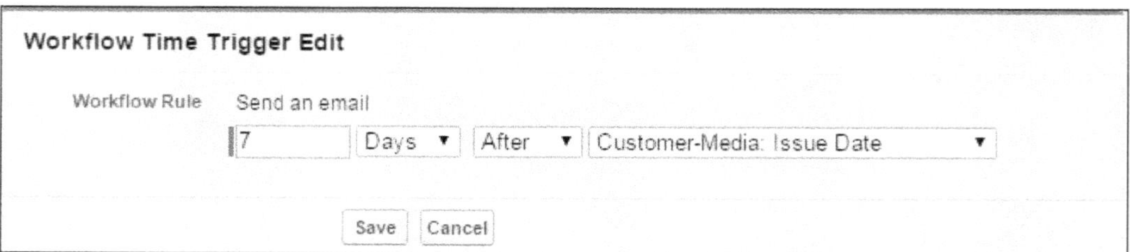

12. Now that we have a time trigger, we can add one of the four actions discussed earlier. For example, we will select send an e-mail as an action:

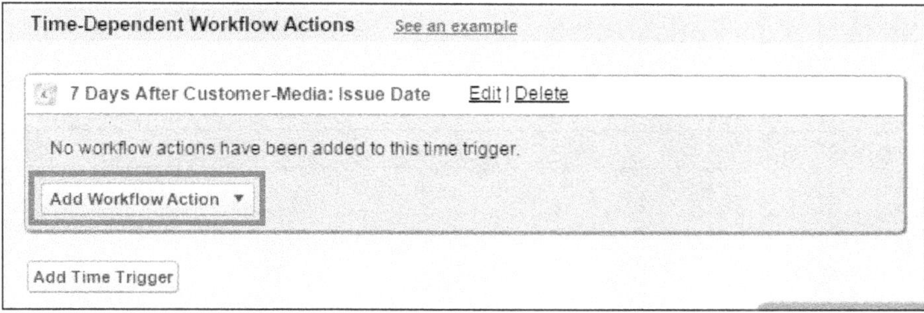

13. On selecting E-mail as an action, a new window opens to configure the e-mail action.

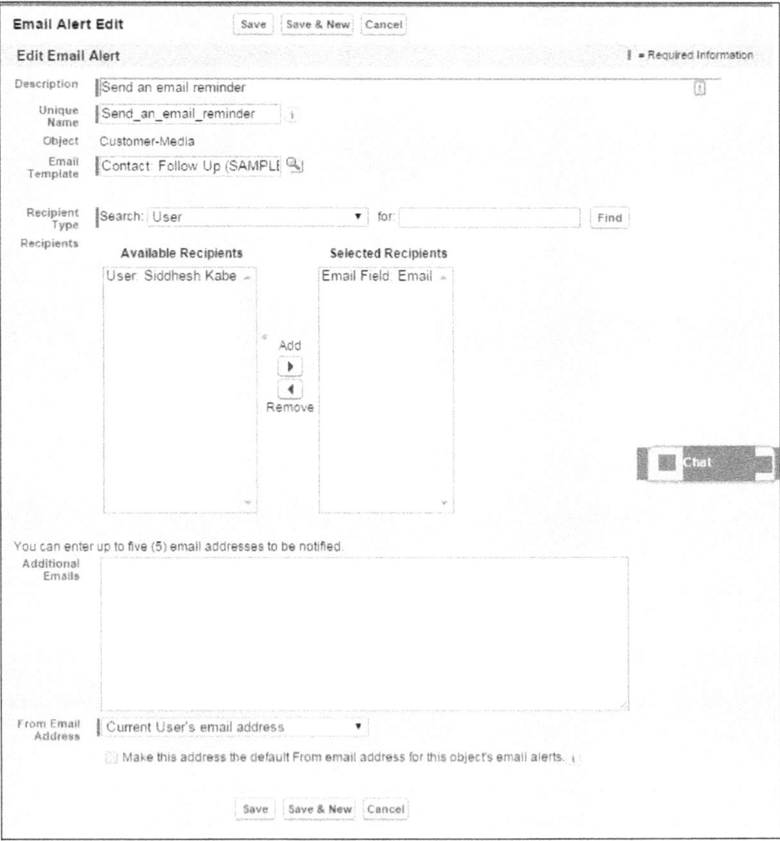

14. We can choose any `email` type field as a Recipient type, and select a template to send an e-mail. Click on **OK** to return to the workflow.
15. Click on the **Done** option to complete the workflow. Once we finish designing the workflow, it has to be activated:

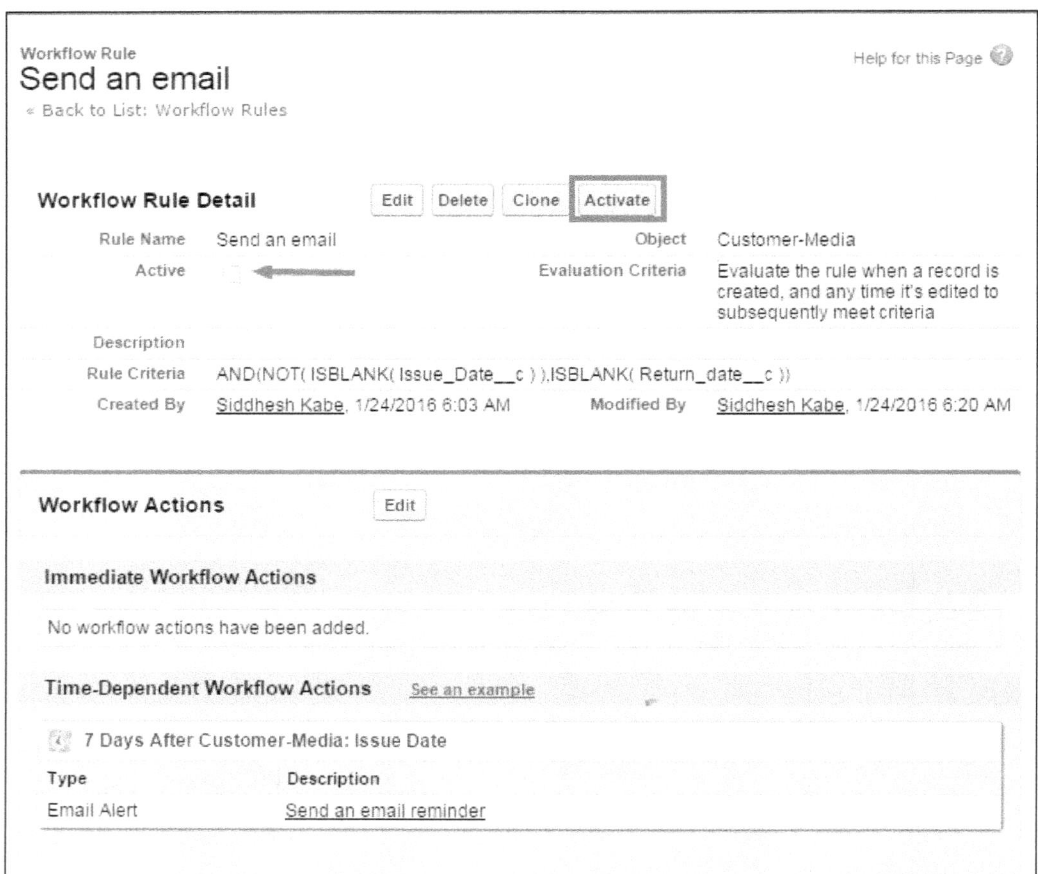

A few things to consider when writing a time-dependent workflow

A time-dependent workflow cannot be used if the Evaluation Criteria is set to Every time a record is created or updated.

> The effects of the workflow cannot be immediately seen; however, pending actions can be monitored using the time-based workflow queue.
>
> To see the queue, navigate to **Administration Setup** | **Monitoring** | **Time-Based Workflow**.

If the record has an action pending in the queue and the workflow is modified and does not meet the criteria, the pending action is canceled. For example, in the preceding example, if the workflow is fired today with the time-dependent action set for seven days later, and if between seven days, the record is changed and it no longer satisfies the entry criteria, the time-dependent action is canceled.

Improving productivity using the automated approval process

Apart from automating the process workflows, Force.com also provides a system to automate the approval process. The difference between workflows and an approval process is that an approval process requires a manual decision between the flows. A typical approval process flow is as follows:

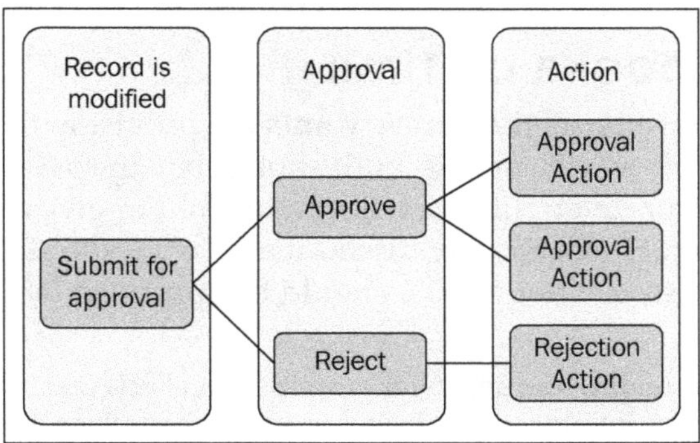

Creating a multi-step approval process

An approval process can be a single step or multiple steps. At every approval stage, we can add a set of actions. The following diagram shows the visualization of a multi-stage approval process:

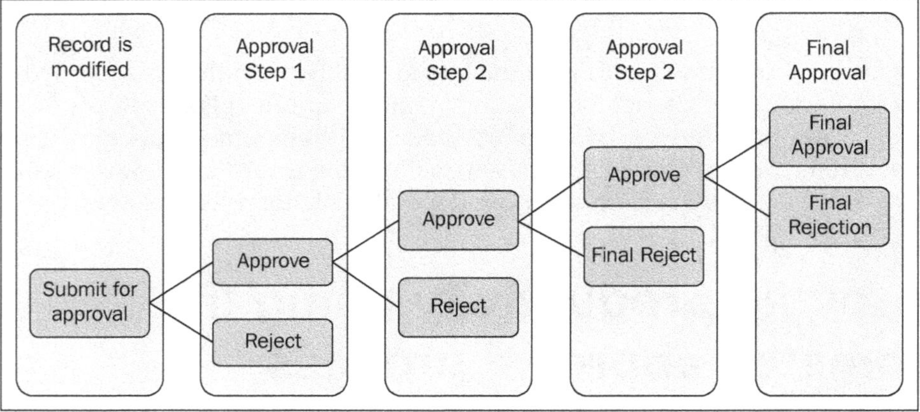

Let's create a multi-step approval process.

Exercise-special circumstances when customers fail to return books on time

Since time is a subjective term, the library wants the provision to provide a discount on the fine collected. However, the discount should be approved by the head librarian and supervisor. Every librarian is empowered to give a discount of up to 5% for every customer. However, any discount above 5% should be approved by the supervisor and any discount above 50% should be approved by the head librarian.

> Before creating the approval process, first check whether all the items required for the approval process are in place. We will define the approval process e-mail template. We need to determine who is submitting an approval to whom. We also need to determine how many approval steps are needed. We will need a new `Discount_on_Fine__c` field of the Percent (2,0) type on the `Customer__c` object for this approval process.

The steps to create an **Approval Process** are as follows:

1. Navigate to **User Name | Setup | App Setup | Create | Workflow & Approvals | Approval Process.**
2. Select the **Customer__c** object for which we need the **Approval Process,** and click on **User Standard Setup Wizard.**
3. Enter the unique name **Customer Discount Approval** and process name, and click on **Next.**
4. Specify the entry criteria. The **Entry Criteria** define which records when submitted for approval should enter this approval process. An object may have multiple approval processes defined; when a record is submitted, each approval process is evaluated in order, and the first one whose entry criteria matches the record uses that approval process. This is exactly how Assignment Rules operate with Leads and Cases. For this example, only those records that have a discount greater than 5% will be entered. Then, click on **Next**:

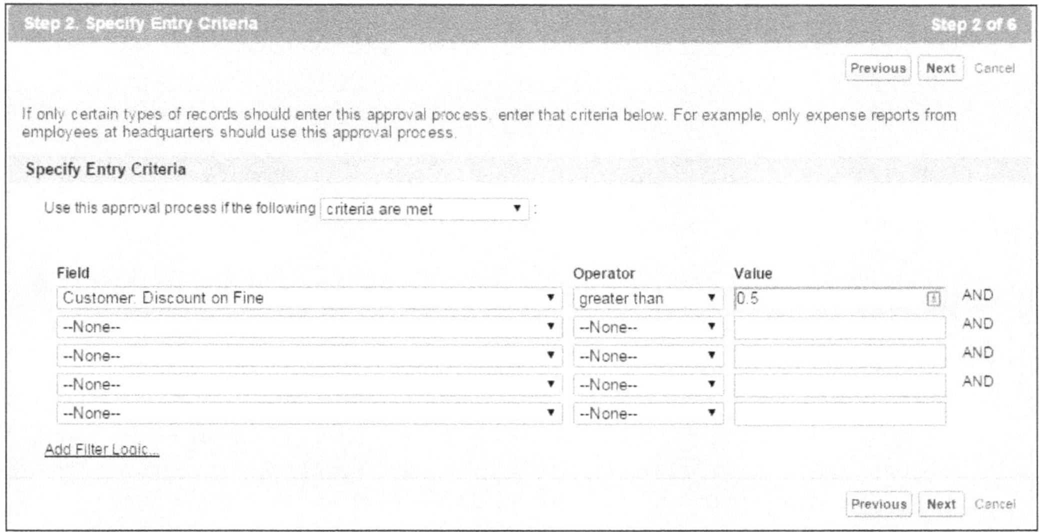

5. In the next step, we can select the field for **Automated Approval Routing**. We can assign the approval process dynamically to the manager of the submitter using this option, as shown in the following screenshot:

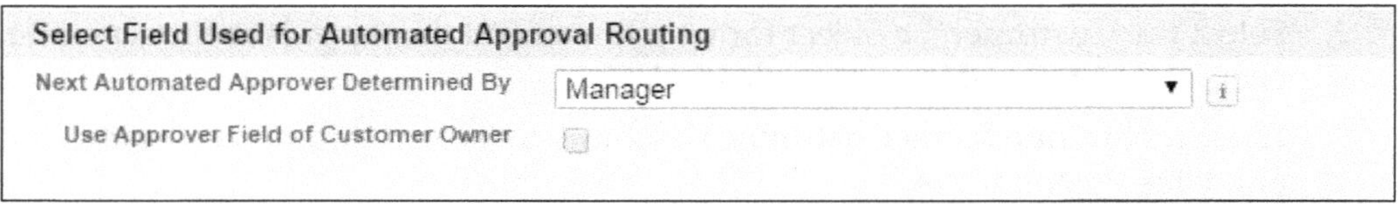

> If the approver is not the direct reporting manager to the submitter or if the Manager field is empty for the user, this option can be set to blank and the approver can be selected on the basis of the step. This process also applies to the multi-step approval process where every stage has a different approver.

6. In the same step, let's select **Record Editability Properties**. When we submit a record for approval, it is automatically locked for editing and can be edited only when it is approved. Using this option, we can allow the approval user to edit the record along with the system administrator. However, the submitter can never edit a record after submission until it is approved, rejected, or recalled. Select **Administrators ONLY ...** and click on **Next**:

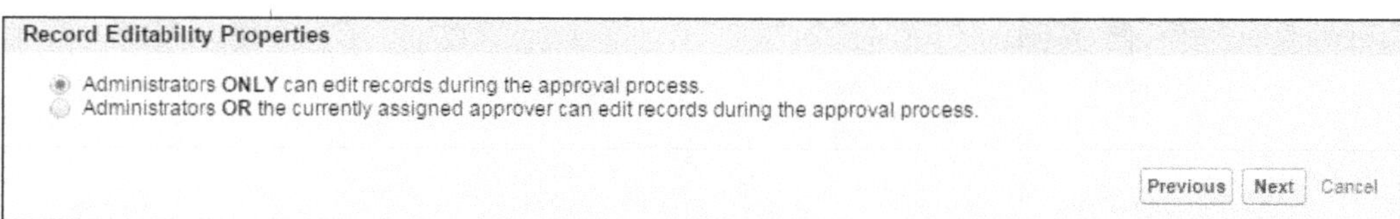

7. In this step, we need to select an **E-mail Template** that can notify the user of the record for approval. As the record moves through the different levels of approval, each approver who can approve the record receives the e-mail. However, for example, if the record does not reach the second approval step, the second approver does not receive this e-mail:

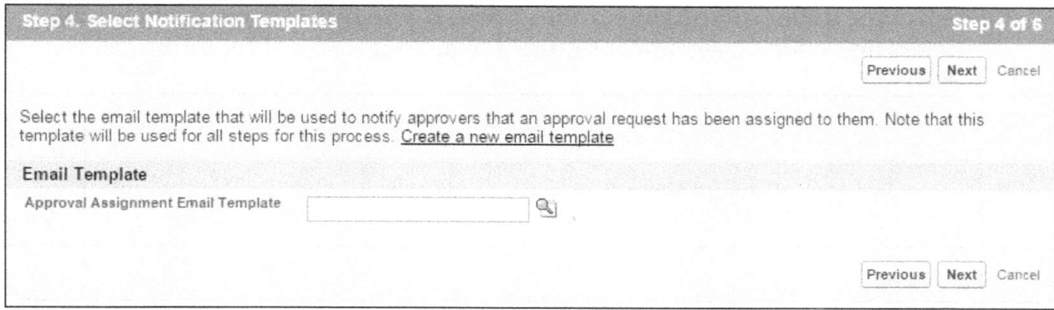

Please ensure that the e-mail template that is selected is available for use.

8. **Select Fields to Display on Approval Page Layout**. This is a quick way to view the record page where the approver will land after clicking on the link through the e-mail. This page should contain all the critical decision-making information. Select the important fields, such as **Discount on Fine** and **Fine** due, and click on **Next**:

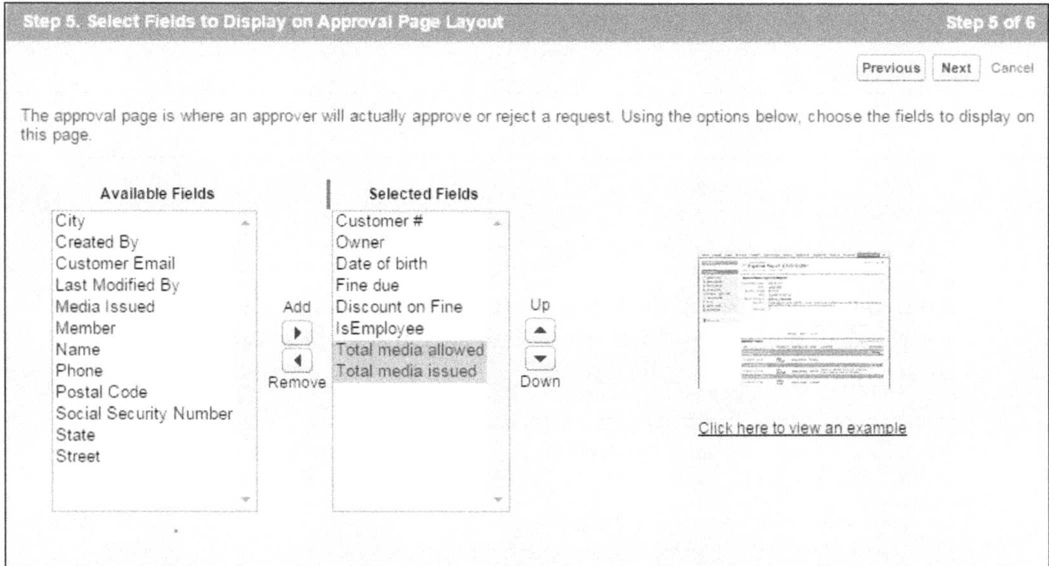

9. Select the initial submitters for the approval process. This option helps us determine which users are authorized to submit a record for approval:

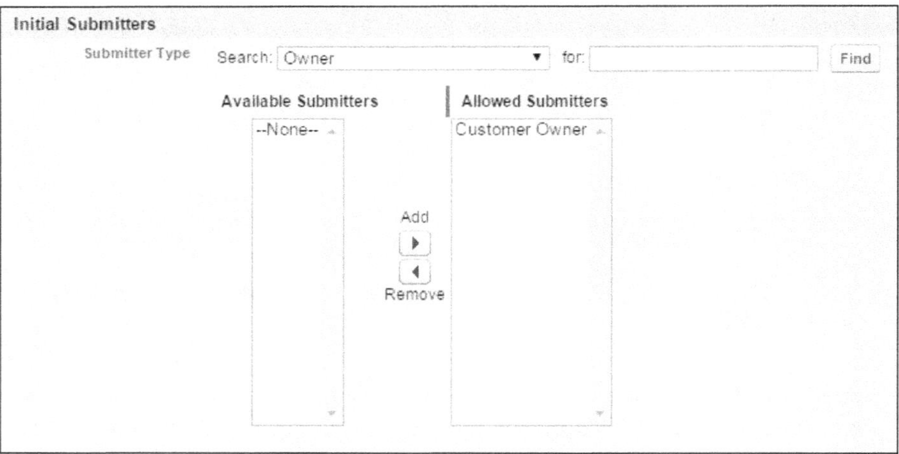

10. Also, in **Submission Settings**, we can select **Allow submitters to recall approval requests**. This option allows users to change their mind and recall the approval request, and then click on **Save**:

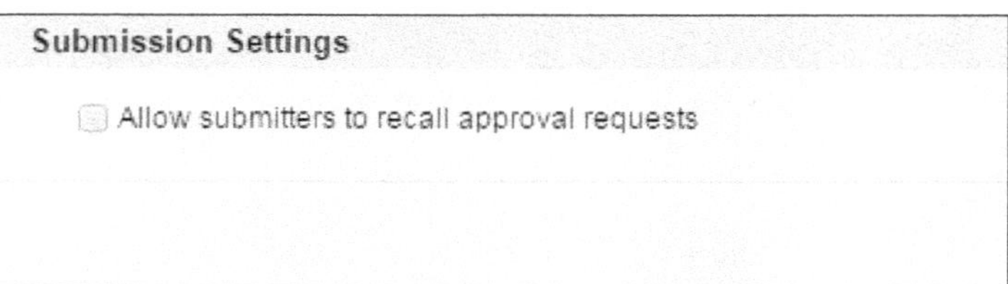

11. After clicking on **Save**, there is a decision box that appears saying that an approval step is to be added immediately. On selecting **Yes**, the wizard to create approval steps will pop up:

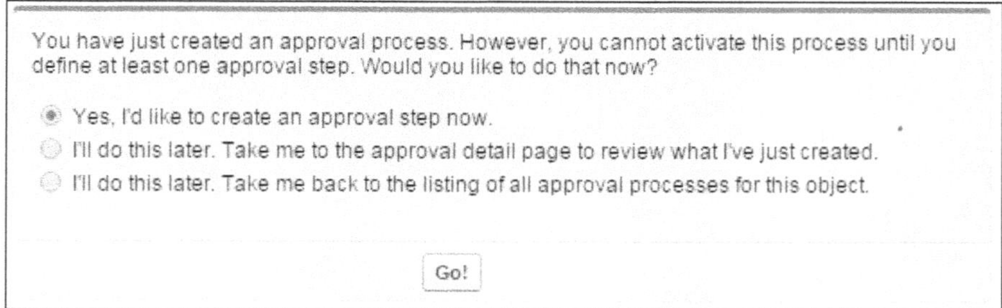

You have just created an approval process. However, you cannot activate this process until you define at least one approval step. Would you like to do that now?
Yes, I'd like to create an approval step now.
I'll do this later. Take me to the approval detail page to review what I've just created.
I'll do this later. Take me back to the listing of all approval processes for this object.
Go!

Creating approval steps

The approval process wizard helps us create an approval process. The next phase in an approval process is the steps where we determine which criteria the approval process should be routed through and to whom. The record filtration in the different steps can be visualized in the following diagram:

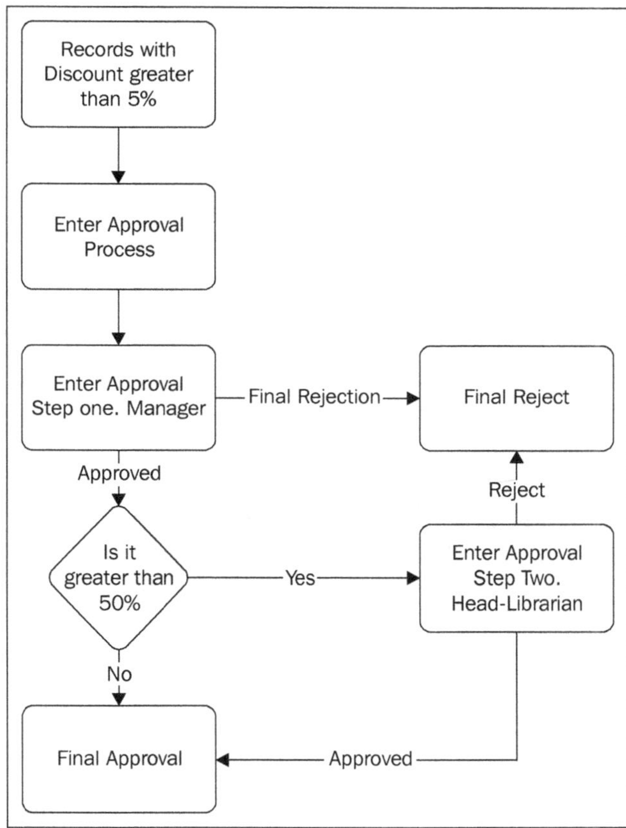

Note that in the *Creating a multi-step approval process* section, we did select the entry criteria for records to enter if greater than 5%; we will again subfilter them or let all the records enter the approval step, depending on the condition. For example, as shown in the preceding diagram, the main entry criteria could be discounted by more than 40 %.

However, there are two different managers to approve the discount from 40 to 50 % and discounts above 50 %; hence, we add further conditions in the approval steps:

1. Go to the **Approval Process** detail page. If we are continuing from the previous steps, then skip the first two steps and proceed to the third step.
2. Click on **New Approval Step**, which will open a wizard.
3. Name the approval process `Discount greater than 5%;` and allocate `1` as a step number, and click on **Next**:

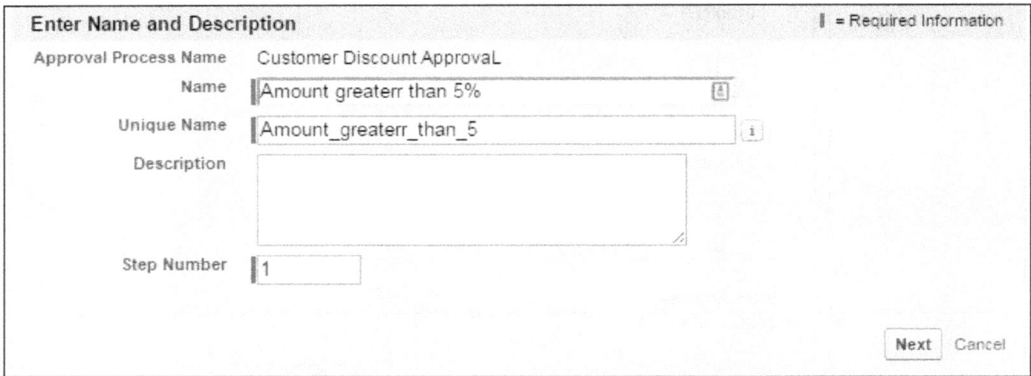

4. **Specify Step Criteria**: If we wish to filter the records for different approval steps or let all the records enter in the step. If we filter the criteria, we need to also mention what to do with the remaining records, that is, auto-approve or reject them. Because for the approval process we have already specified the criteria, all the records that enter this step will be greater than 5%; hence, all the records should enter this step:

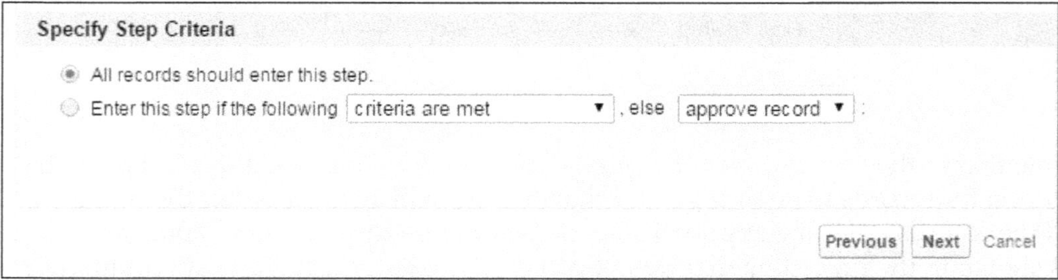

5. **Select Approver**: We have to select the approver for the record in this case. Apart from going to the manager for approval, we can assign the record to a queue of users or we can also let the user choose the approver manually. We will select **Manager** as the approver:

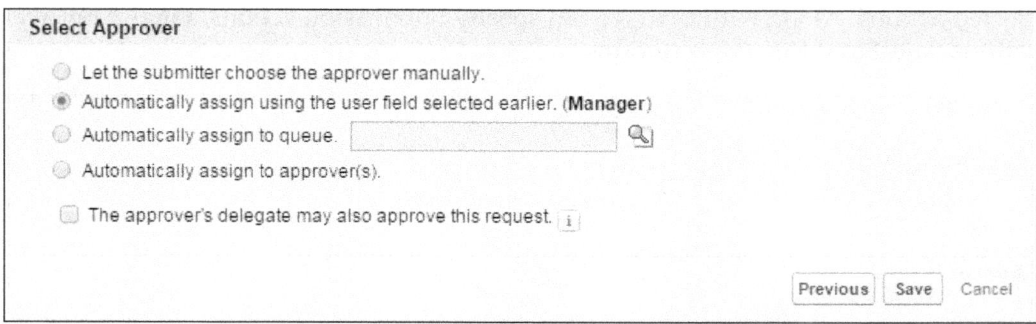
Select Approver
Let the submitter choose the approver manually.
Automatically assign using the user field selected earlier. (Manager)
Automatically assign to queue.
Automatically assign to approver(s).
The approver's delegate may also approve this request.
Previous
Save
Cancel

Also, we can directly specify the user or users who can approve the record. If the approval is assigned to multiple users (by selecting **Automatically assign to approver(s))** or if we select the checkbox for the delegate to approve the record, the manager's delegate can also approve it. This is called the **delegated approval process**.

6. This step gives us the option of jumping directly to adding the approval or rejection action to the step. The actions are similar to those of workflow actions, and we will come to that in the next section. Go to the **Approval Process** detail page to see the work that we did.

You have just created an approval step. You can optionally specify workflow actions to occur upon approval or rejection of this step. Would you like to do that now?

- Yes, I'd like to create a new approval action for this step now. Task
- Yes, I'd like to create a new rejection action for this step now. Task
- No, I'll do this later. Take me to the approval process detail page to review what I've just created.

Go!

Approval actions

An approval process uses the same actions as that of a workflow. However, we can add actions at every step in the approval process. If there are five steps, each of them will have two sets of actions each: one for approved actions and the other for rejected actions. Along with that, we can specify Submission actions, **Final Approval Actions**, and **Final Rejection Actions**:

We can specify the default actions that can occur when the record is:

- **Submitted**: By default, Force.com adds a new type of action to this step, which is a record lock. However, we can modify this action and unlock the record. This happens when a record is submitted for approval; a possible action would be a field update for **Status from Open to Under Approval**.
- **Approved**: These actions are executed when the record is approved in a step and is still in the approval process. Possible actions can be updating the status to **Approved by XYZ** or **Under XYZ approval**.
- **Rejected**: These actions are executed when the record is rejected in a step and is still assigned to someone else. Possible actions can include an e-mail alert sent to the submitter stating that it has being rejected.
- **Finally approved**: The default final approval action is to **Lock** the record. It is recommended that the record remains locked to prevent the user from editing. These actions are executed at the end of the approval process when the record is finally moved out of it. Possible actions can be updating the **Status** to **Approved** and an e-mail alert sent to the submitter confirming about the approval.
- **Finally rejected**: The default final rejection action is to **Unlock** the record. These actions are executed when the record is finally rejected with comments from the rejecter.
- **Recall action**: When a record is recalled, it is automatically unlocked. If the submitter has a change of heart once the record is submitted for approval, he can recall the record. This is possible only if we specify that the submitter can recall the record.

We can specify the action to any of the preceding steps. The actions are similar to workflow actions, and we can also reuse the existing workflow actions in the approval process.

A parallel approval step

A parallel approval step has many approvers in a single step. The approval process can be assigned to more than one approver; in this case, we have two scenarios:

- All the approvers need to approve the record unanimously
- A single person in the group can approve the record

A common scenario would be if you need to get an approval for an amount of more than 10,000 for a project; it will go to the project manager as well as the finance manager for approval. Both the approvals are required.

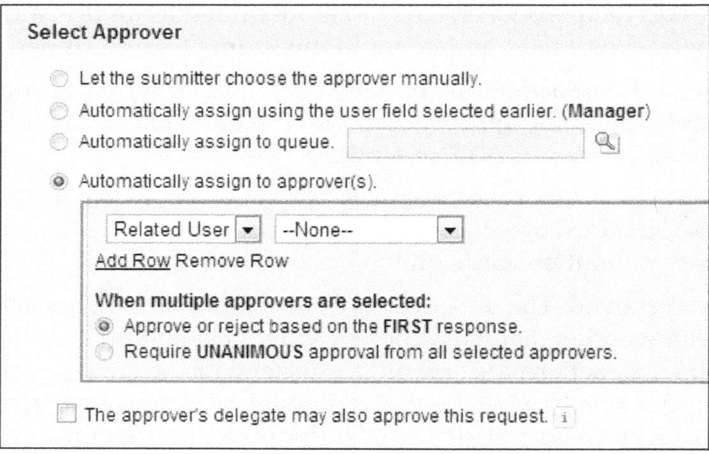

To create a parallel approval process, first create an approval process, as mentioned earlier. Then, perform the following steps to create the parallel approval step:

1. Go to the **Approval Process detail** page. If we are continuing from the previous steps, then skip the first two steps and proceed to the third step.
2. Click on **New Approval Step**, which will open a wizard.
3. Give the approval process a valid name and a valid step number, and click on **Next**.
4. **Specify Step Criteria**: If we wish to filter the records for different approval steps, let all the records enter in the step, or if we filter the criteria, then also mention what to do with the remaining records, that is, auto-approve or reject them.
5. **Select Approver**: Select **Automatically assign to approver(s)** so that we can directly assign the user or the related user.
6. Now, we can specify whether we need a unanimous approval from the user or a single approver is enough.

Comparing workflows and approval processes

Both workflows and approval processes help us automate business processes. Let's quickly have a recap of both:

Workflow rules	Approval process
Workflow rules are triggered immediately and automatically after saving	The record has to be sent for approval manually by clicking on **Submit for approval**
Workflow actions are executed immediately or are time-dependent	There is a separate action for each step of the approval process
They have a single set of criteria and action	This is a multi-step process
They are completely automated	This requires a manual decision at every stage

This covers automating a business process using workflows and approvals. It is worth noting that the records can be approved from any of the following places:

- In the chatter feed of the approver
- On the submitter's profile page
- In the chatter feed of the approval request record
- In the chatter feed of anyone following the approval request record, including the submitter
- In the company filter of every user with access to the approval record
- Users can opt out from seeing the approval post in their personal feed; however, they can still see it on the object chatter feed

In the following section, we will give an overview of the monitoring tools available for us to monitor running processes in the system.

Debugging and monitoring the process

Logs are used to record error and backend processes that are running in the organization. They store the following process information:

- Workflow and approval processes
- Assignment rules
- Escalation rules
- Auto-response rules
- Apex Script errors
- Resources used by Apex Script

Types of logs

There are two types of logs:

- Debug logs
- System logs

The debug log

We use the debug log to debug and troubleshoot workflows and approval.

Debug logs are stored separately and can be retained. They are stored on the basis of particular users only. We can download, view, and manage the debug log for users when **Debug Logs** are enabled for a user from the **Setup** menu. The next 20 actions will be logged, each resulting in a log file. An action may load a URL, such as clicking on a tab or clicking on a button. So, for example, if a user navigates to the **Account** tab, clicks on the **New** button, then clicks on the **Save** button, three logs will have been generated and the counter will have reduced from 20 to 17. Once all are exhausted, the administrator simply needs to enable logging for that user again. All of the validation rules, workflow rules, field updates, Apex, and so on that occur in response to page loads or button clicks are included in the **Debug Log** file generated. There is a limit of 2 MB per log and 50 MB per organization.

To set up a debug log, navigate to **Setup** | **Administration Setup** | **Monitoring** | **Debug Logs**:

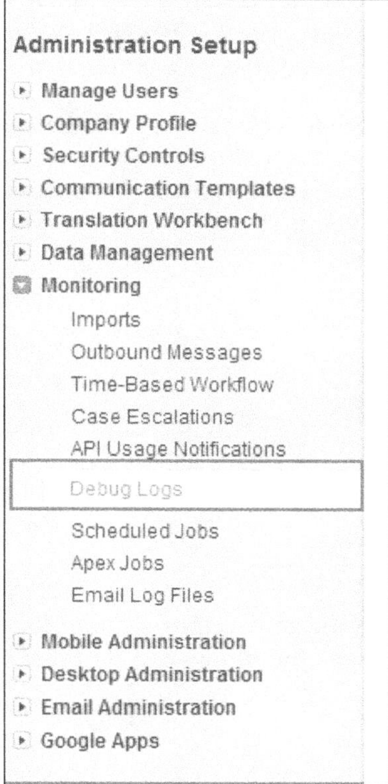

Click on **New** and add the user name to monitor in the box:

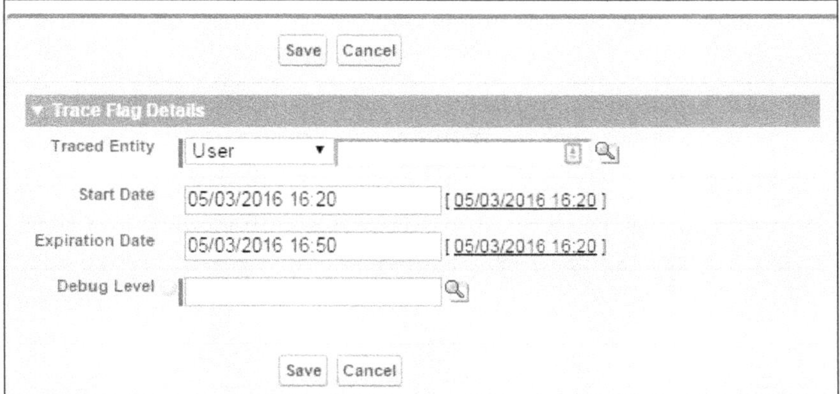

The Developer Console

The Developer Console auto-enables Debug Logging for the current user and makes it easy to reference the generated log files in the **Logs** tab of the Developer Console. As long as the Developer Console is open, the logs will continue to be collected regardless of the 20-log limit normally imposed when enabled via the Setup menu.

To start the system log, navigate to **Your name** | **Developer Console** in the top header of the page. The advanced developer console provides you with good tools to monitor and modify your system from the backend:

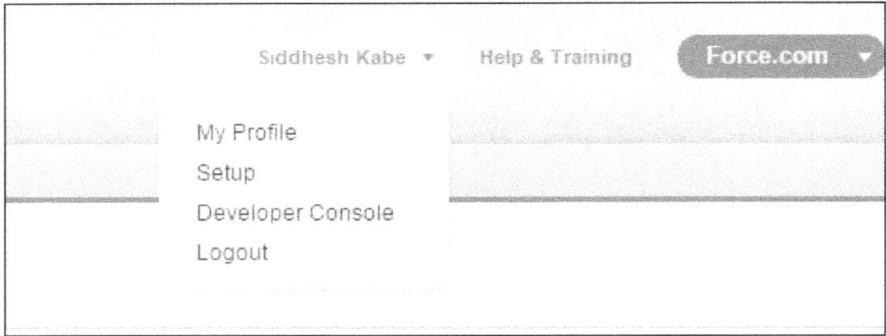

The system log will pop up on the screen. The system log will monitor processes as long as they are open, whereas the debug log will record 20 logs irrespective of whether it is opened or not.

Summary

In this chapter, we covered the basics of logic services provided by Force.com. The controller and the business logic are the most powerful tools behind every application. Using the Force.com powerful point-and-click mechanism, we can actually solve most of the critical business problems and automate the processes.

Thus, we complete creating the model-view-controller architecture on Force.com. We learned the basics of creating the model views and building the logic.

In the further chapters, we will proceed toward the fundamentals of building multiple user applications. We will discuss how to set up security and access control to data for users. We will discuss the data loader and massive data operations on Force.com.

Test your knowledge

Q1 Which one of the following cannot be viewed in debug logs?

1. Workflow formula evaluation results
2. Assignment rules
3. Formula field calculations
4. Validation rules
5. Resources used by Apex Script

Q2 Which of the following do we get as part of logic as a service out-of-box offering? [Select any three]

1. A data warehouse
2. An approval process
3. Workflow rules
4. Validation rules

Q3 Only a particular user with the right profile should be able to submit a record for approval. How do you achieve this?

1. Add this condition to the entry criteria
2. Choose the initial submission action
3. Add this condition to the approval step entry criteria
4. Add this condition as a rejection action

Q4 If the approval process has three parallel approvers in the first step, when will it move to the next step? Select any two options.

1. A unanimous approval is required and all the approvals are there
2. Majority approval is required and an approval majority is there
3. A unanimous approval is required and an approval majority is there.
4. The first approval is there and a unanimous approval is not required

Q5 Under what circumstances is a workflow rule triggered?

1. Automatically when the record is saved
2. When the user submits it for a workflow
3. When the manager submits it to a workflow

Q6 Which one of the following can't be a final rejection action in the approval process?

1. Locking the record
2. An outbound message
3. Deleting the record and sending it to the Recycle Bin
4. An e-mail alert

Q7 Using an approval process, an organization has configured the application to have the first step of the process require approvals from three different hiring managers.

Select the two possible approval choices based on multiple approvers for an approval step.

1. Approve or reject based on the first response
2. Require majority approval from all the selected approvers
3. Require x out of y approvals from all the selected approvers
4. Require a unanimous approval from all the selected approvers

Q8 You have created a time-based workflow rule. Choose from the following two ways to check whether the workflow actions are getting fired or not:

1. Check the time-base workflow queue
2. Check whether the workflow throws any error on the screen.
3. In the debug log, set yourself as a user and then check the debug log.

Q9 Which workflow evaluation rule doesn't support a time-dependent workflow?

1. When a record is created or when a record is edited and did not previously meet the rule criteria
2. Every time a record is created or edited
3. Only when a record is created

Q10 In MVC, a data model refers to?

1. Custom fields
2. Custom tabs
3. Workflow rules

Q11 In a Master-Detail relationship scenario where the fields of the parent object need to be displayed in the related list, how will a developer design this?

1. The cross-object formula field
2. A workflow rule
3. A validation rule
4. An assignment rule

Q12 In a recruiting application, a position that is of the "Critical" type should not be open for more than 14 days. How will you develop the business logic to cater to this?

1. A time-dependent workflow action to send an e-mail to the owner after 14 days
2. A time-dependent workflow action to send the record for review to the owner after 14 days
3. A time-dependent workflow action to send an e-mail to the owner before 14 days
4. A time-dependent workflow action to close the position after 14 days

5
Data Management

We have seen how to create different objects, fields, and relationships. We can now create a page layout for the objects and add business logic. Now that we have the backbone of the application, it's time to add data. Force.com provides us with some really efficient tools to manage, manipulate, and clean data.

In this chapter, we are going to learn:

- How to import large datasets using the data loader
- How to import data using the Data Import Wizard
- How to execute the data loader via the command line
- The different Salesforce IDs and why we use them

The basics of data operations

When an application migrates from the legacy system to Salesforce.com, a tremendous amount of data is present in the legacy system. This legacy data is crucial for maintaining the continuity in the business, and it can be exported from a legacy system in CSV format and then imported into Salesforce for further use. Similarly, data from Salesforce can be exported and shifted to a data center to create backups.

Difference between 18 and 15-character record IDs

The Force.com platform uses two different types of record IDs to identify each record. When we open a record in Salesforce, it uses a 15-character ID; however, when we extract the data from the backend, it uses an 18-character ID.

The 15-character ID is case-sensitive, while the 18-character ID is not case-sensitive. The 18-character ID is used to migrate data from legacy systems or spreadsheets that do not recognize case-sensitive IDs. Functions such as VLOOKUP in Excel do not recognize case-sensitive IDs, and hence, there is a risk of data corruption. Therefore, we use the case-insensitive 18-character ID.

The record ID can be obtained using any one of the following three methods:

- By analyzing the URL of the record detail page that contains the 15-character ID
- By running a report on the object, which will return the 15-character ID
- By downloading the ID using the data loader and fetching the 18-character ID
- Administrators can also create formula text fields using the `CASESAFEID()` function to get the 18-character ID

Getting the record ID from the URL

The easiest way to obtain the record ID is to fetch it from the URL. Whenever we open the **Detail** page of a record, we can see the ID of the record.

Let's take a look at the **Record** ID of the opportunity object. The URL of the detail page of the opportunity object is shown in the following screenshot:

The instance name is the server on which the organization resides. Salesforce is a multi-tenant environment, and so, multiple companies or *orgs* are hosted in the same instance. The record ID is unique for every record in the organization.

Record ID

The record ID in the Salesforce organization is case sensitive. So, `00690000003zRfq` is not equal to `00690000003ZRFQ`. Further, the record ID comprises two parts, as shown in the following screenshot:

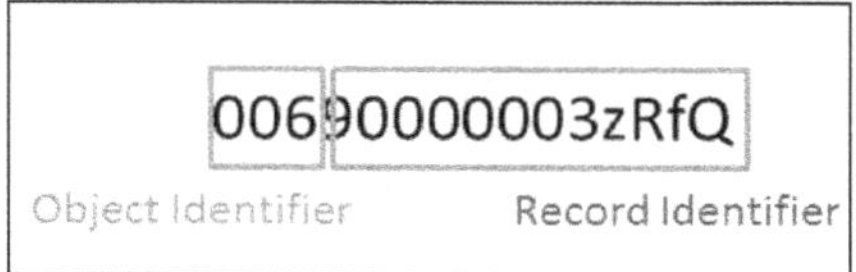

The first three characters of the record ID are the object identifiers, while the remaining characters identify the record. The following table shows us the three character prefixes and the objects that they are associated with:

Prefix	**Object Name**
001	Account
003	Contact
005	User
006	Opportunity
00e	Profiles
00Q	Leads
00T	Tasks
00U	Event
015	Document
01t	Product
500	Case
701	Campaign
800	Contract

URL manipulation

The URL can be manipulated to open a new page, an edit page, or a list view for the record. This is useful for quickly navigating to the desired page or adding a shortcut bar to the browser.

Adding a `/o` to the Object URL prefix will open the object tab, as shown in the following screenshot:

https://ap1.salesforce.com/001/o

Instance name Salesforce Server URL Record ID

Adding `/e` will open the **New** page of the object.

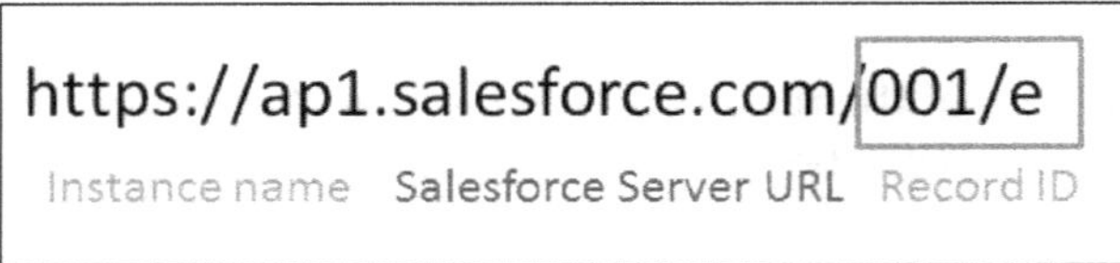

Similarly, when we add the record ID instead of the object identifier to the URL, we can navigate directly to the detail page or the edit page of the record.

Relationships - masters first

When we load data, we need to load it in the order of dependencies; for example, before we insert `Opportunities`, we must first insert the `Account` records.

Another example is to load **Opportunity Line Items**. We must first load both the parent records of Opportunity as well as **Price Book** and its **Price Book Entries**.

Modifying system fields

Salesforce automatically manages the system fields, such as **Created Date**, **Last Modified Date**, **Last Modified by**, and **Created by**. Normally, we are unable to set or change these values for audit integrity purposes. However, an administrator can contact Salesforce Support to enable the *Create Audit Fields* feature for a limited time to allow these fields to be set on the create operation only.

To find more details about how to create **Audit Fields**, go to `https://help.salesforce.com/apex/HTViewSolution?urlname=Considerations-before-having-Create-Audit-Fields-enabled&language=en_US`.

Features of modifiable system fields

Some of the important features of modifiable system fields are as follows:

- The fields can be modified only once in the lifetime of the initial insert.
- They are accessible through the API, that is, the data loader.
- All custom objects can have modifiable system fields; however, not all standard objects can have modifiable fields.
- Account, opportunity, contact, lead, case, task, and event can have modifiable fields.
- The fields are read-only for existing records. If you need to change these system fields for the existing records, then you must export the data, delete the Salesforce copies, then reimport the new data.

The CRUD operations

We can perform four different data manipulation operations using the API. The data is inserted in CSV format. The records to be manipulated are created as rows and the field API names are created as columns.

The `INSERT` operation allows us to insert bulk data into an object. The records are inserted without a `RecordID`.

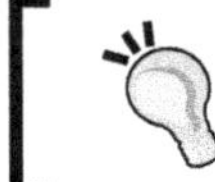

We can map individual fields to Force.com; however, to save time, we can initially extract a single record with the selected fields and use it as a template to quickly map other fields.

The `UPDATE` operation updates the record on the basis of the Record ID. If we do not provide the Record ID, the update operation will fail. The `DELETE` operation requires the Record ID and deletes those records. Unlike the traditional SQL systems, we cannot directly provide a delete query, such as `DELETE FROM` account `WHERE name = 'Acme'`. Instead, we must first query for the Acme account and then issue a delete for that ID.

We also have a `UPSERT` operation, which is a combination of insert and `Update` operations. The records that need to be updated are provided with the Record ID or External ID, and the records that do not have any Record IDs are inserted. As compared to traditional SQL databases, `UPSERT` is analogous to the `MERGE` statement, which will update a record that matches the criteria else insert a new record if no match is found. The `UPSERT` operation helps avoid duplicates based on IDs or external IDs. If more than one record is matched, an error is reported.

External IDs

When we are migrating data from an external system, we can link it with Salesforce records using an external ID. A custom field can be marked as an external ID to identify the primary keys of the legacy system. The `Text`, `number`, and `e-mail` fields can be flagged as external IDs.

Fields marked as external IDs are indexed and are available on all the objects that can have custom fields. External ID fields are searchable and appear in search queries.

An object can have up to seven external ID fields.

Exercise-migrating data from the legacy system

The general library wishes to migrate the media information from the spreadsheets they are currently using. They have a field called **Media Number** in the spreadsheet, which is a unique identifier (a primary key) in the current system. Migrate the data into the media object and avoid duplicates.

To migrate the data from the spreadsheet, we first need to create an external ID field in the media object. We discussed how to create a custom field in the object in *Chapter 2, Creating a Database on Force.com*.

Create a **Media_number** field in the media object in Salesforce; the field can be a text field. Check the flag for the external ID to flag it. While loading the data, use the **Media_number** field and use upsert to load the data.

Data loading tools

We can easily import the external data into Salesforce from any system that can save data in the comma delimited text format (`.csv`).

Salesforce offers two main methods to import data:

- **Data Import Wizard**: This is accessible through the Setup menu and allows us to import data to common standard objects as well as to custom objects. We can import up to 50,000 records at a time.

- **Data Loader**: This is a client application that can import up to five million records at a time, of any data type, either from files or a database connection. It can be operated either through the user interface or the command line.

When to use the Data Import Wizard	When to use Data Loader
• We need to load fewer than 50,000 records • The Data import wizard supports the object that we need to import • The data can be imported manually	• We need to load 50,000 to five million records • The Data Import Wizard does not support the object that we need to import • We need to schedule regular automated data loads

Using the Data Import Wizard

Once you have created an export file and cleaned up the data for import, follow these steps to import data using the **Data Import Wizard**:

1. To start the wizard, perform the following steps:
    - From **Setup**, go to **Administration Setup** | **Data Management** | **Data Import Wizard**.
    - Click on **Launch Wizard!**
2. Choose the data that you want to import from the following:
    - We can import accounts, contacts, leads, and solutions from the **Standard Object** tab and other objects from the **Custom Objects** tab.
    - Next, we need to specify whether we want to add new records, update existing records, or add and update records simultaneously.
    - Specify matching and other criteria. We will be matching records using their Salesforce ID.
    - In the last section, we will specify the file that contains the data.
    - Choose the character encoding method for your file. Most users will not need to change their character encoding.

- Click on **Next**.

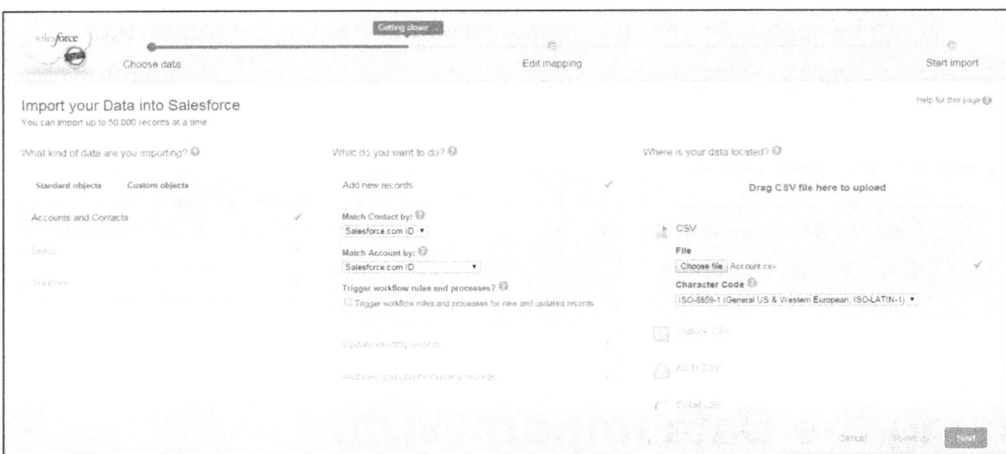

3. On the next screen, we are going to map the data fields to the Salesforce data fields.
4. The Data Import Wizard automatically tries to map as many data fields as possible to the standard Salesforce data fields. If some fields are unmapped, we need to map them manually:

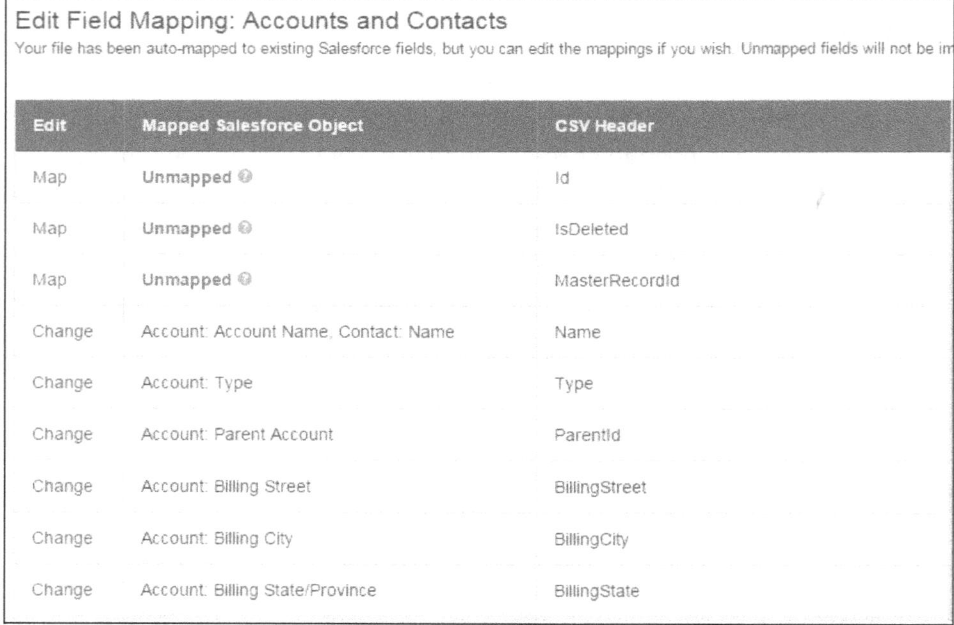

Edit Field Mapping: Accounts and Contacts
Your file has been auto-mapped to existing Salesforce fields, but you can edit the mappings if you wish. Unmapped fields will not be im
Edit
Mapped Salesforce Object
CSV Header
Map
Unmapped
Id
Map
Unmapped
IsDeleted
Map
Unmapped
MasterRecordId
Change
Account: Account Name, Contact: Name
Name
Change
Account: Type
Type
Change
Account: Parent Account
ParentId
Change
Account: Billing Street
BillingStreet
Change
Account: Billing City
BillingCity
Change
Account: Billing State/Province
BillingState

5. The fields that are unmapped are highlighted in **RED** in the second column. We can click on the **Map** link on the left-hand side of the page to manually map these fields.

   Select the Salesforce field to the map the column with:

   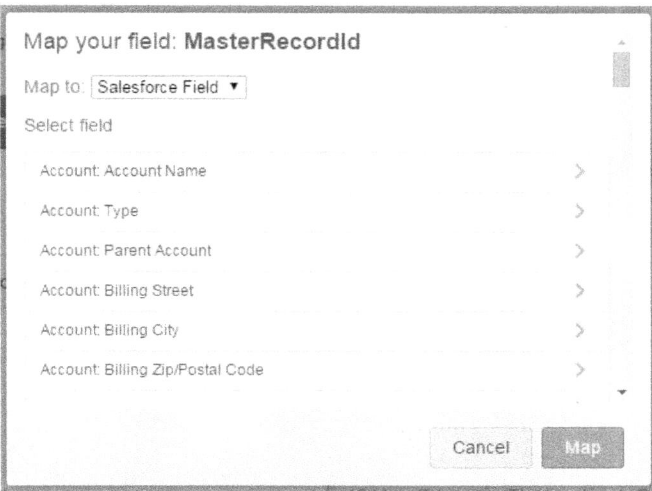

   To change the field mapping that Salesforce has already mapped, click on the **Change link**. Then click on **Next**

6. To start the import, perform the following steps:

On the next screen, the Import wizard will highlight the mapped fields and unmapped fields. It will also highlight the errors, if there are any, in the data. If everything is correct, click on **start import**:

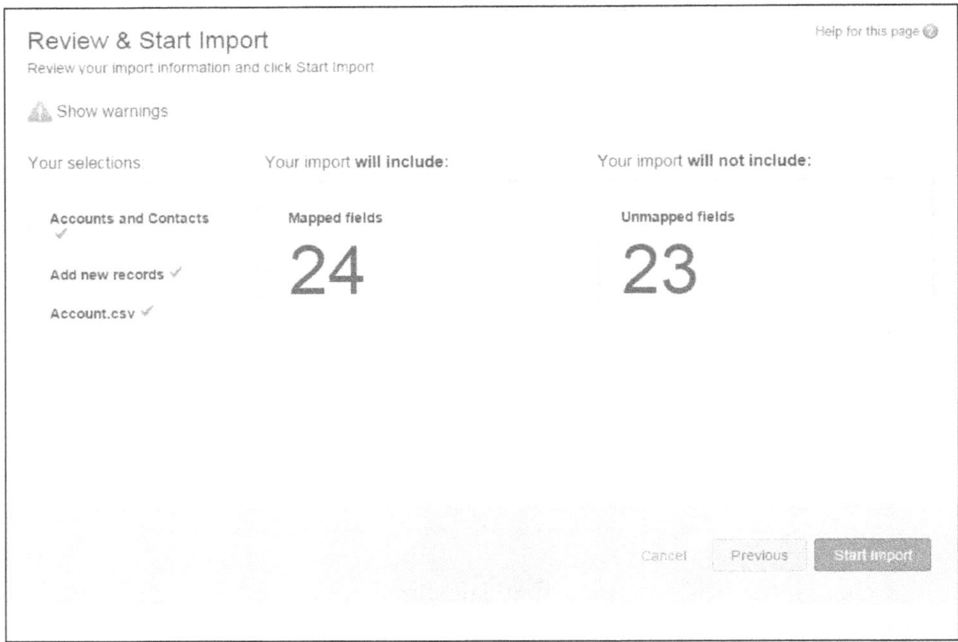

Apex data loader

The Apex data loader is a utility used to upload data to the organization. We can load any object that has **API_Access**. Unlike other tools, the data loader is not a cloud-based tool, but a desktop utility built for systems running on desktop systems. Some features of the data loader are as follows:

- The Apex data loader is available in unlimited edition, enterprise edition, and developer edition orgs
- It supports the **CSV** (**Comma Separated Value**) format to load data and export data
- It is a useful tool for backing up and archiving your office data
- The data loader also runs on the command line

Some salient features of the data loader are listed as follows:

- The Apex data loader is an API-based tool used to load Salesforce data
- We can load more than 50,000 records using it and also schedule data loads
- Data can be exported and mass deleted
- The Apex data loader can run from the command line
- We can export data for backup and mass delete
- We can also schedule the data loading at regular intervals
- Data can be imported and exported using CSV and JDBC

Downloading the data loader

Unlike the other features of Force.com, the data loader is not completely on the cloud. We need to physically download and install it on the machine to use it. To obtain and install the data loader, perform the following steps:

1. Navigate to **User name** | **Setup** | **Data Management** | **Data Loader**.
2. Download the **Data Loader**.
3. Launch **Install Shield Wizard** and follow the instructions.

Install the data loader in the machine before proceeding to the next section. In the next section, we will be loading data.

Using the data loader

The data loader helps us export data for backup, insert data, delete, and hard delete the data, as shown in the following screenshot:

Let's export some opportunities for the purpose of an example:

1. Click on **Export** on the **Apex Data Loader**.
2. If you are not logged in, it will ask for a login. Ensure that you append the security token to the password, as shown in the following screenshot, and click on **Next**.

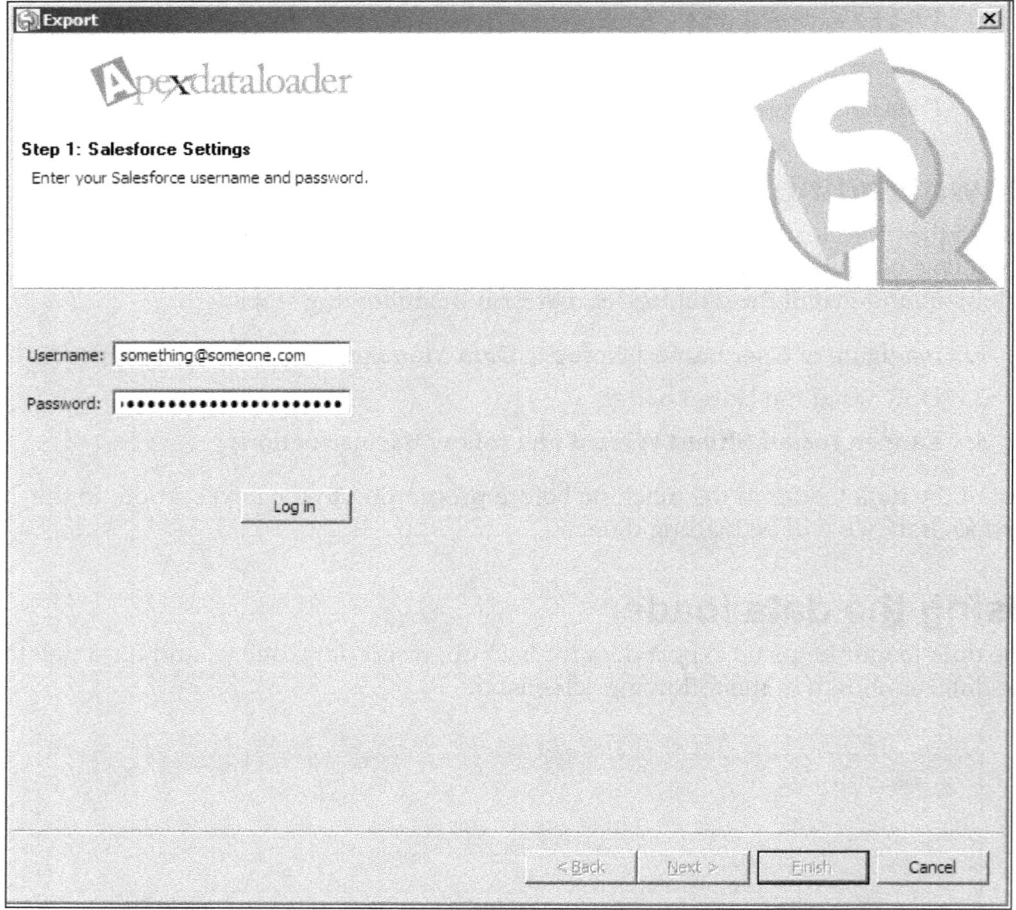

3. Select the object to extract the data from and the folder in which the data should be extracted. Ensure that you give the filename as `.csv`, as shown in the following screenshot, and click on **Next**.

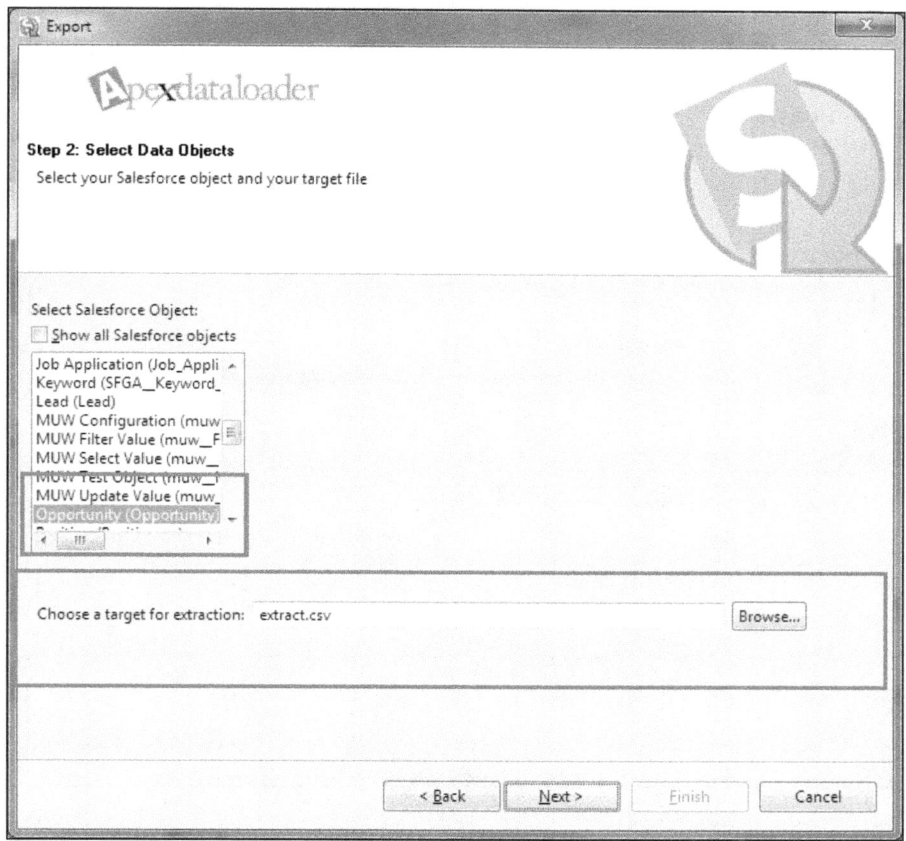

4. Prepare the query, as shown in the next screenshot. Select the fields to be downloaded from the field chooser situated on the left-hand side of the screen. We can add conditions to the query using the condition box on the right-hand side of the screen.
5. Don't forget to click on the **Add condition** button to add the condition to the query.

6. The final query is formed in the wide input textbox, which includes the fields and the conditions:

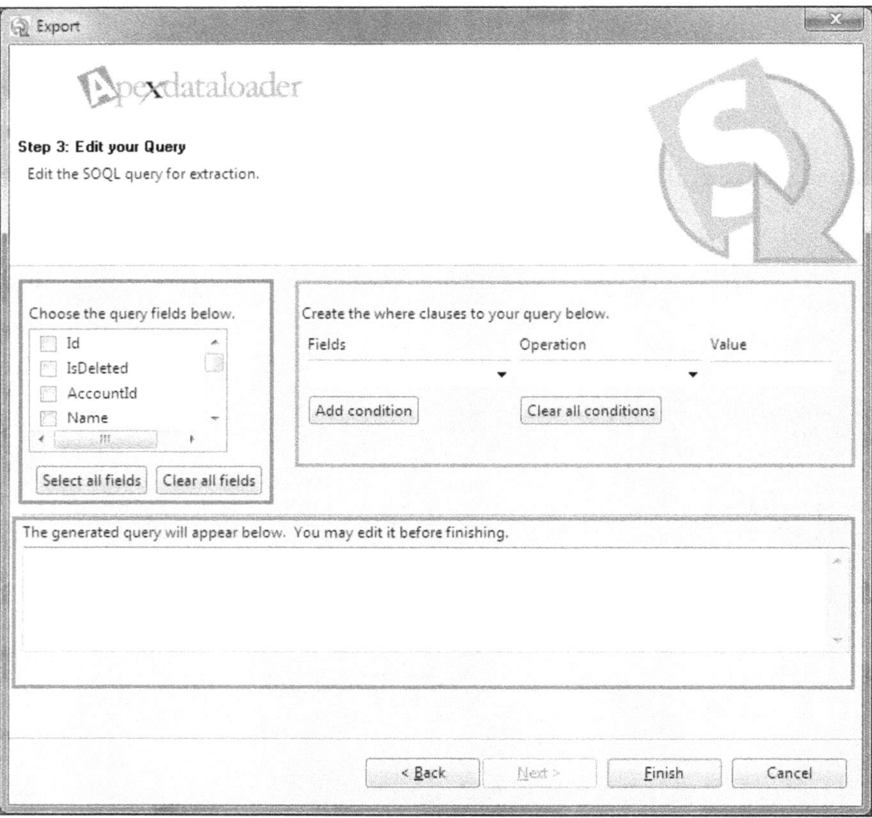

7. Click on **Finish**, and it will start extracting. If there are any errors, the final report will show two files: `success.csv` and `error.csv`.
8. Error files will have the reason for the error in the last column.
9. The finished data will be extracted to the file.

Upserting data

Now that we have exported the data, let's try to upsert the data. We are going to use the same export file as a template to upsert new records. It is easier to map fields on an exported file because Salesforce can automatically map the records.

Perform the following steps to upsert the data:

1. Click on the **Upsert** button on the main screen of **Data Loader**, select the object to upsert, and click on **Next**:

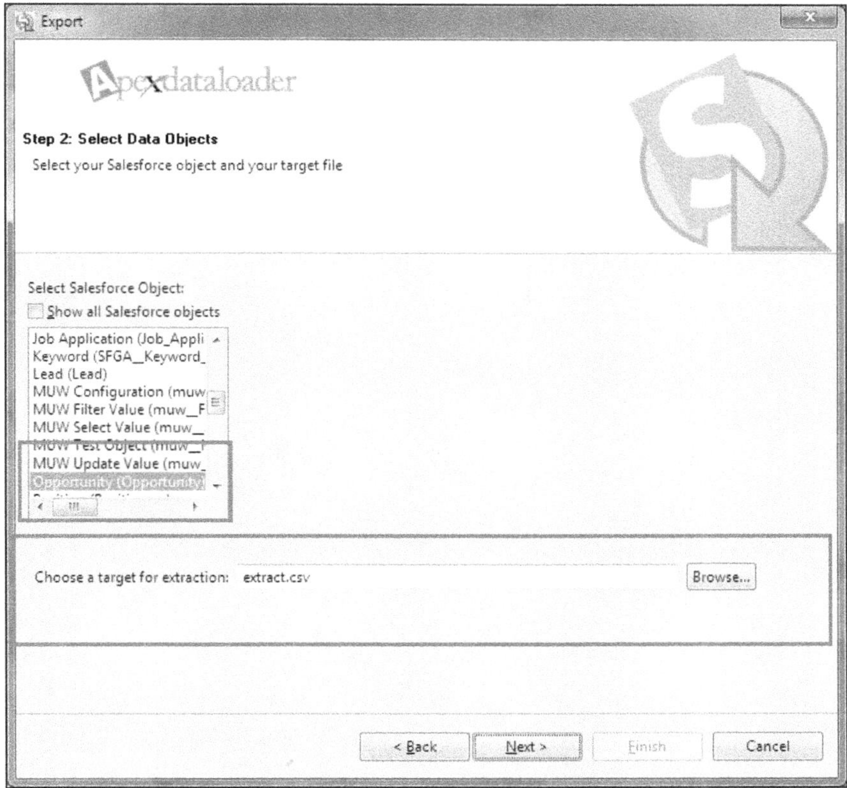

2. On the next screen, choose the matching ID. If there is an external ID field defined in the drop-down menu, there will be an option to select the external ID. This ID is used to determine the duplicates before loading.

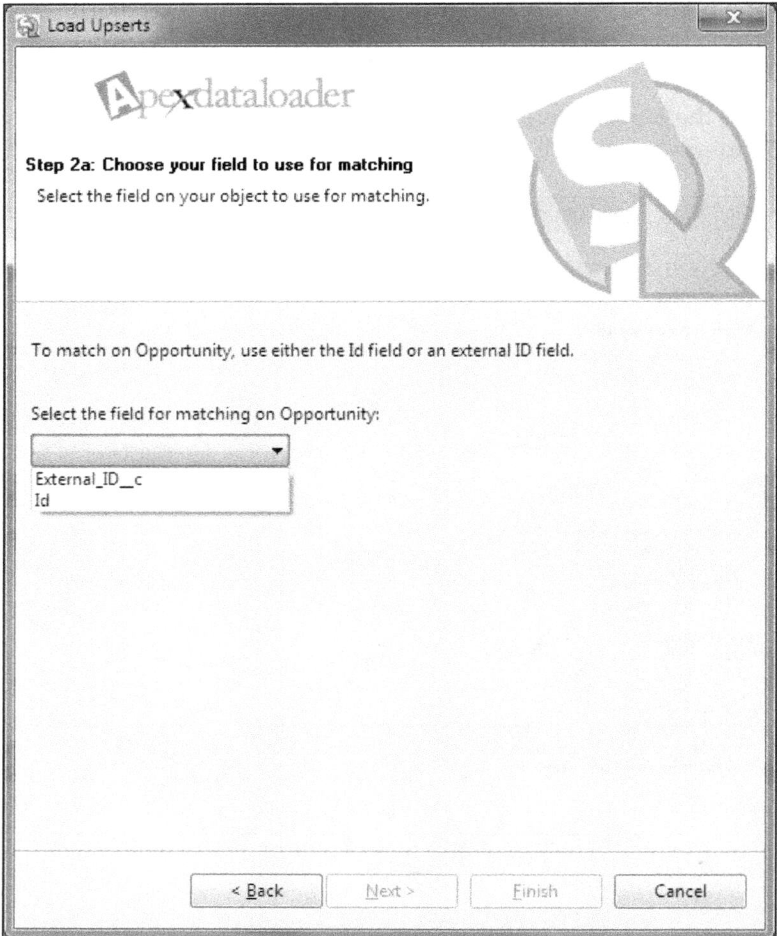

3. On the next page, we prepare the mapping to map the fields in the CSV file to the fields in the object. As shown in the following screenshot, click on **Create or Edit a map**. We can also save this map for future use.

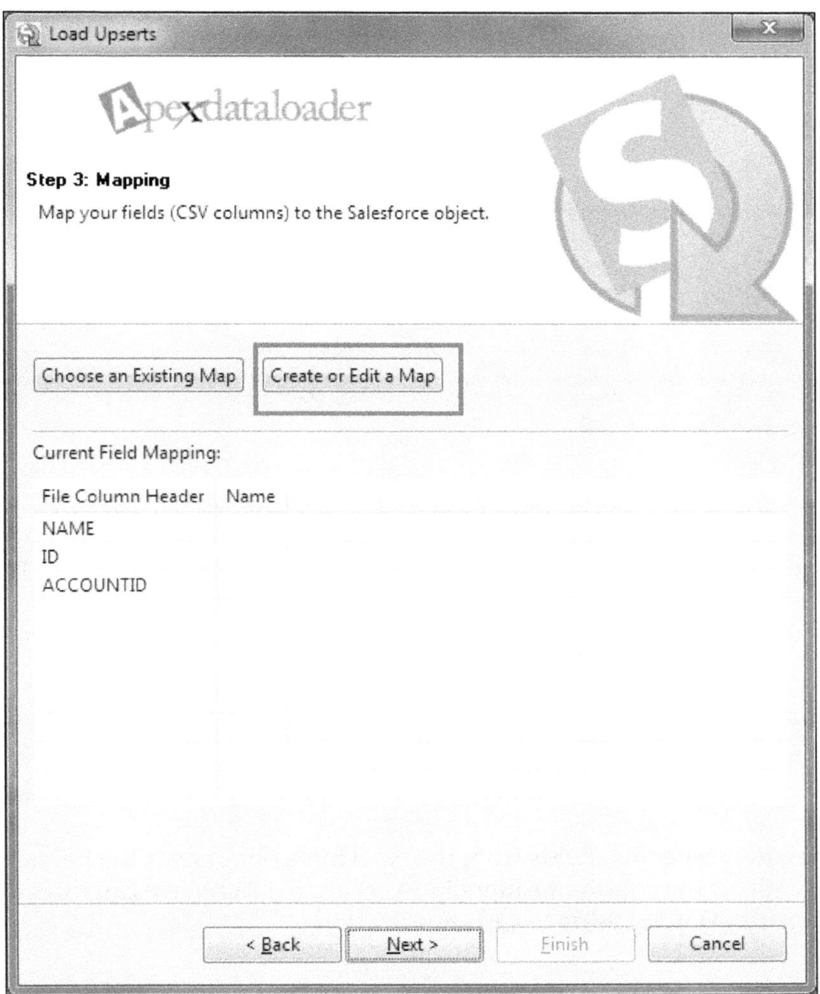

4. As shown in the following screenshot, we can map the Salesforce fields displayed on the top to the fields in Excel displayed at the bottom:

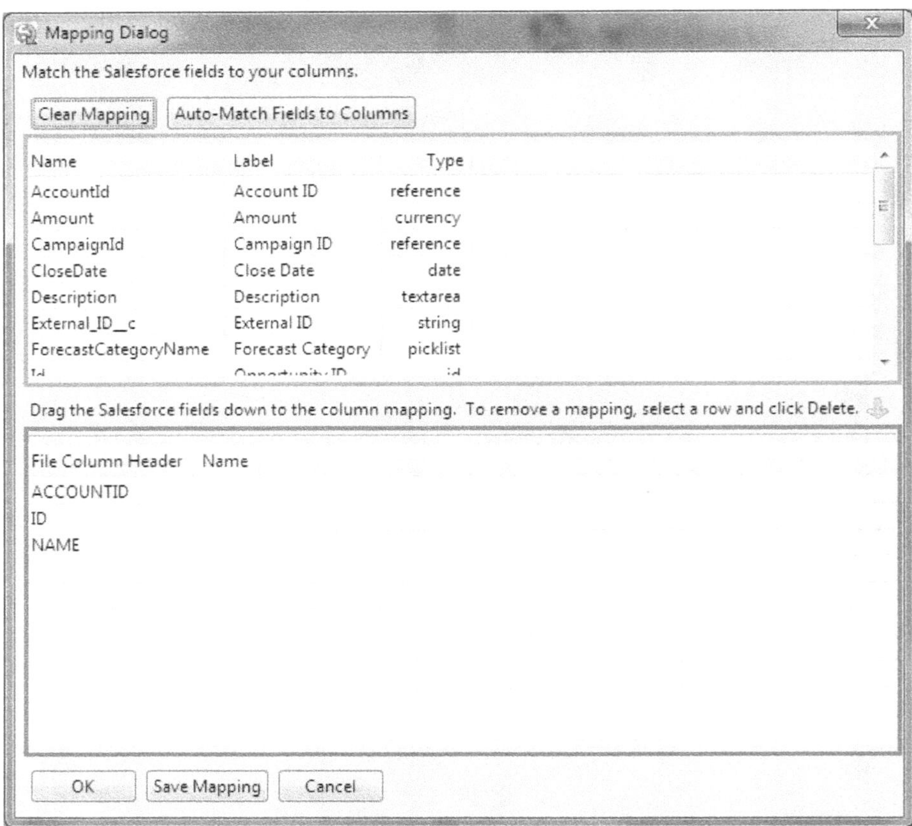

5. Drag the respective fields from the Salesforce object over the fields from the CSV file. If the column headers in Excel are the same, we can directly click on the **Auto-Match Fields to Columns** button.

6. We can also save the mappings in an external file for future use. Finish the mappings and click on **Next**:

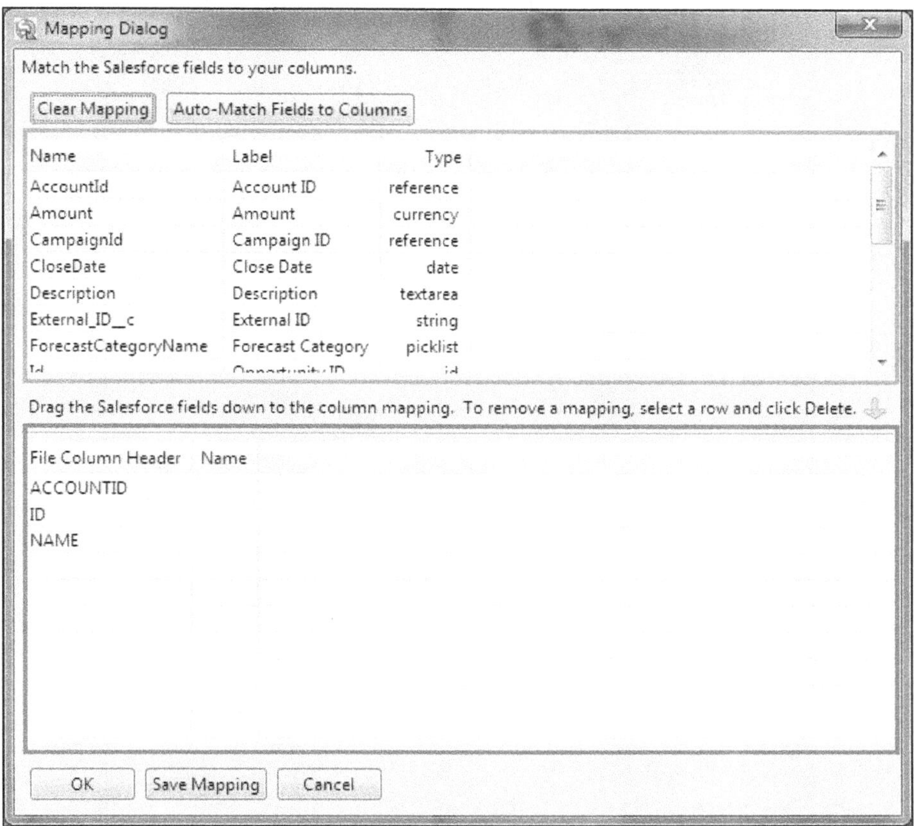

7. The wizard asks you to choose a directory in the next screen. This directory is where the success and error files are created. If some new records are inserted, the success file comes with the ID of these new records while the error file comes back with the error code:

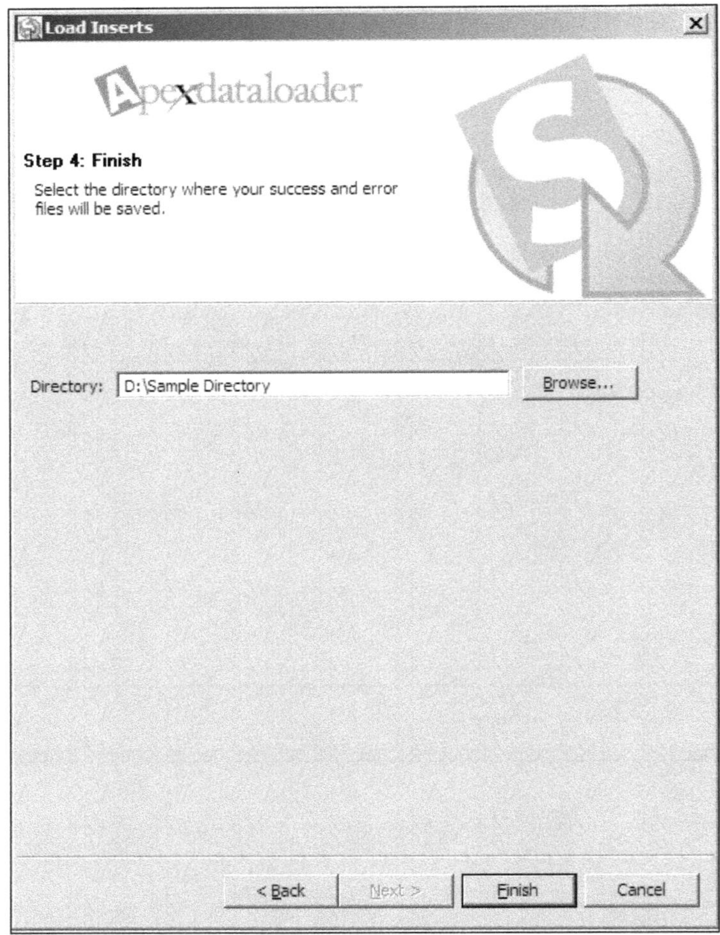

8. Select the **Directory** and click on **Finish**.

Thus, we have seen the commands of export and upsert using the data loader. The commands of insert and update are very similar to upsert. However, they won't allow mapping with an external ID. The operations of delete and update require a Salesforce ID.

Setting up the data loader

By default, the data loader is configured to operate using some default parameters. We can further configure it as per our requirements to improve performance.

The data loader by default works only with the production organization. To make it operable with the sandbox, we need to modify some parameters. Let's configure the data loader for the sandbox operation.

Go to **Settings** | **Settings in the Data Loader**. A new window will open, as shown in the following screenshot:

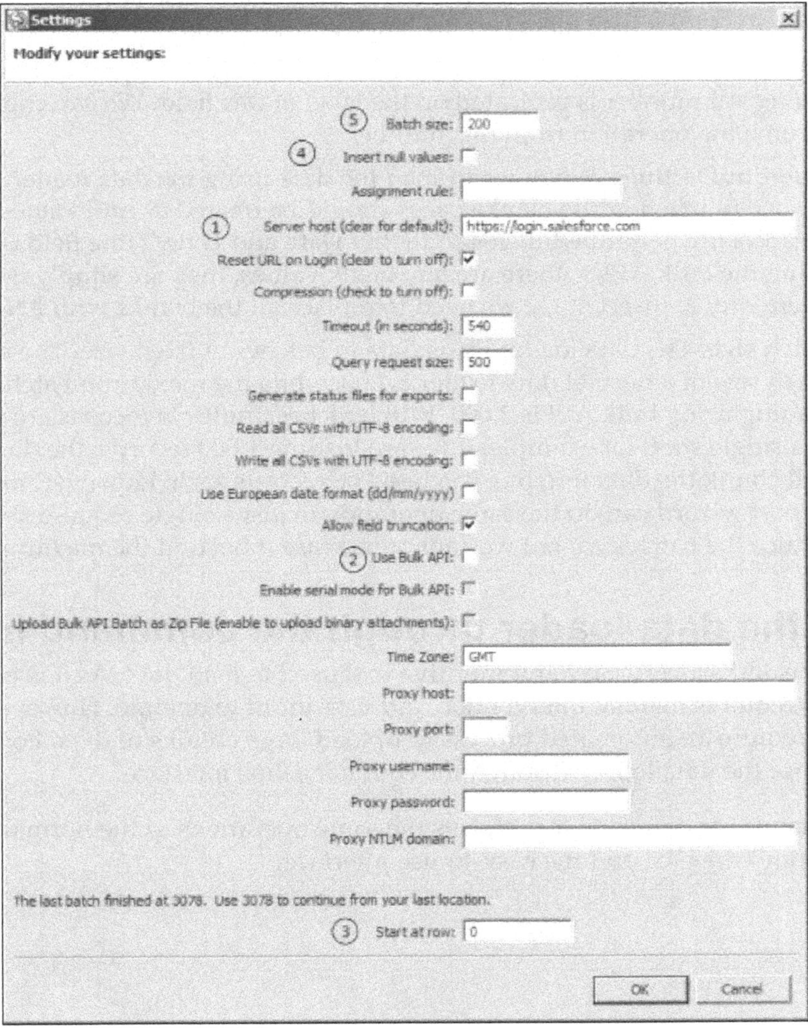

There are five major configuration changes that we need to keep in mind while setting up the **Data Loader**. Let's take a look at each one of them:

1. **Server host (clear for default)**: The server host is the endpoint URL where the data loader should be connected. By default, the server host would be `https://login.salesforce.com`. This endpoint URL is used when we upload data to the production organization or the free developer edition. However, when we upload data to sandbox, we need to change it to `https://test.salesforce.com`.
2. **Use the bulk API**: By default, the maximum **Batch size (5)** is `200` while uploading using the data loader; however, if the data is large, we can use the bulk API, which increases the batch size to `2,000`.
3. **Start at row**: If our batch operations are suddenly interrupted at any point, the record number is indicated on the label of this field. We can choose to resume the operation from this number.
4. **Insert null values**: When we upload the data using the data loader, we need to specify whether the blank spaces should be treated as null values. This is especially helpful while inserting the **Date** and **Date/Time** fields. When using the bulk API, if there are any blank values, they are simply ignored. Therefore, to insert `NULL`, we need to replace all the blanks with **#NA**.
5. **Batch size**: The data loader loads data in batches of fixed size. The maximum batch size of a normal data loader is 200, while the maximum batch size of loading using bulk API is 2,000. With batches, multiple records are inserted in a single shot; for example, if we are loading 1,000 records, the data loader will chunk the data into five batches, 200 records each. However, the data import wizard can do the same operation in just a single request. We can reduce the batch size, but we cannot increase it beyond the maximum limit.

Using the data loader through the command line

The data loader is a very easy and intuitive tool used to load data. As it is easy to use, it also requires manual intervention and user input to operate. However, many times, we require an automated process to upload large chunks of data. For these cases, we use the data loader through the command-line interface.

The command-line data loader performs the same operations as the normal data loader without the GUI and the easy-to-use interface.

Configuring the command-line data loader

Before we fire up the data loader with the command-line interface, we need to configure it so that it can perform the desired operations.

The main configuration file is the `config.properties` file, which is located in the `Data Loader` folder. The default location of the data loader is `c:\Program Files\salesForce.com\Apex Data Loader 35.0`.

For help with using the command line, the data loader provides the `-help` command.

As the command-line data loader runs on Command Prompt, we have very few options to customize and format the commands during the operation. To overcome this, we prepare some files that store the basic commands and configuration needed to run the data loader from the command line. Let's take a look at some of the files used in the operation.

Preparing the process-conf.xml file

The `process-conf.xml` file contains a description for every potential process that can be called from the command line. Each of these processes is referred to as a Process Bean. A sample `Process-conf.xml` file is shown in the following screenshot:

```
<!DOCTYPE beans PUBLIC "-//SPRING//DTD BEAN//EN" "http://www.springframework.org/dtd/spring-beans.dtd">
<beans>
    <bean id="accountMasterProcess"
          class="com.salesforce.dataloader.process.ProcessRunner"
          singleton="false">
        <description>AccountMaster job gets the Customer record updates from ERP (Oracle financials) and uploads them to salesforce using
        'upsert'.</description>
        <property name="name" value="accountMasterProcess"/>
        <property name="configOverrideMap">
            <map>
                <entry key="sfdc.debugMessages" value="true"/>
                <entry key="sfdc.debugMessagesFile" value="c:\dataloader\samples\status\accountMasterSoapTrace.log"/>
                <entry key="sfdc.endpoint" value="https://login.salesforce.com"/>
                <entry key="sfdc.username" value="user@mycompany.com"/>
                <!-- password below has been encrypted using key file, therefore it will not work without the key setting: process.encryptionKeyFile
                the password is not a valid encrypted value, please generate the real value using encrypt.bat utility -->
                <entry key="sfdc.password" value="5555555555555555"/>
                <entry key="process.encryptionKeyFile" value="c:\dataloader\samples\conf\sample.key"/>
                <entry key="sfdc.timeoutSecs" value="600"/>
                <entry key="sfdc.loadBatchSize" value="200"/>
                <entry key="sfdc.externalIdField" value="Oracle_Id__c"/>
                <entry key="sfdc.entity" value="Account"/>
                <entry key="process.operation" value="upsert"/>
                <entry key="process.mappingFile" value="c:\dataloader\samples\conf\accountMasterMap.sdl"/>
                <entry key="dataAccess.name" value="queryAccount"/>
                <entry key="dataAccess.type" value="databaseRead"/>
                <entry key="process.initialLastRunDate" value="2005-12-01T00:00:00.000-0800"/>
            </map>
        </property>
    </bean>
```

The section marked in the outer rectangle is a single process bean that holds the data operation. The following are its main properties:

- `Name`: This is used to identify the bean in the `config.properties` file and when we call it from the command-line interface, for example, `accountMasterProcess`.
- `sfdc.entity`: The Salesforce object that is the target of the actions. The value of this property is case-sensitive. For example, **Account** (note: Capital A).
- `process.operation`: This attribute identifies the type of operation, for example, `insert`, `upsert`, `update`, and so on.
- `process.mappingFile`: This attribute identifies the mapping between the fields in the source file (`dataAccess.name`) and the Salesforce object. This mapping file is an `.sdl` file. This file can be easily created from the GUI of the data loader.
- `dataAccess.type`: This attribute identifies the operation to be performed on the source file. For example, if we are using the ODBC data source, the property will read `databaseRead`; if we are including data from CSV, the property will be `CSVRead`.
- `sfdc.username`: This stores the Force.com login name for the command line run. If there is no owner name record specified, this will be the new owner.
- `sfdc.password`: The configuration file is stored as a plain text on the machine; storing the password in the file is not a good and secure way. `sfdc.password` and `process.encryptionKeyFile` serve the purpose of encrypting the password for added security. To generate the key and the encrypted password, the data loader provides the `Encrypt.bat` utility with its installation. We will take a look at the `Encrypt.bat` file in the next section.

These are the entities in the `process-conf.xml` file. This file has to be prepared every time we need to perform an operation. If we need to perform multiple operations in one go, the entire `<bean> </bean>` should be repeated with all the parameters inside it.

After we configure the desired files, we are now ready to run the operation. To run the command-line job, the data loader comes with a `process.bat` file kept in the `Data loader folder\bin\` folder.

To run the batch process, we run the `process` using the name of the command as input, `process ../accountMasterProcess`

In this case, `process` is the command given to run the data loader and `accountMasterProcess` is the name given to the ID in the `Bean` attribute.

Encrypting a password using Encrypt.bat

To log in to the Salesforce.com organization, we need to specify the password in the `config.properties` file. For security purposes, the password should be stored after encryption so that no unauthorized person can read it.

Salesforce provides us with the `encrypt.bat` utility, which encrypts the password from the plain text. The utility is available at the `Data loader folder\bin\encrypt.bat` default location.

`encrypt.bat` runs in the command line and supports the following commands:

- `Generate a key`: This command generates a key from the text we provide. Usually, we should provide the password with the security code in plain text format to generate an encrypted key.
- `Encrypt text`: This command performs the same operation as generating a key; it can only be used to encrypt the general text provided.
- `Verify encrypted text`: This command matches plain text and the encrypted password and prints a success or failure message.

Troubleshooting the data loader

If there is some error in the operation of the data loader, we can access the log files of the data loader. The two log files are as follows:

- `sdl.log`: This contains a detailed chronological list of data loader log entries. Log entries marked as INFO are procedural items, such as logging in to Salesforce. Log entries marked as ERROR are problems, such as a submitted record missing a required field.
- `sdl_out.log`: This is a supplemental log that contains additional information not captured in `sdl.log`. For example, it includes log entries for the creation of proxy server network connections.

These files are present in the `temp` folder of the system running on Microsoft Windows and can be accessed by entering `%TEMP%\sdl.log` and `%TEMP%\sdl_out.log` in the **Run** dialog box.

Other data manipulation wizards

Force.com provides us with some special data manipulation wizards that are used for some specific operations. The mass transfer records wizard is used to change the ownership of multiple users. The mass delete record wizard helps us delete multiple records in a single operation. Let's take a look at these two wizards in detail.

Mass transfer records

When we upload data records into the system, they can be directly associated with the owner of the record; however, if the owner is not specified, then the records are associated with the person who uploads the record. In this case, it becomes tiresome to change the users for every record, especially when the records are large in number.

To solve this problem, Force.com provides us with the mass transfer of records tool. It is a simple cloud-based utility that changes the ownership of the record from one owner to another. Let's see how to mass transfer the records from one user to another.

The mass transfer of records tool requires the `Mass transfer` permission for the profile, and edit and read permissions for the records being transferred. These permissions are available on the profile of the user.

To mass transfer records, perform the following steps:

1. Navigate to **User Name | Setup | Administrative Setup | Data Management | Mass Transfer Records,** as shown in the following screenshot:

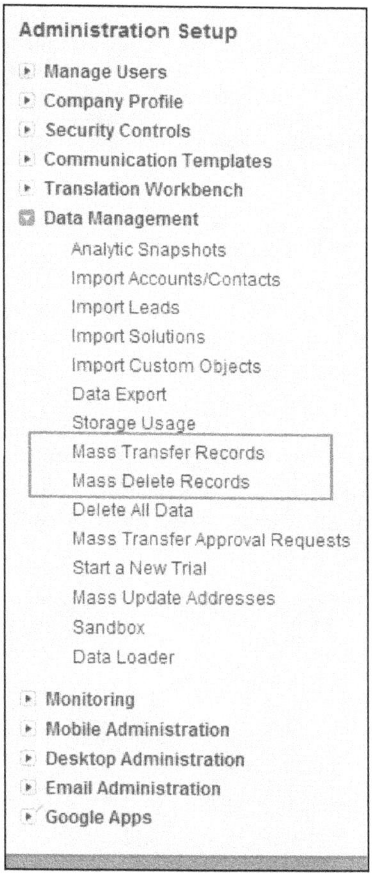

Administration Setup
Manage Users
Company Profile
Security Controls
Communication Templates
Translation Workbench
Data Management
Analytic Snapshots
Import Accounts/Contacts
Import Leads
Import Solutions
Import Custom Objects
Data Export
Storage Usage
Mass Transfer Records
Mass Delete Records
Delete All Data
Mass Transfer Approval Requests
Start a New Trial
Mass Update Addresses
Sandbox
Data Loader
Monitoring
Mobile Administration
Desktop Administration
Email Administration
Google Apps

2. Select the object to be transferred. For example, let's select the Media object and transfer the records from one user to another, as shown in the following screenshot:

Mass Transfer

- Transfer Accounts — Transfer multiple accounts from one user to another
- Transfer Customers — Transfer multiple customers from one user to another
- Transfer Leads — Transfer multiple leads from one user to another
- Transfer Locations — Transfer multiple locations from one user to another
- Transfer Media — Transfer multiple media from one user to another

As mentioned earlier, we need the **Edit** and **Read** permissions on the object records that are being transferred; only those objects for which we have those permissions will be seen on the page.

3. Select the user who we want to transfer the records from and the user who we want to transfer the records to. If we do not select the user to transfer records from, all the records filtered by the filters can be transferred. Click on **Find**:

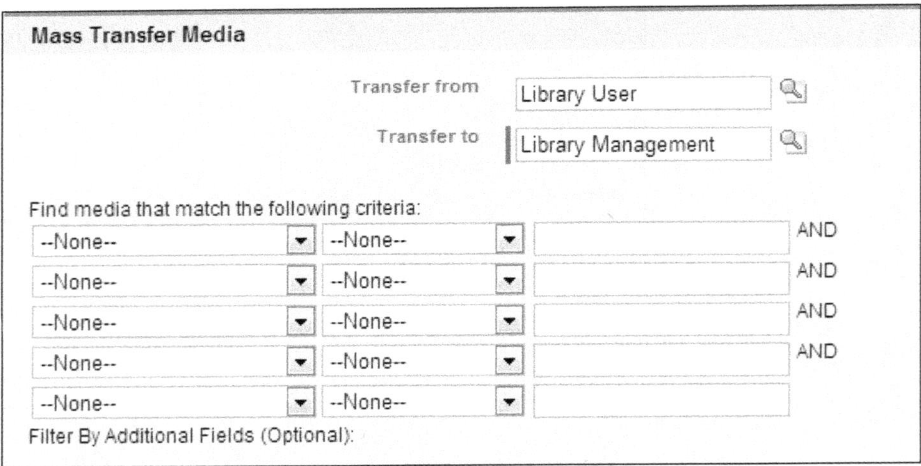

4. On the basis of the search criteria, the records to be transferred will appear below the search box, as shown in the following screenshot. Select the records that you want to transfer and click on the **Transfer** button.

Mass Transfer Accounts

Transfer from

Transfer to

Transfer open opportunities not owned by the existing account owner

Transfer closed opportunities

Transfer open cases owned by the existing account owner

Transfer closed cases

5. The records are transferred immediately.

When we transfer standard objects, such as `Account`, we get additional options to transfer related records from the object, such as transfer opportunities and transfer cases, along with the `Account` object, as shown in the following screenshot:

Mass delete records and delete all data

Some of the other data operations include deleting the organization database using the mass delete wizard and deleting all the data.

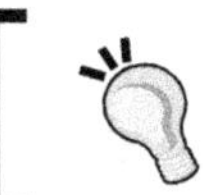

Warning: Deleting all data has no undo option; it formats the organization.

The mass delete wizard helps us delete data from the organization. To mass delete records from the standard objects, perform the following steps:

1. Navigate to **User Name** | **Setup** | **Administrative Setup** | **Data Management** | **Mass Delete Records,** as shown in the following screenshot:

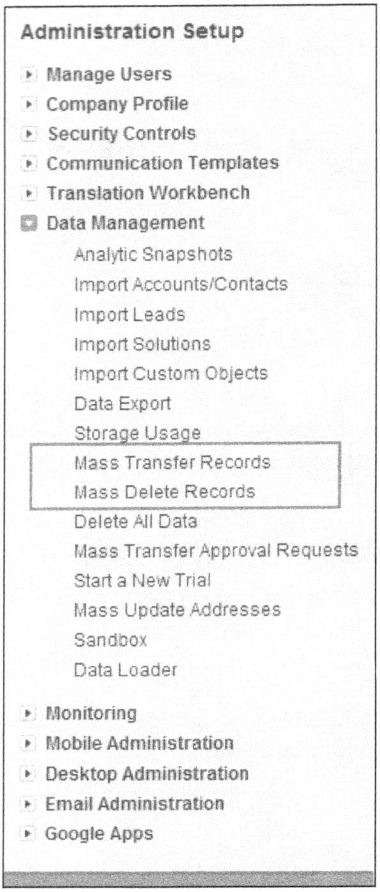

Administration Setup

- Manage Users
- Company Profile
- Security Controls
- Communication Templates
- Translation Workbench
- Data Management
    - Analytic Snapshots
    - Import Accounts/Contacts
    - Import Leads
    - Import Solutions
    - Import Custom Objects
    - Data Export
    - Storage Usage
    - Mass Transfer Records
    - Mass Delete Records
    - Delete All Data
    - Mass Transfer Approval Requests
    - Start a New Trial
    - Mass Update Addresses
    - Sandbox
    - Data Loader
- Monitoring
- Mobile Administration
- Desktop Administration
- Email Administration
- Google Apps

2. For now, the **Cloud Mass Delete Record** tool only allows the mass deletion of standard objects. Let's try to delete a few accounts as an example. Select the `Account` object for mass deletion.

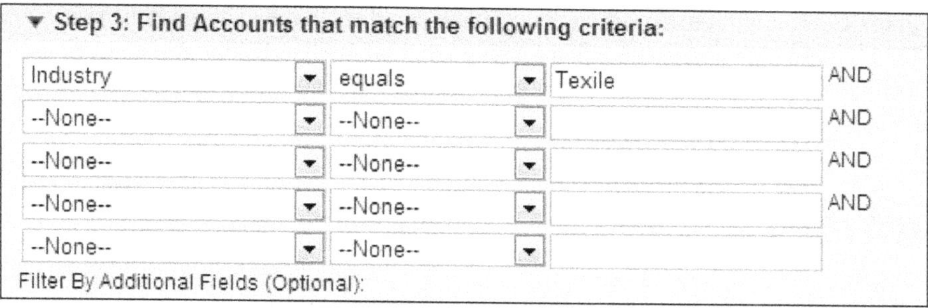

3. On the next page, we get a complete single page wizard for mass account deletion. The first two steps are for information; step 3 is an account filter, as shown in the previous screenshot. The data filters are used to filter out the data for deletion.

▼ Step 4: Choose to delete Accounts with Closed-Won Opportunities

☐ Delete Accounts that have associated Closed/Won Opportunities. (If not checked, those Accounts will not be deleted.)

▼ Step 5: Choose to delete Accounts with another owner's Opportunities

☐ Delete Accounts that are associated with Opportunities owned by someone else. (If not checked, those Accounts will not be deleted.)

- Accounts with associated cases will not be deleted.
- Accounts with associated active Self-Service users will not be deleted.
- Accounts with activated contracts will not be deleted.
- Partner Accounts with Partner users will not be deleted.

4. The next two steps in the wizard are additional information while deleting the records, as shown in the previous screenshot. These steps are unique to the **Account** object and other standard objects will have different steps.
5. A final checkbox confirms whether it is a hard delete or soft delete. If we choose to permanently delete the records, they cannot be recovered. Use this option only if you are absolutely sure you want to delete these records.

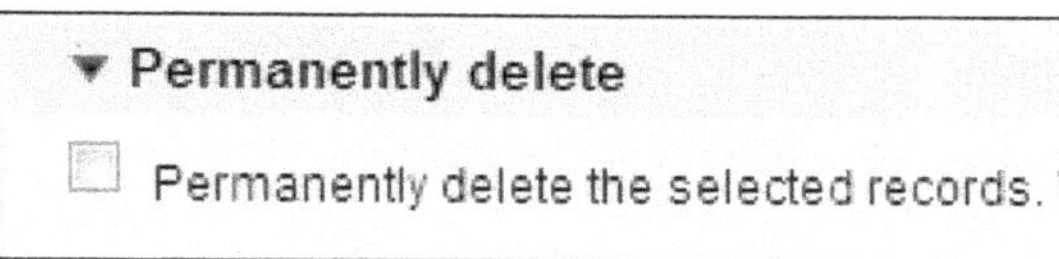

Data storage limit

The storage limit of the organizations depends on the number of licenses and the types of licenses we have. With Professional and Enterprise user licenses, we get 20 MB/user with a minimum storage of 1 GB, and unlimited user licenses get 120 MB/user. It is highly recommended that we periodically delete the data to remove unwanted records. Additional storage can be purchased in blocks of 50 MB and 150 MB from Salesforce.com.

Summary

In this chapter, we have seen operations on the crucial Salesfoce data. We have learned the two ways provided by Salesforce to perform massive data operations.

The data loader is a client application for the bulk import or export of data. Use it to insert, update, delete, upsert, or extract Salesforce records. Similarly, we have web-based import wizards, which are available in the **Data Management** menu in the setup. We have seen when to use which. We now have an understanding of the data operations. In the upcoming chapter, we will build the application online and learn how to share the data between users.

Test your knowledge

Q1 Out of the following, what are the capabilities of the data loader? (Choose three)

1. Insert more than 50,000 records.
2. Insert, delete, and update records for custom objects
3. Insert records to different objects in a single operation
4. Run a batch process

Q2 The library wants to import updated titles of the media items from their external servers every night at 1 p.m. in an automatic nightly build. What can be used for this scenario?

1. The import wizard
2. The data loader
3. The data loader using Command Prompt
4. None of the above

Q3 The library wants to update the records in the system. What do they need in the CSV file before the update?

1. The Salesforce record ID
2. Any unique name for the record
3. External ID

Q4 By using which tool can the developer change the data model of a Salesforce organization? (Read carefully)

1. Data loader
2. Administrator setup
3. Cloud-based data wizard
4. Other

Q5 If you wanted to load the users of the library system in Salesforce using the import wizard, what issues would you face?

1. Can't load custom objects through the import wizard
2. Can't load users through the import wizard
3. Can't load around 50,000 records through the import wizard

Q6 An organization wants to leverage the import wizard to import different types of data. What type of data cannot be imported through the wizard?

1. Accounts and contacts
2. Leads
3. Custom objects
4. Users

Q7 The system administrator has created a new custom object and application. This individual now needs to populate the new object with 1,000 records that are formatted in a CSV file. Is the import wizard appropriate for this task?

1. Yes
2. No

6
Analytics and Reporting

Salesforce provides us with an intuitive and advance report builder than can help us create reports and graphs on the data inside the CRM.

By the end of this chapter, we should be able to:

- Identify which report type is suitable for business requirements
- Create custom reports
- Create graphical dashboards
- Schedule a dashboard for automatic refresh
- Set up an analytical snapshot

In the previous chapters, we learned how to build an application on Force.com. We have seen how to load data in Salesforce. Now, it is the time to generate reports and dashboards.

Let's get started with it.

Reports

Reports are useful to display large amounts of data. They are used for conditional reporting on a subset of data; for example, a report of all the books purchased in the last quarter. A report enlists all the data that we want to fetch and can be filtered, grouped, or displayed as a chart. Reports are stored in different folders that are shared between users. The folder can be hidden, made private, or made available to the whole organization.

Creating a report

We can create custom reports on the standard and custom objects. To create a report, navigate to the **Reports** tab in the **Sales** application.

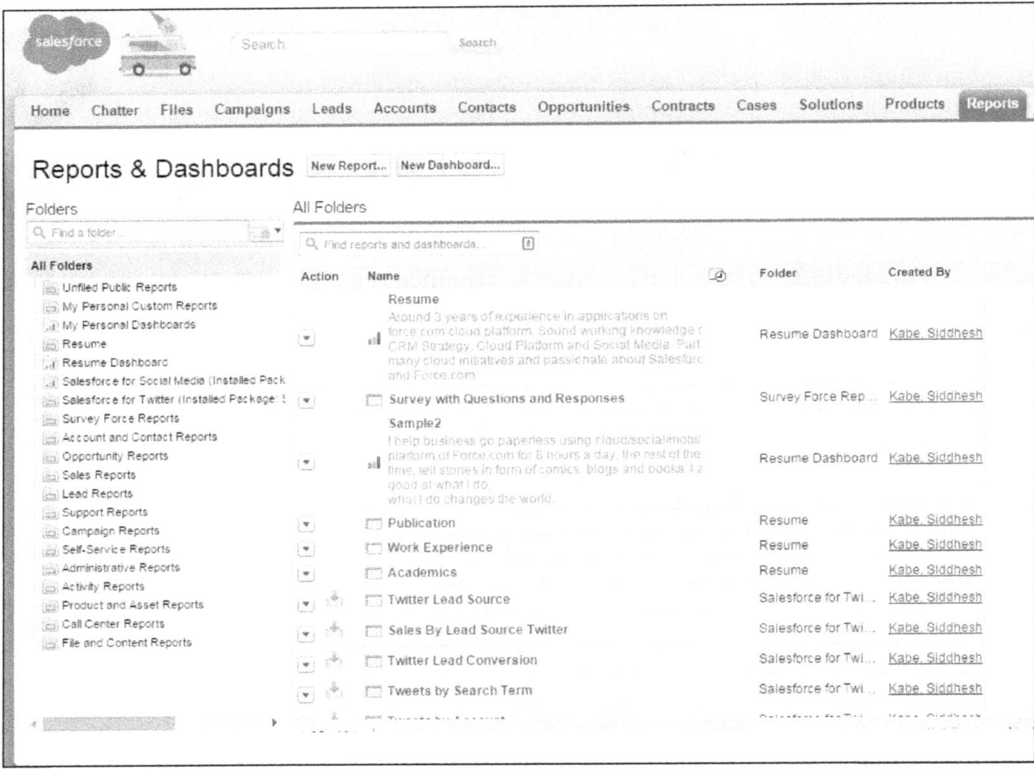

Creating a new report

To create a new report, click on the **New Report** button to open the advance report builder.

Selecting a report type

When we open the advance report builder, the first step is to select a report type. A report type is a Salesforce object along with a related object that determines the data that will be displayed on the report. We can also define a custom report type.

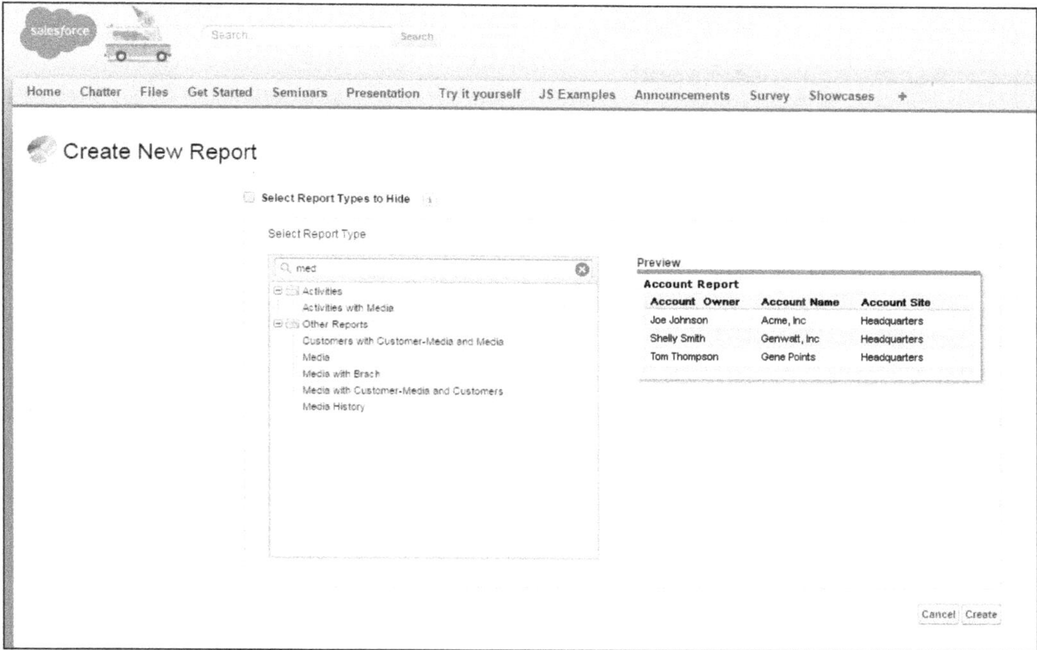

Choosing a report format

The next step to build a report is to choose the right format. There are four types of formats to choose from. Let's take a look at them one by one:

1. **Tabular reports**: Tabular reports are similar to a spreadsheet; they consist of an ordered set of fields in columns with each matching record listed in a row. This type of report show tabular data without subtotals or aggregation. They are useful to represent detailed data of objects for auditing purposes. However, with large amounts of data, they are not very useful. For example, a list of all accounts created in your organization:

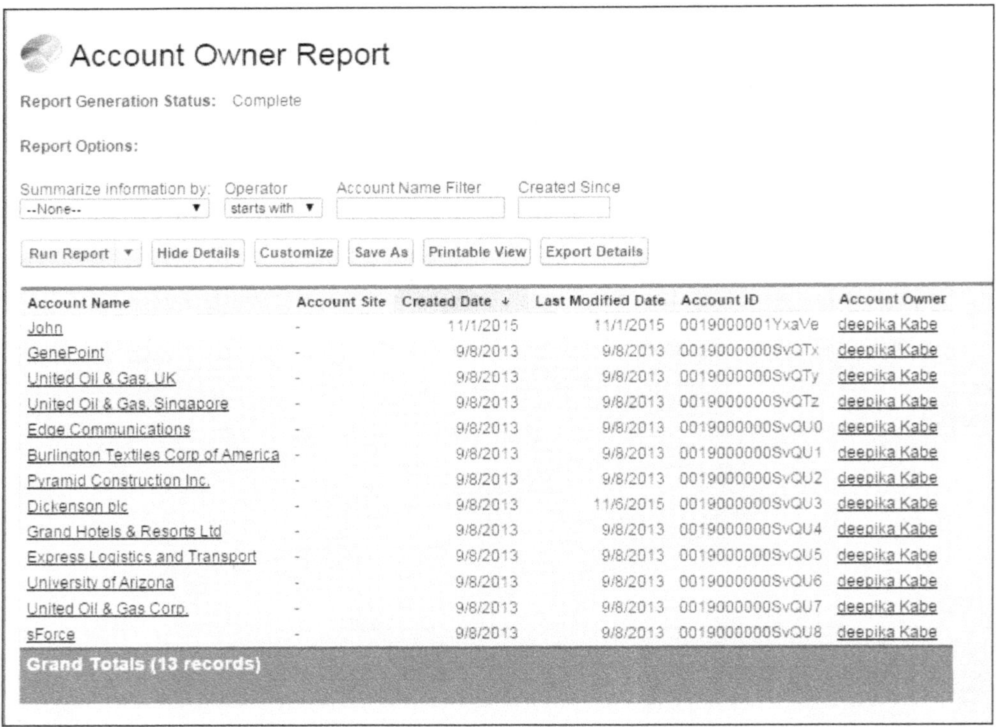

Account Name	Account Site	Created Date ↓	Last Modified Date	Account ID	Account Owner
John	-	11/1/2015	11/1/2015	0019000001YxaVe	deepika Kabe
GenePoint	-	9/8/2013	9/8/2013	0019000000SvQTx	deepika Kabe
United Oil & Gas, UK	-	9/8/2013	9/8/2013	0019000000SvQTy	deepika Kabe
United Oil & Gas, Singapore	-	9/8/2013	9/8/2013	0019000000SvQTz	deepika Kabe
Edge Communications	-	9/8/2013	9/8/2013	0019000000SvQU0	deepika Kabe
Burlington Textiles Corp of America	-	9/8/2013	9/8/2013	0019000000SvQU1	deepika Kabe
Pyramid Construction Inc.	-	9/8/2013	9/8/2013	0019000000SvQU2	deepika Kabe
Dickenson plc	-	9/8/2013	11/6/2015	0019000000SvQU3	deepika Kabe
Grand Hotels & Resorts Ltd	-	9/8/2013	9/8/2013	0019000000SvQU4	deepika Kabe
Express Logistics and Transport	-	9/8/2013	9/8/2013	0019000000SvQU5	deepika Kabe
University of Arizona	-	9/8/2013	9/8/2013	0019000000SvQU6	deepika Kabe
United Oil & Gas Corp.	-	9/8/2013	9/8/2013	0019000000SvQU7	deepika Kabe
sForce	-	9/8/2013	9/8/2013	0019000000SvQU8	deepika Kabe
Grand Totals (13 records)					

2. **Summary**: A summary report is used to summarize a group of data, view subtotals, and create charts. They can be used as the source report for a dashboard. For example, the report of **Opportunities** based on the **Stage** they are in:

Grouped By: Stage
Sorted By: Stage ↑

Opportunity Name	Lead Source	Amount	Expected Revenue	Close Date	Next Step	Probability (%)	Fiscal Period	Age	Created Date
Stage: Prospecting **(2 records)**									
Pyramid Emergency Generators	Phone Inquiry	$100,000.00	$10,000.00	8/19/2011	-	10%	Q3-2007	875	9/8/2013
Sales	-	$100.00	$10.00	11/2/2015	-	10%	Q4-2015	91	11/1/2015
Stage: Qualification **(1 record)**									
Dickenson Mobile Generators	Purchased List	$15,000.00	$1,500.00	8/19/2011	-	10%	Q3-2007	875	9/8/2013
Stage: Needs Analysis **(1 record)**									
United Oil Plant Standby Generators	-	$675,000.00	$135,000.00	8/19/2011	-	20%	Q3-2007	875	9/8/2013
Stage: Value Proposition **(2 records)**									
Express Logistics Portable Truck Generators	External Referral	$80,000.00	$40,000.00	8/19/2011	-	50%	Q3-2007	875	9/8/2013
Grand Hotels Guest Portable Generators	Employee Referral	$250,000.00	$125,000.00	8/19/2011	-	50%	Q3-2007	875	9/8/2013
Stage: Id. Decision Makers **(3 records)**									
Grand Hotels Kitchen Generator	-	$15,000.00	$9,000.00	8/19/2011	-	60%	Q3-2007	875	9/8/2013
GenePoint Lab Generators	-	$60,000.00	$36,000.00	8/19/2011	-	60%	Q3-2007	875	9/8/2013
Edge Emergency Generator	-	$35,000.00	$21,000.00	8/19/2011	-	60%	Q3-2007	875	9/8/2013
Stage: Perception Analysis **(1 record)**									
Express Logistics SLA	External Referral	$120,000.00	$84,000.00	8/19/2011	-	70%	Q3-2007	875	9/8/2013
Stage: Proposal/Price Quote **(2 records)**									
University of AZ Installations	Employee Referral	$100,000.00	$75,000.00	8/19/2011	-	75%	Q3-2007	875	9/8/2013
United Oil Refinery Generators	-	$270,000.00	$202,500.00	8/19/2011	-	75%	Q3-2007	875	9/8/2013
Stage: Negotiation/Review **(2 records)**									
United Oil Installations	-	$270,000.00	$243,000.00	8/19/2011	-	90%	Q3-2007	875	9/8/2013
United Oil Office Portable Generators	-	$125,000.00	$112,500.00	8/19/2011	-	90%	Q3-2007	875	9/8/2013

3. **Matrix**: A matrix report is used to group and summarize data by both rows and columns. This report can be used as the source report for dashboard components. This type of report is used to compare related totals, especially if there are large amounts of data to be summarized and to compare values in several different fields. For example, a report of the opportunities sorted by **Stage** on the rows and by **Type** on the columns:

		Type				
Stage		-	Existing Customer - Upgrade	Existing Customer - Replacement	New Customer	Grand Total
Prospecting	Record Count	2	0	0	0	2
Pyramid Emergency Generators		1				
Sales		1				
Qualification	Record Count	0	0	0	1	1
Dickenson Mobile Generators					1	
Needs Analysis	Record Count	0	1	0	0	1
United Oil Plant Standby Generators			1			
Value Proposition	Record Count	0	2	0	0	2
Express Logistics Portable Truck Generators			1			
Grand Hotels Guest Portable Generators			1			
Id. Decision Makers	Record Count	1	1	1	0	3
GenePoint Lab Generators		1				
Grand Hotels Kitchen Generator			1			
Edge Emergency Generator				1		
Perception Analysis	Record Count	0	1	0	0	1
Express Logistics SLA			1			
Proposal/Price Quote	Record Count	0	2	0	0	2
University of AZ Installations			1			
United Oil Refinery Generators			1			
Negotiation/Review	Record Count	0	2	0	0	2
United Oil Installations			1			
United Oil Office Portable Generators			1			
Closed Won	Record Count	0	11	0	7	18
Edge SLA			1			
United Oil Installations			1			
GenePoint SLA			1			

4. **Joined Report**: A joined report is used to join multiple subreports together. Each report thus joined has its own set of columns, sorting, and filtering. We can also join reports from different data types. For example, a report of **Cases** by **Status**, as shown in the following screenshot:

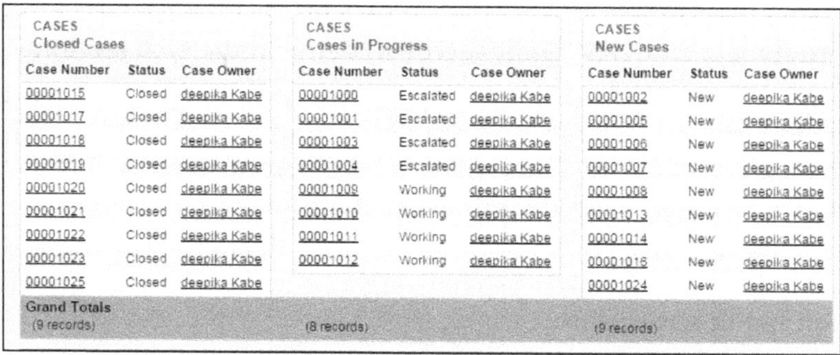

CASES Closed Cases			CASES Cases in Progress			CASES New Cases		
Case Number	Status	Case Owner	Case Number	Status	Case Owner	Case Number	Status	Case Owner
00001015	Closed	deepika Kabe	00001000	Escalated	deepika Kabe	00001002	New	deepika Kabe
00001017	Closed	deepika Kabe	00001001	Escalated	deepika Kabe	00001005	New	deepika Kabe
00001018	Closed	deepika Kabe	00001003	Escalated	deepika Kabe	00001006	New	deepika Kabe
00001019	Closed	deepika Kabe	00001004	Escalated	deepika Kabe	00001007	New	deepika Kabe
00001020	Closed	deepika Kabe	00001009	Working	deepika Kabe	00001008	New	deepika Kabe
00001021	Closed	deepika Kabe	00001010	Working	deepika Kabe	00001013	New	deepika Kabe
00001022	Closed	deepika Kabe	00001011	Working	deepika Kabe	00001014	New	deepika Kabe
00001023	Closed	deepika Kabe	00001012	Working	deepika Kabe	00001016	New	deepika Kabe
00001025	Closed	deepika Kabe				00001024	New	deepika Kabe
Grand Totals (9 records)			(8 records)			(9 records)		

Customizing the report

The new report builder is a quick and painless way of creating amazing custom reports. The following screenshot shows the layout of the report builder:

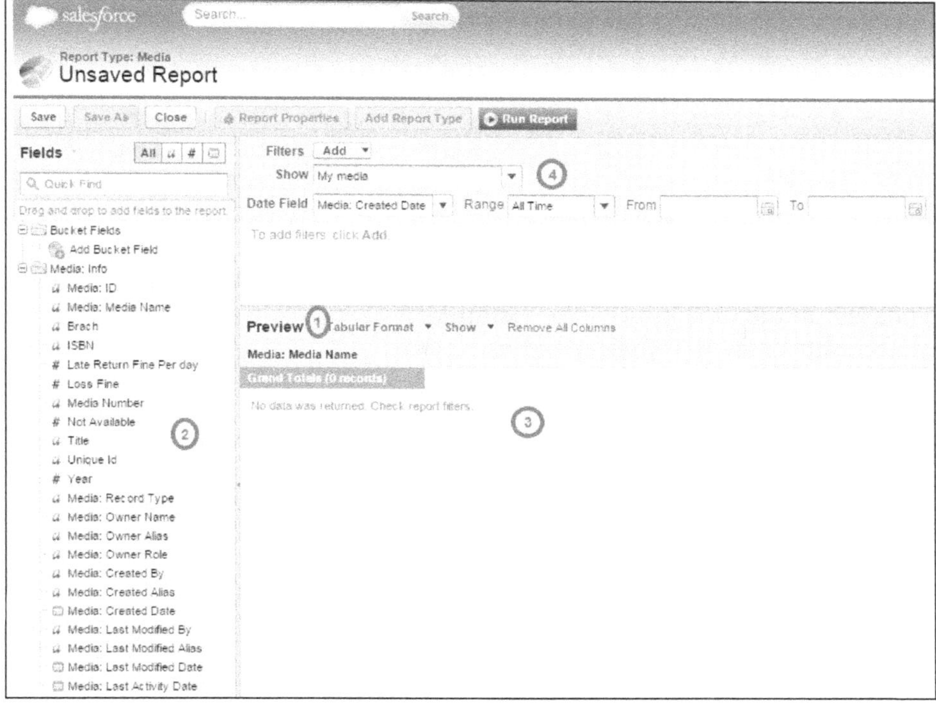

The advance report builder has the following four important sections:

1. To begin with, we select the right format of a report. Each type of report brings a new section to customize the report based on the format. For example, a summary report gives us an option to summarize the data. The joined report has a section to create a block. We will take a look at the different features of each report type in detail in the next section.
2. The sidebar on the left displays the list of all the fields of the object selected in the report type. We can drag the fields from the left sidebar as the columns on the main panel, which are marked by the number three. We can use the field filters on the top of the sidebar to filter the view of fields.
3. The main stage gives us an option to reorder the fields as columns. We can also sort the report by choosing a column to sort, as shown in the following screenshot:

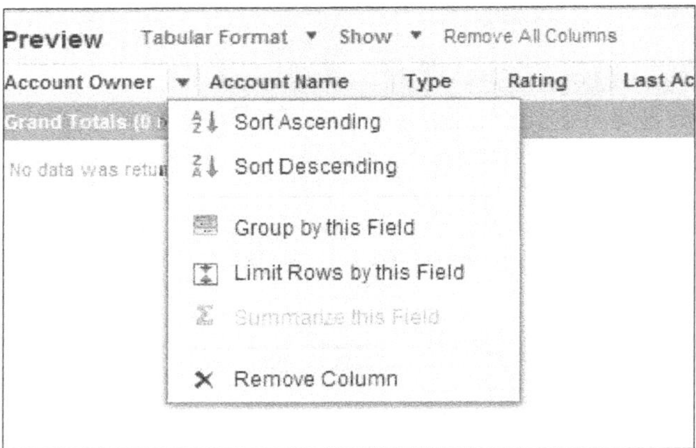

4. The filter panel on the top of the stage gives us the option to filter values based on the time period. For example, we can create a report for all the accounts opened in the current fiscal year:

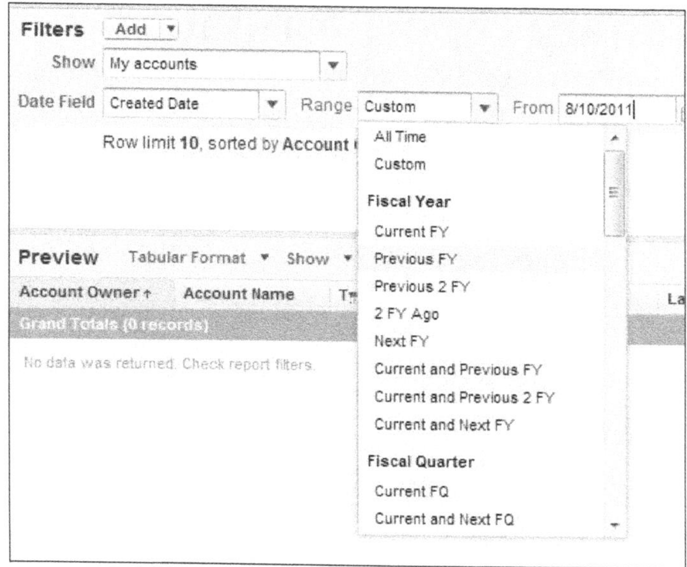

We can also set additional filters for data by clicking on **Add** | **Field Filter**, as shown in the following screenshot:

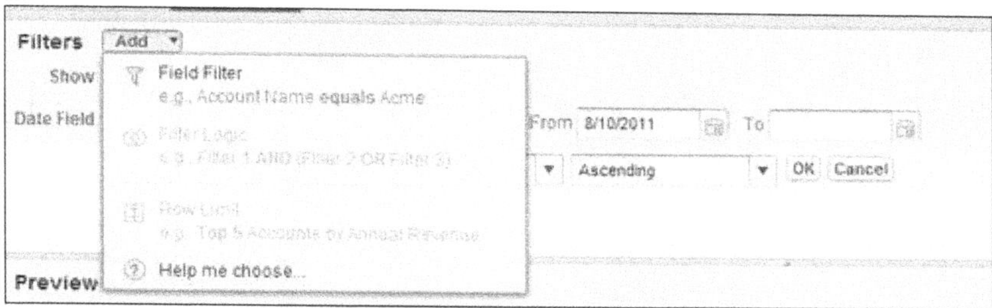

Field filters let us filter the data rows based on the rules defined in this section; for example, the account name begins with Smith or the account city is San Francisco.

The preceding steps are used to generate a generic tabular format. The other formats of the reports have a few additional steps that we will take a look at in the next section.

The summary report format

The following screenshot shows the additional block for the summary report format:

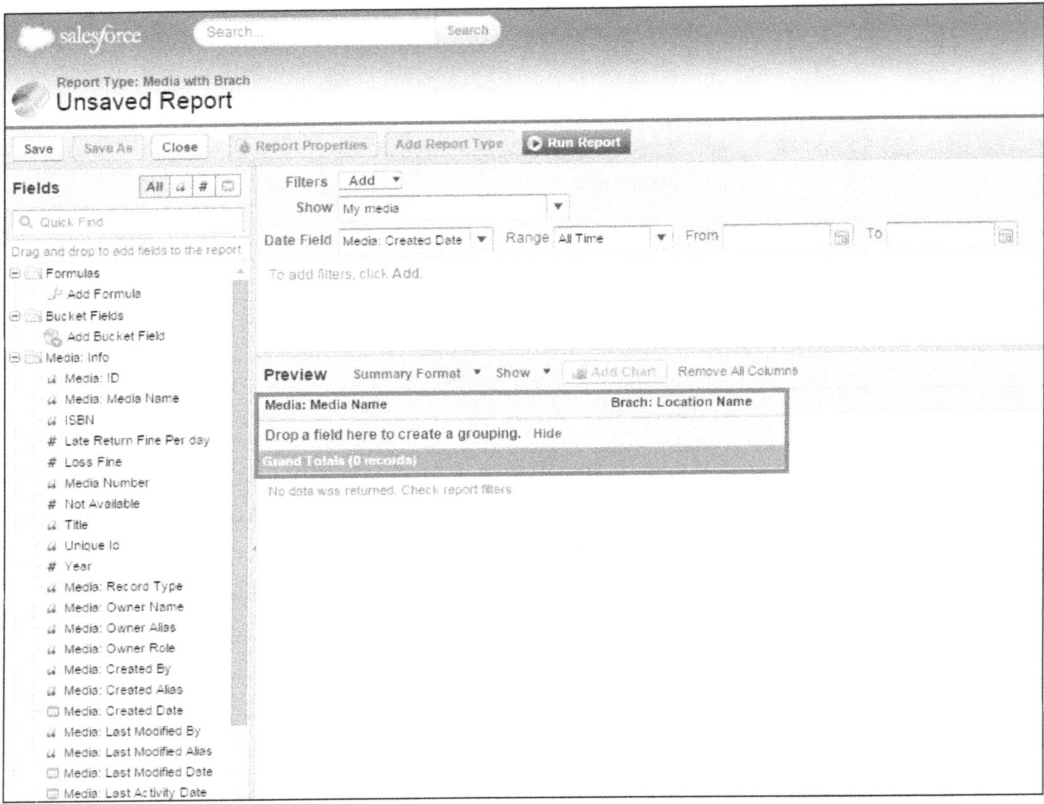

When we choose a summary report, we get an additional panel to drag a field to be summarized. The data in the report is summarized with that field.

The matrix report format

When we select a matrix format report, we get a similar grouping section for the row, as shown in the following screenshot:

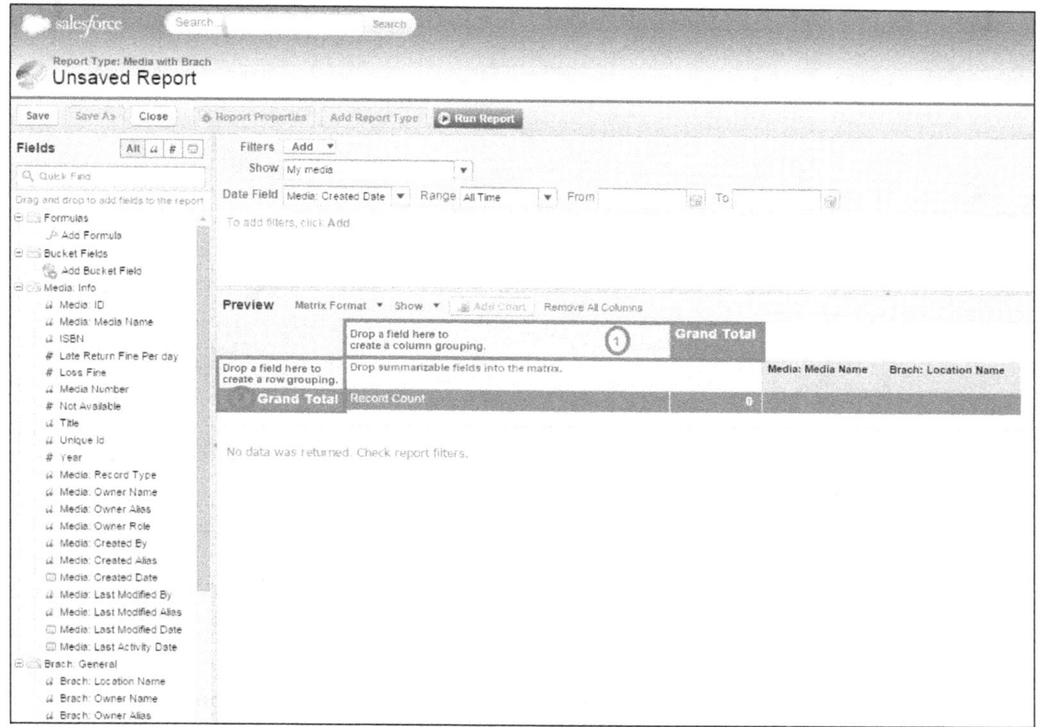

A matrix report creates two groupings on the basis of rows and columns.

The joined report format

We can use the joined report that can display two separate tabular reports. The joined report is created in blocks with each block representing a separate report. We can have different filters for each report as well as common fields to summarize them. For example, we can compare the **List of Open Opportunities** by the **Type of Account**.

When we create a joined report, the report opened on the preview pane becomes block number 1. We can label each block separately for an easy understanding. Let's take a look at the report builder while creating a **Joint Report**.

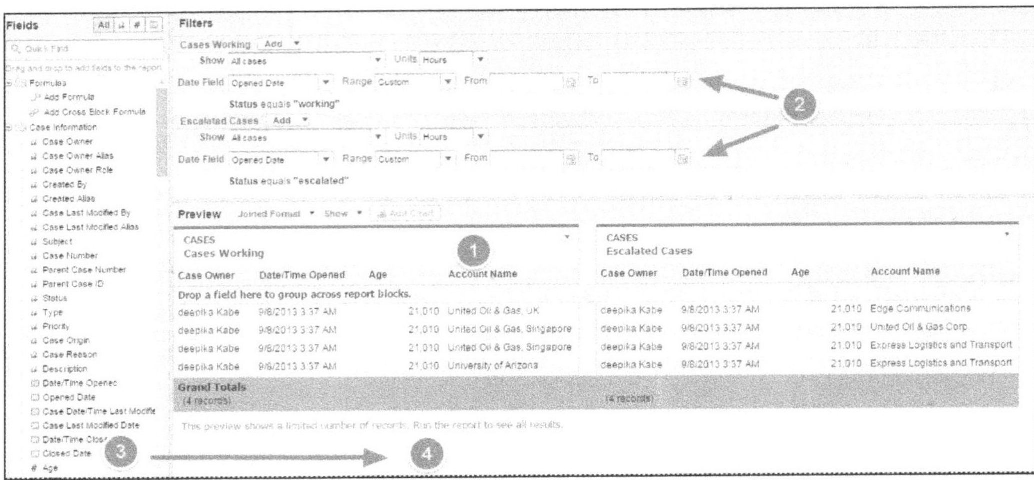

1. On the preview pane marked by number 1, we can see different blocks. The first block is the original report that was a summary report. We can label different blocks in the header (**1**).
2. Each block comes with a separate filter, which is useful to compare data. Here, in the example, we need to set filters for Working Cases and Escalated Cases (**2**).
3. To add new blocks, we drag the field from the sidebar onto the preview pane outside the existing blocks (**3** and **4**).
4. We can also summarize both the reports based on a common **Summary** field.

Adding charts

We can add custom charts to the **Summary**, **Matrix**, and **Joint Reports** using the **Add Chart** button, as shown in the following screenshot:

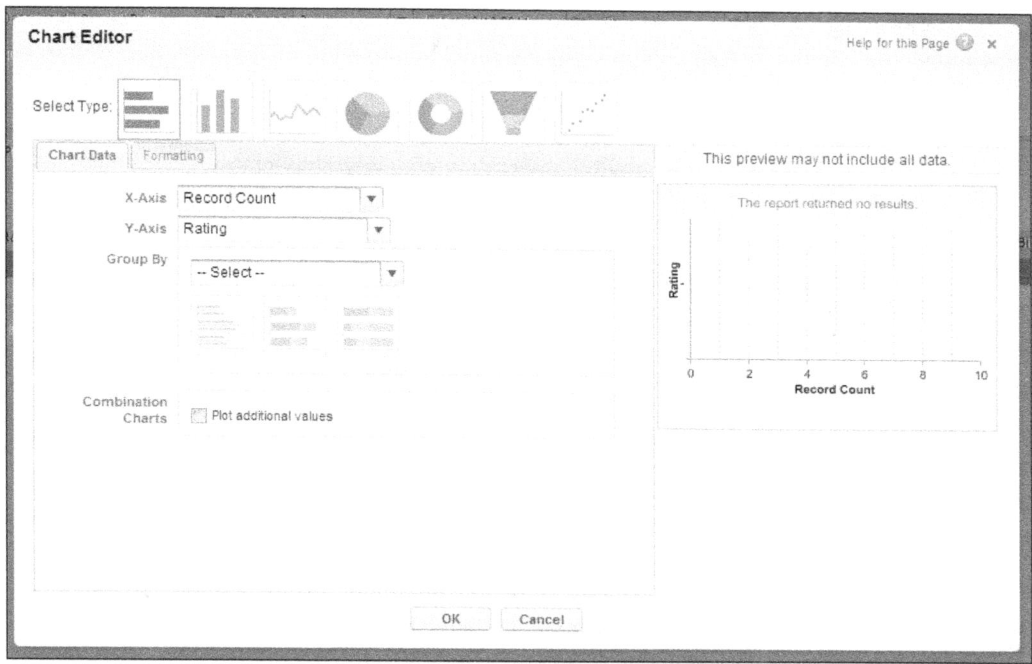

We will take a look at the options used to customize charts while creating dashboards in the next section. One final thing remaining at this point is to run the report and watch it go live.

Remember that the preview of the report does not contain live values, and we won't get a proper report until the report is run.

Report options

Once the report is generated, we get the following options:

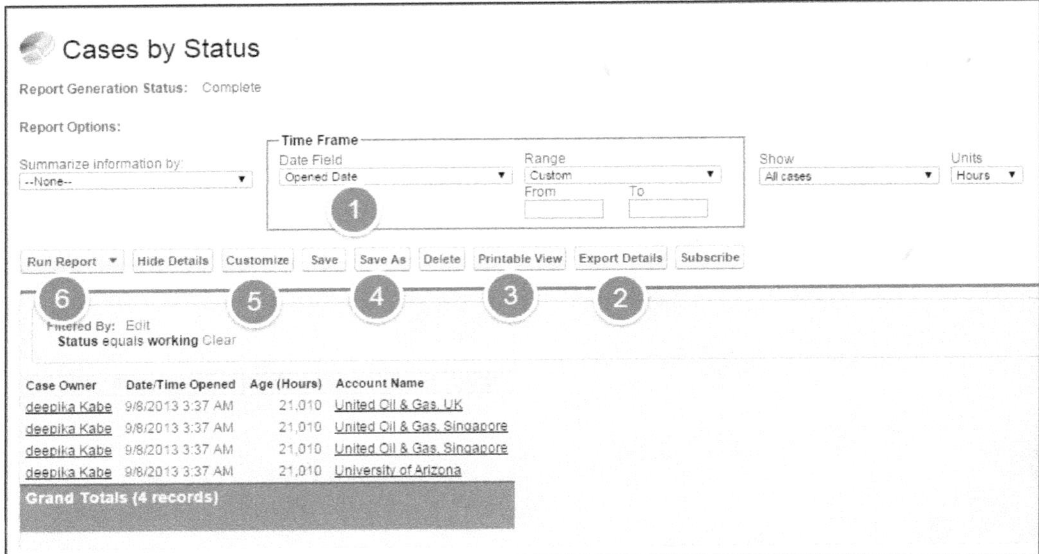

When we save the report, there are a few more options available to drill down and summarize the data. The numbers correspond to the numbers on the previous screenshot:

1. Changing the time frame: We can change the time frame once the report is generated. This overrides the time frame set while customizing the report.
2. We can export and download the report once it is generated.
3. The report is generated as a plain text output using printable view.
4. The report can be saved as a copy using the **Save As** option.
5. Customize opens the report builder again.
6. When we select **Run Report**, it caches the data that was available in the system. Whenever there is a change in the data or after a particular period, we can run the report again to recalculate the value.

Scheduling a report

We can schedule the report to run at a particular time and e-mail it to the participants. The report once scheduled will run automatically at the time and recalculate the values without the need for manual intervention.

To schedule a report, first follow all the steps and generate a report. On the report page, as shown in the following screenshot, select the arrow beside the run report. In the drop-down menu, select the **Schedule Future Runs...** option.

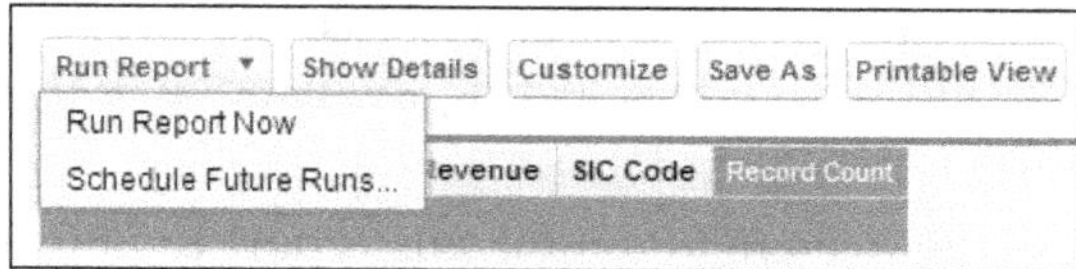

If the report is not saved, it will open the save report dialog box. Save it and continue. If the report is saved, it will open the next page, as shown in the following screenshot:

Media Customer

Schedule Report

Save Report Schedule Cancel

Running User Hector Barbossa (1)

Email Report To me To me and/or others...

(2) If you plan to email the scheduled report to other users, ensure it is in a public folder that is shared with all intended recipients.

Search: Public Groups for: Find

Select From --None--

Add Remove

Send Email To User: Hector Barbossa

Schedule Report (3)

Frequency Daily Weekly Monthly Every weekday Every day

Start 11/26/2011 [11/26/2011]

End 12/26/2011 [11/26/2011]

Preferred Start Time Find available options... (4)

Exact start time will depend on job queue activity.

Save Changes Save report modifications with this schedule Discard report modifications

(5) Save Report Schedule Cancel

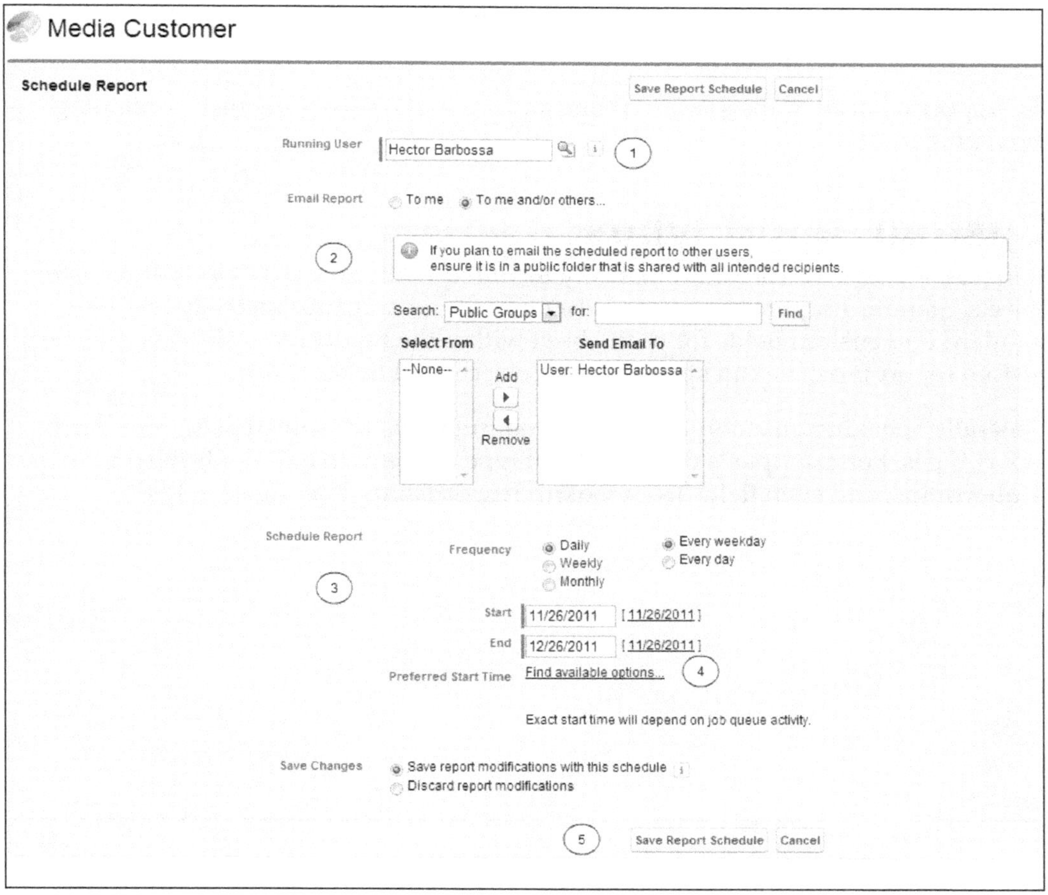

Let's take a look at the numbers marked on the preceding screenshot in detail:

1. Select a user to run the report. The report will be filtered on the basis of the data access to this user. If the user is at the top of the hierarchy than the recipient, they can view the data not accessible to them. Hence, we have to exercise caution when selecting the user so that we don't provide unauthorized access.
2. Select the appropriate users to e-mail this report to. If more than one user is in the delivery list or it is sent to a public group, we need to save this report in the public folder where all the recipients will have access to it.
3. Select the date and schedule for the report.
4. The time depends on other scheduled reports queued by other users. The exact time is also determined by the availability of bulk queues.
5. Save the schedule report.

The report will run at the specified time and we will receive an e-mail containing the report.

Custom report types

Standard report types are automatically included with standard objects and custom objects. Standard report types cannot be customized and automatically include standard and custom fields for each object within the report type. However, using a custom report type, we can specify which objects and fields to use.

Generally speaking, most organizational requirements are solved using standard report types. For example, a custom report type is useful to add fields from lookup relationships, and even fields from lookup relationships from those fields.

To set up a custom report type, we execute the following steps:

1. Navigate to **Setup** | **App Setup** | **Create** | **Report Types,** and click on new **Custom Report Type**:

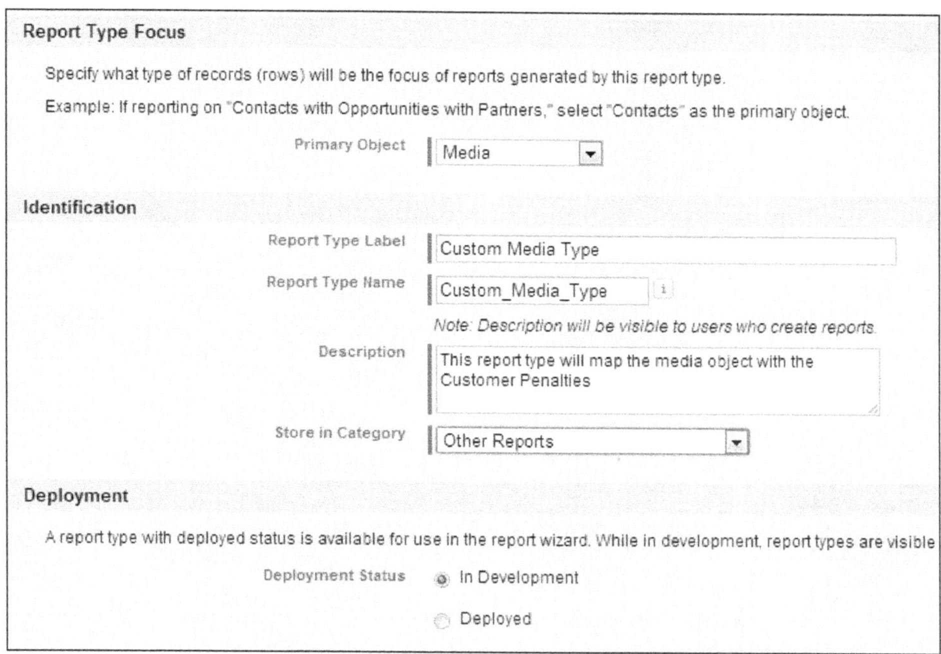

2. Define a custom report type by `name`, `description`, `primary object`, `development status`, and the `category` to store it in, as shown in the following screenshot, and click on **Next**.

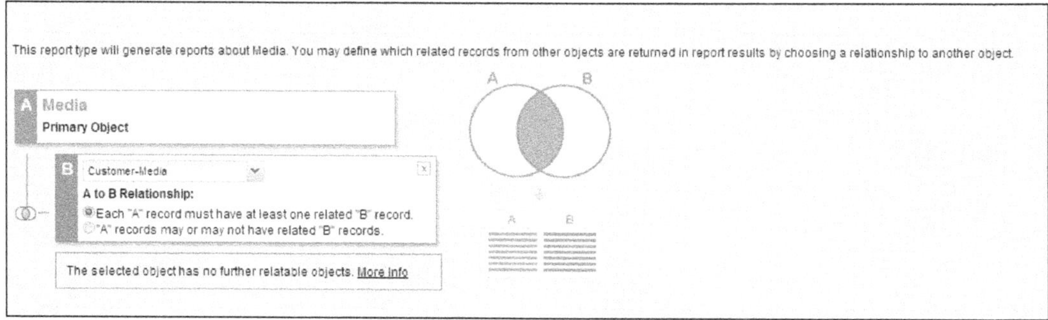

This report type will generate reports about Media. You may define which related records from other objects are returned in report results by choosing a relationship to another object.
A
Media
Primary Object
B
Customer-Media
A to B Relationship:
Each "A" record must have at least one related "B" record.
"A" records may or may not have related "B" records.
The selected object has no further relatable objects. More Info
A
B

3. Choose the objects for the custom report type. The objects are available on the basis of the primary object's relationships with the other objects. Only the objects with a lookup or `master-child` relationship with the primary object are seen in the list. Save the relationship.

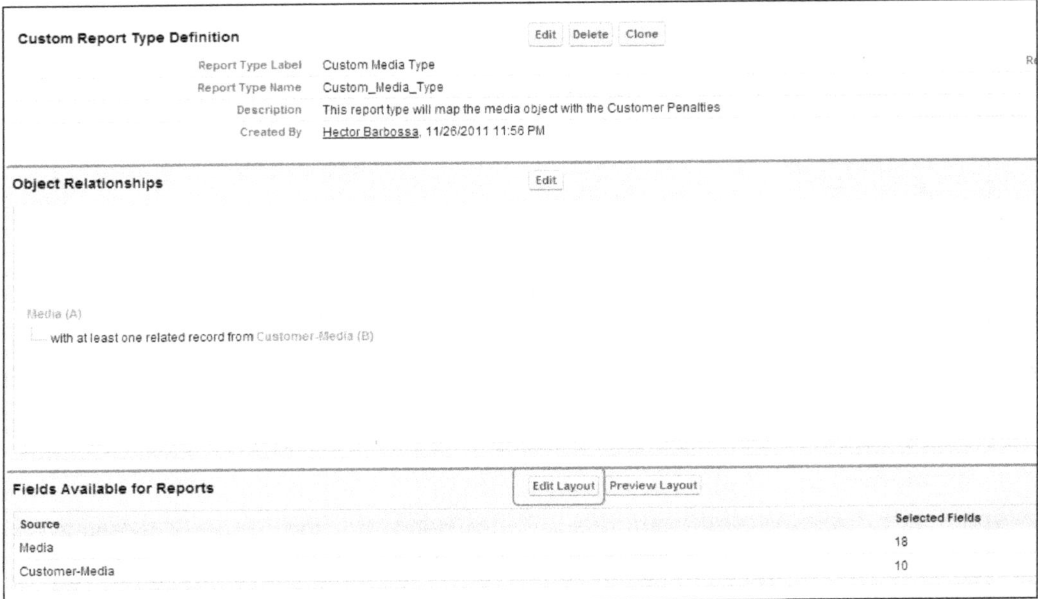

4. On the custom report type page layout related list, click on the **Edit Layout** button, to view the same as in the following screenshot:

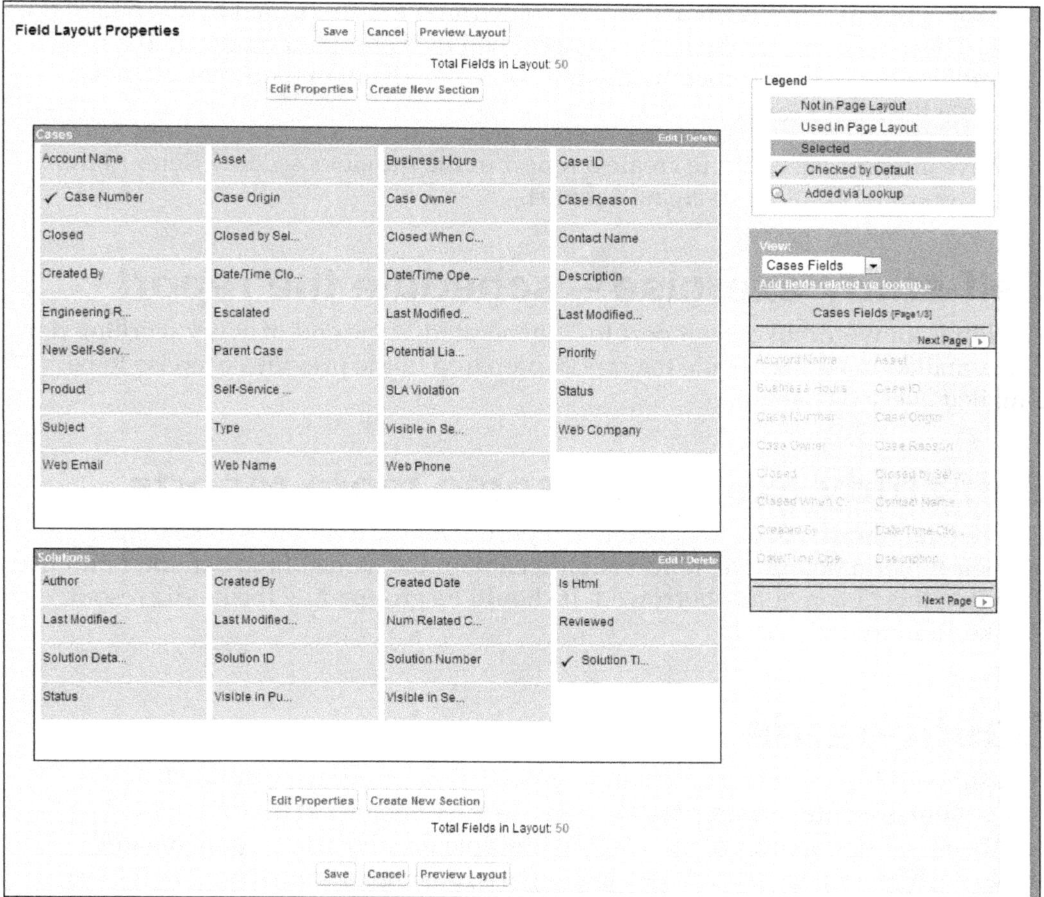

5. On the edit layout, we can specify which standard and custom fields a report can display when created or run from the custom report type. Once added, select **Preview Layout** to check whether the correct fields are added.
6. The custom record type will be available in the report type while creating reports.

Self-study exercise – create a report

The general library needs to get an inventory check of all the media items that are available presently in the library and are scheduled to be returned by the end of the week. The availability of the item is determined by a checkout on the media object. The report should be grouped by the type of the media item (books or movies). Generate the report for it.

We have already seen how to create a report in the previous section. Refer to the section on report builder to create a report.

Self-study exercise – schedule the report

The librarian would like the report to be generated at the end of every working day and e-mailed to her. Schedule the report prepared in the previous exercise to be e-mailed every day at 5 p.m.

Self-study exercise – some more reports

The general library needs to generate a report of all the defaulters to be displayed on their bulletin board. The report should contain the name of the defaulter and the item that the customer has borrowed. It should be grouped by the media resource (books and movies).

Dashboards

A dashboard is a visual representation of data. Behind every dashboard component is a data form report. We can use the same report in different dashboard components. We can display multiple dashboard components in a single dashboard page layout. Just like reports, dashboards are stored in folders. If the users have access to the folder, they can have access to the dashboard; however, to access each individual component, they need access to the reports.

Displaying graphical charts using dashboards

Now that we have seen how to create reports, it is time to use these reports and create a graphical representation. A dashboard is a single snapshot view of the reports using charts. We will use the point-and-click dashboard builder to create charts for our reports.

Dashboards can contain up to 20 components. They visualize the data of multiple reports on a single page. The dashboard can take a snapshot of the entire organization in a single view. They can also be scheduled for e-mail distribution.

The following screenshot is an example of a dashboard that shows information about the education and experience of a person:

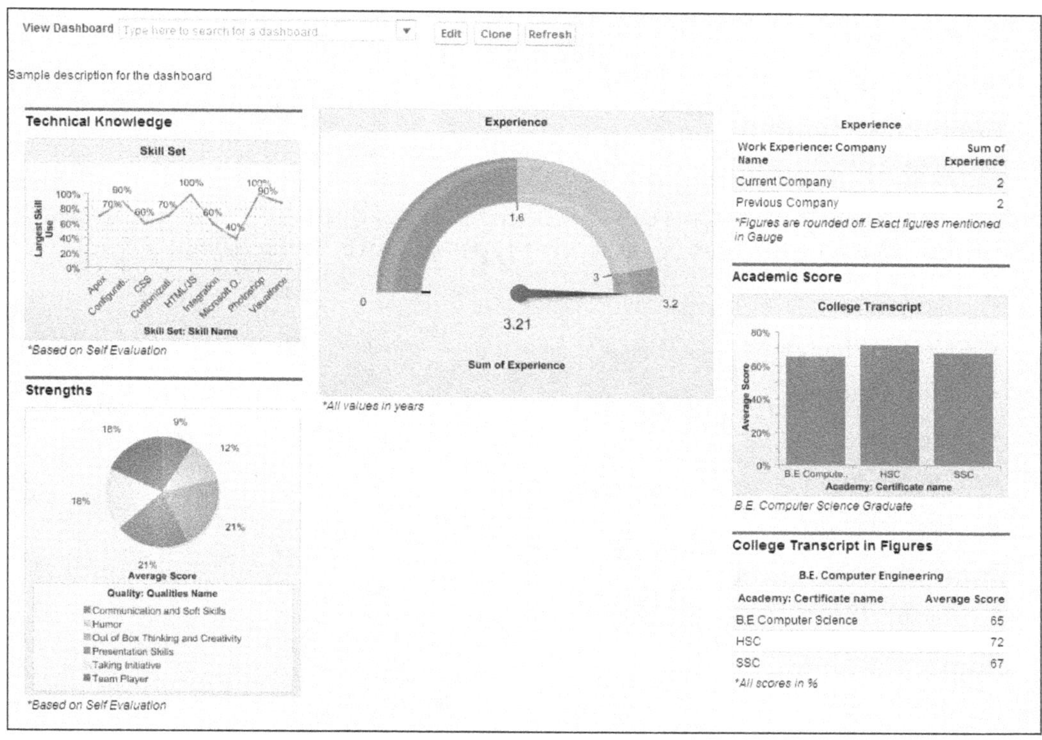

The dashboard builder

The dashboard builder is the cloud utility used to build stunning dashboards of charts. It has easy-to-use drag-and-drop features.

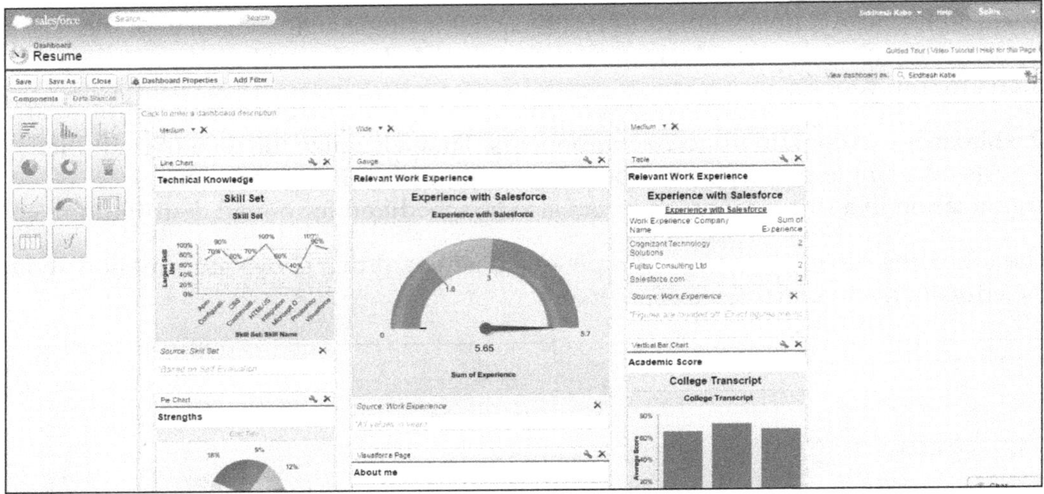

On the left-hand side panel, we can choose the types of available charts to create a dashboard from. We can add the following types of charts to the dashboard:

- Bar chart
- Vertical bar chart
- Line chart
- Pie chart
- Donut chart
- Funnel chart
- Scatter chart
- Gauge meter
- Tabular chart
- Metric chart

Along with the charts, we also get an option to include a custom Visualforce chart component in the dashboard. This enables us to use third-party charting APIs such as the Visualforce charting API or Google Charts on the dashboard.

Let's quickly take a look at the dashboard features and see how to link them to reports:

1. A dashboard can have three columns at a time. The columns can be narrow, medium, or wide. To add graphs to the column, simply drag the graph from the left-hand side panel onto the column.
2. **Data Sources** are the reports and **Visualforce Pages** that provide the data for the graphs:

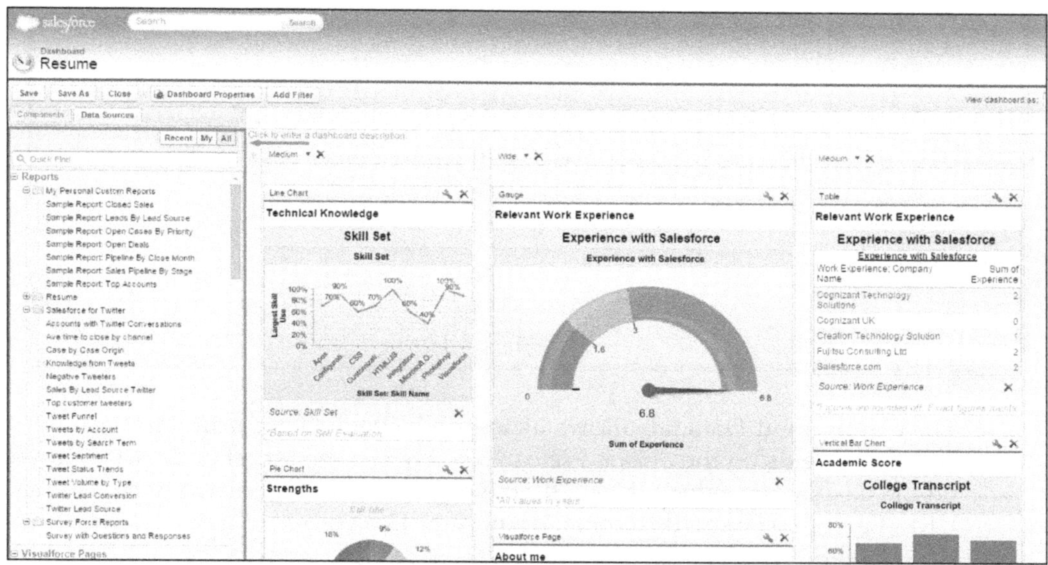

For a report to appear in the list, it should either be a summary or matrix report and grouped by at least one column. To add the data source to the chart, drag the data source over the chart that we dragged in the previous step.

3. Each chart has a different configuration. We can choose the color scheme for the groups and the data points. The columns that come on rows and the other options are shown in the following screenshot:

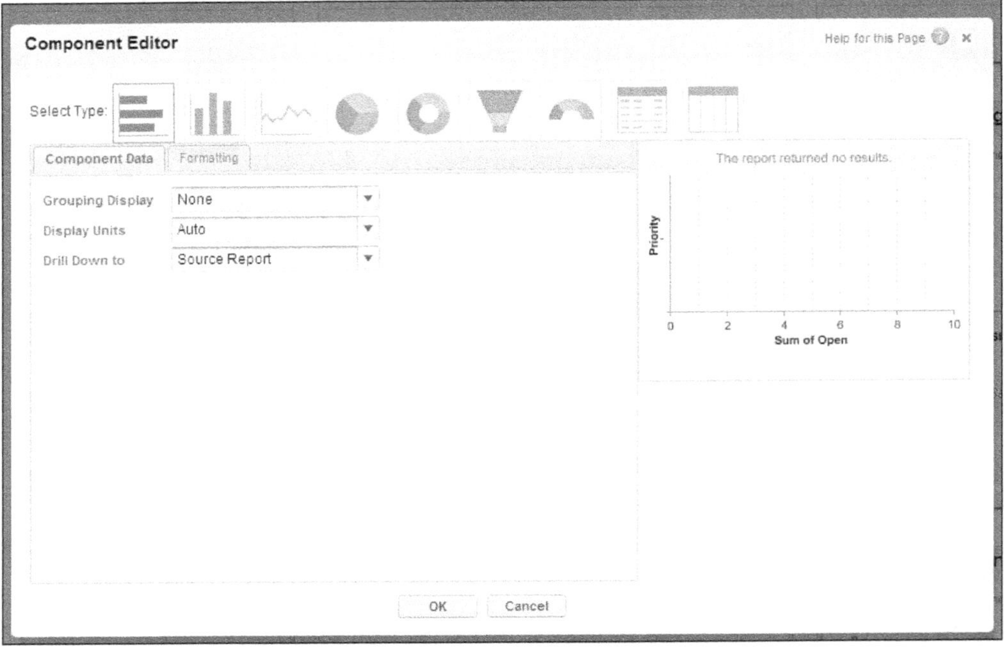

The **Component Data** tab allows us to group the data according to the summary fields on the object. We can also choose the target of the drill down on the dashboard, which is usually the report, the record object or a custom URL. Each chart has a different **Component Data** tab.

Formatting options allow us to choose background gradients, text colors, and so on to make the chart more attractive. Some charts may also have special options.

Combination charts

Combination charts plot multiple data in a single chart. Each set of data is based on a different field, so we can quickly and easily compare values in different charts. The sample combination chart is shown in the following screenshot:

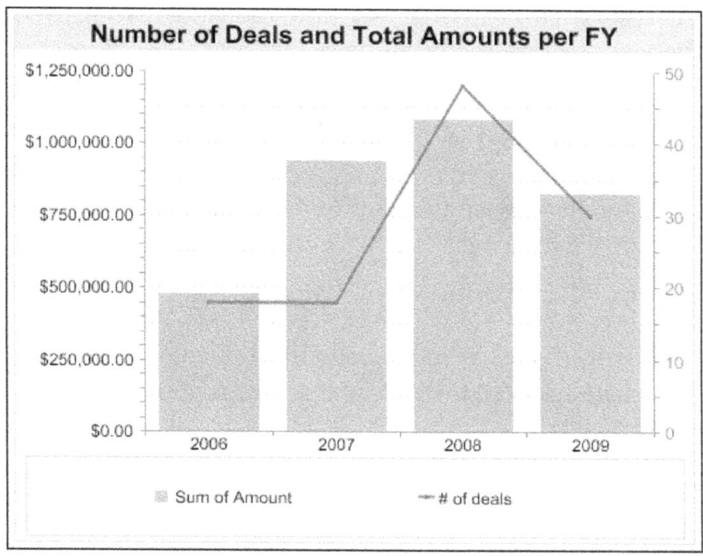

We can create the following combinations of charts:

- Line chart on bar graph
- Line chart on line chart
- Bar graph on bar graph

Line charts can be normal or cumulative. Bar graphs can be horizontal or vertical.

Dashboard security

The access to the reports and dashboards is not controlled by profiles/roles directly but through folder sharing. However, access to the underlying data still adheres to sharing rules and profile permissions. Each dashboard folder has a setting that controls the access level for the user.

There are three basic types of access levels for every user:

1. **Viewer Access**: With this access, you can view the data in the report and dashboard only. You cannot modify the data; nor can you delete it.
2. **Editor Access**: This allows a user to edit the report or dashboard.
3. **Manager Access**: This can do everything the viewer and editor access can do simultaneously controlling other users' access to the folder.

Creating a dashboard folder

Salesforce provides us with a `My Personal Dashboard` folder, which has sharing access to only one user. If we wish to create a separate dashboard for a group of users, we have to create a folder with the correct sharing rights on it.

To create a dashboard folder, perform the following steps:

1. Go to the dashboard list view (the **Dashboard** tab).
2. Select the **Create new folder** link on the top, as shown in the following screenshot:

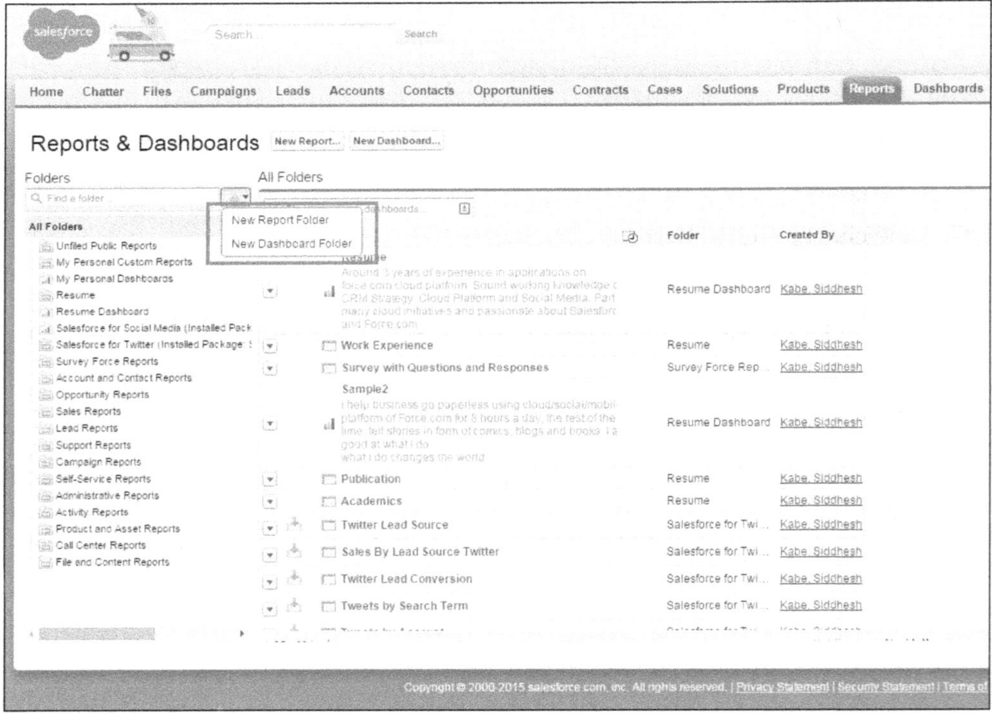

The dashboard list view will always open in the most recent folder that was accessed.

3. On the pop-up screen, enter the relevant **Dashboard Folder Label**, and select the **Public Folder Access** type:

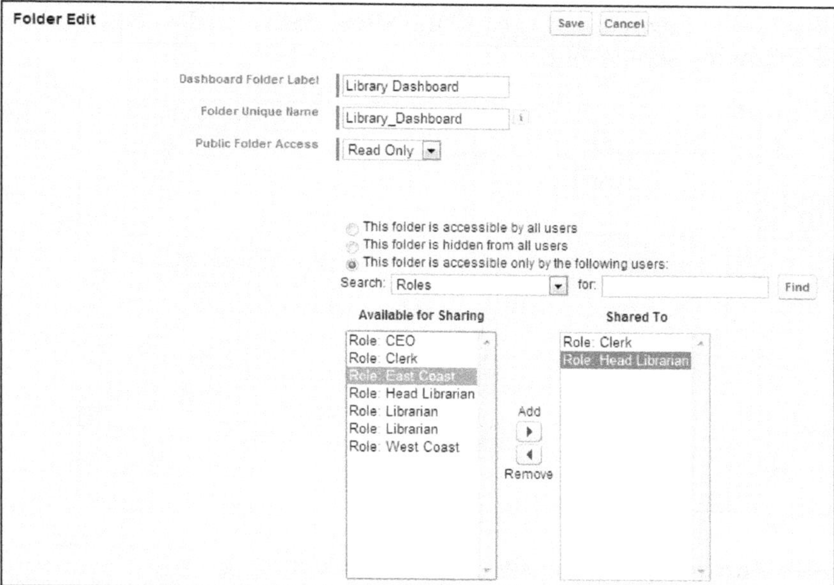

The access type can be **Read Only** and **Read/Write**. The third section lets us choose the relevant users for the folder. The folder if created as hidden from all the users is only accessible to the user who created it. The third option lets us select specific users who can access the folder.

4. Fill in the details and save the folder. The folder can be seen in the tab list.
5. Now, if we save the dashboard in this new folder, it will be shared with the users who have access to it.

Dashboard running user

The running user of the dashboard is the user on whose perspective the data is displayed on the dashboard. For example, if the **Running User** is the manager, any user who can see the dashboard can see what the manager can see on it irrespective of the sharing rules.

Alternatively, we can create a dynamic dashboard that changes the data according to the user who opens it.

To create dynamic dashboards, perform the following steps:

1. From the **Dashboards** tab, create a new dashboard or edit an existing one.
2. Click on the down arrow next to the **View dashboard as** field, as shown in the following screenshot:

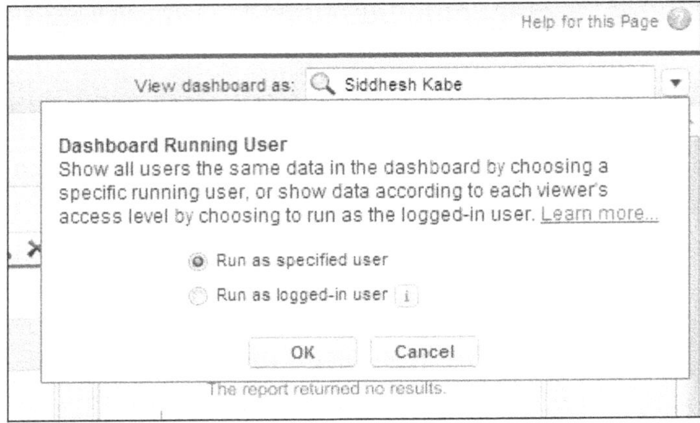

3. Select **Run as logged-in user** and click on **OK**.
4. **Save** the dashboard.

The `dashboard` folder controls who sees the dashboard, while the runner user controls what is displayed on the dashboard.

Scheduling a dashboard refresh

We can also schedule for the dashboard to refresh at particular intervals.

This feature is available only for EE and UE users.

To schedule a dashboard refresh, perform the following steps:

1. On the **Dashboards** tab, select a dashboard using the **View Dashboard** field.
2. Click on **Refresh** and choose **Schedule Refresh**, as shown in the following screenshot:

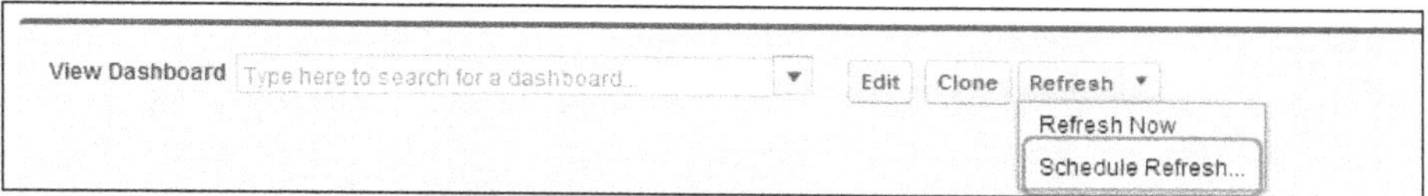

3. The **Schedule Refresh** option will open another page, as shown in the following screenshot:

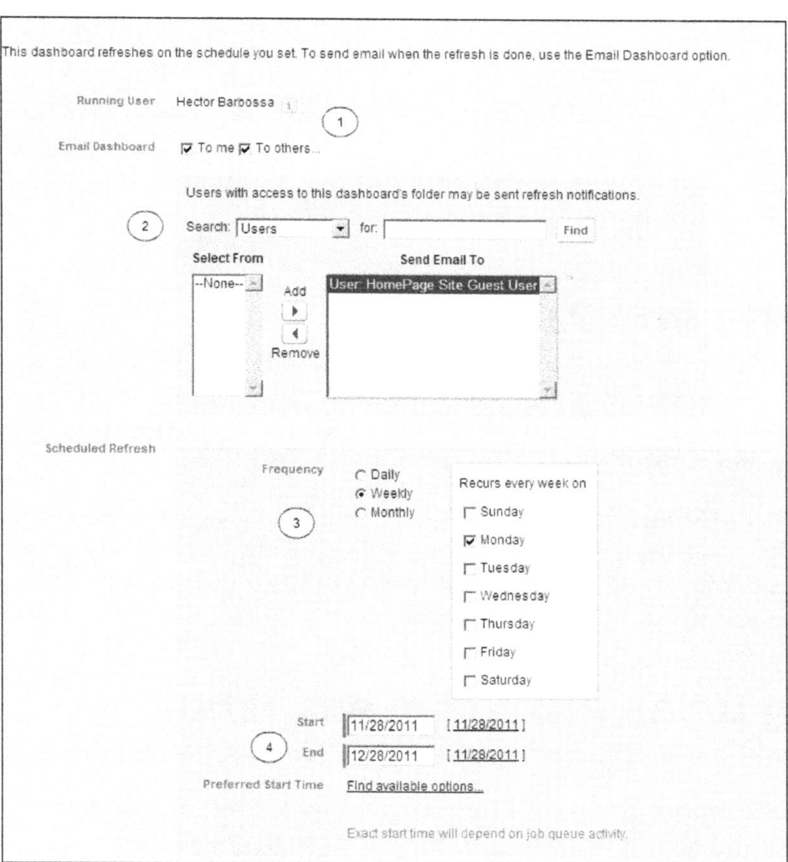

The following steps correspond to numbers on the preceding screenshot:

1. Select the appropriate users to e-mail this report to. If more than one user is in the delivery list or it is sent to a public group, we need to save this dashboard in the public folder where all the recipients will have access to it.
2. Select the frequency of scheduling the refresh, which can be daily, weekly, or monthly.
3. Select the start and end date for the refresh. Find the available options for the appropriate time. The time is dependent on other scheduled dashboards queued by other users. If there is a dashboard scheduled to get refreshed at one time, the time won't be available to refresh again.
4. Click on **Save**.

The dashboard will be delivered in the inbox at the refresh interval.

Self-study exercise — create a dashboard

The general library wants to view their operation on a single dashboard. We have already created some reports in the previous exercise. Create a library dashboard with all the components for the users to access.

Analytic snapshot

An analytic snapshot is used to run a report on historical data. We can save tabular or summary report results to fields on a custom object, and then map those fields to the corresponding fields on a target object. We then schedule when to run the report to load the custom object's fields with the report's data.

For example, the library manager can set up an analytic snapshot that reports on the books that have been checked out every day at 5:00 p.m. and store the data in a custom object. The library manager can then spot the trends in book issuing and the readership.

Setting up an analytical snapshot

Before we set up an analytical snapshot, we require the following two things:

- **Source report**: The source report is the custom report created using the report builder. It can have columns of more than one object.
- **Target object**: The target object is the custom object that contains fields that are similar to columns in the report.

We need to make sure all the columns in the report map with the fields are in the target object. The fields should be created in the target object.

If you need help in setting up the report or the object, refer to the *Chapter 5, Data Management*. Once these two are in place, let's proceed to set up the analytical snapshot:

1. Go to **User Name** | **Setup** | **Administration Setup** | **Data Management** | **Analytic Snapshots**.
2. Click on **New Analytic Snapshot** and give it an appropriate name:

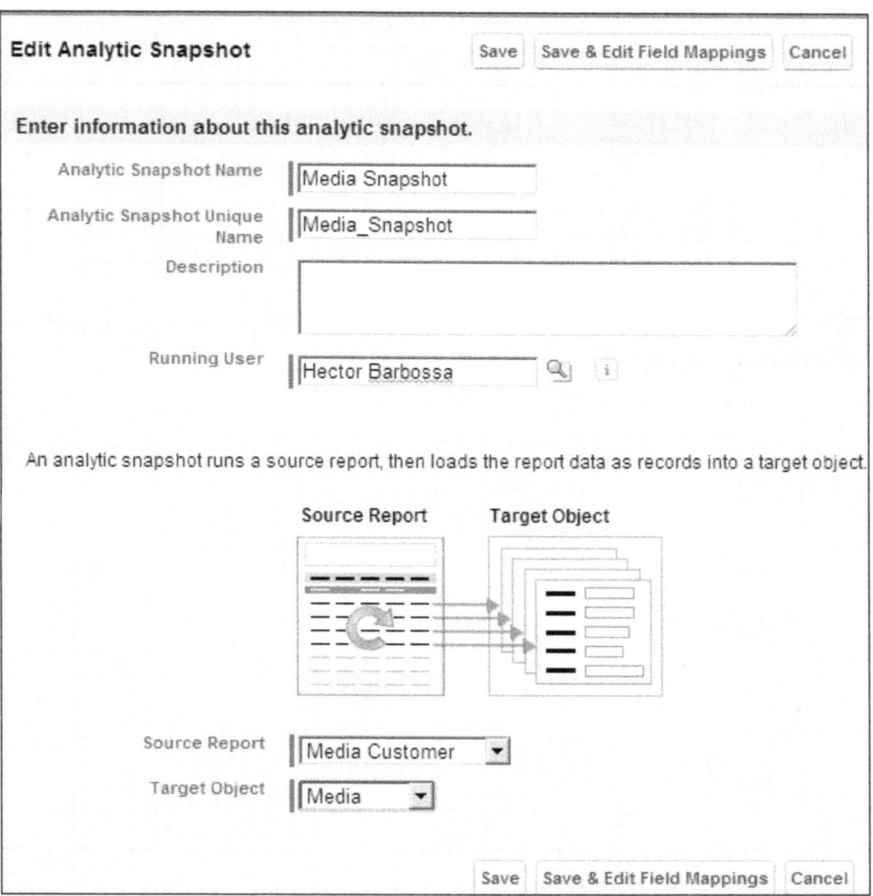

3. As shown in the preceding screenshot, the data loaded in the object will be based on the sharing settings for the running user.
4. Select the target object and the source report; now, click on **Save** and **Edit Field Mappings**. The mapping page allows us to map the fields from the report to the fields in the object.
5. If the source report is a summary report, select the level of grouping, as shown in the following screenshot:

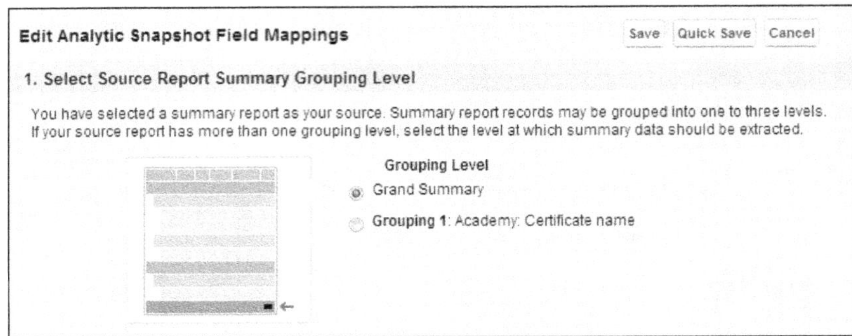

6. Map the fields from the source report to the target object, as shown in the following screenshot:

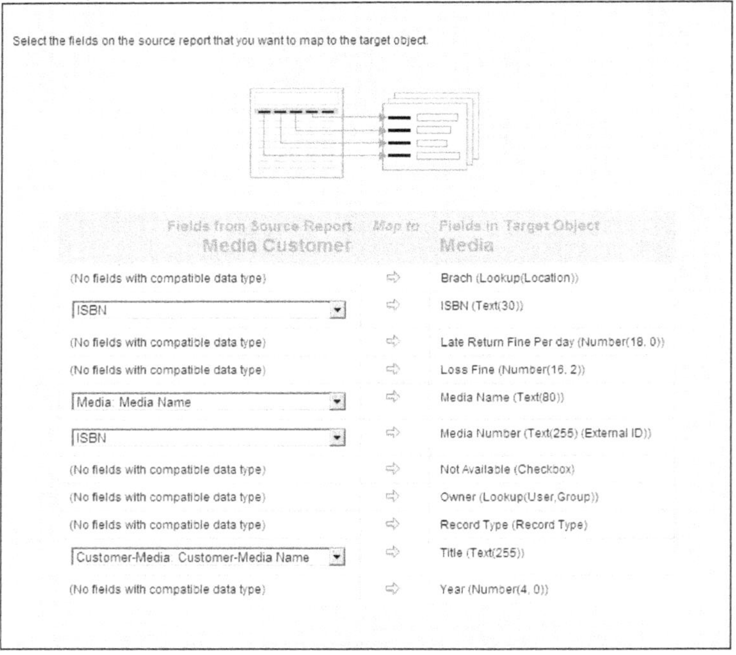

7. Click on **Edit** on the **Schedule Analytical Snapshot** related list, as shown in the following screenshot:

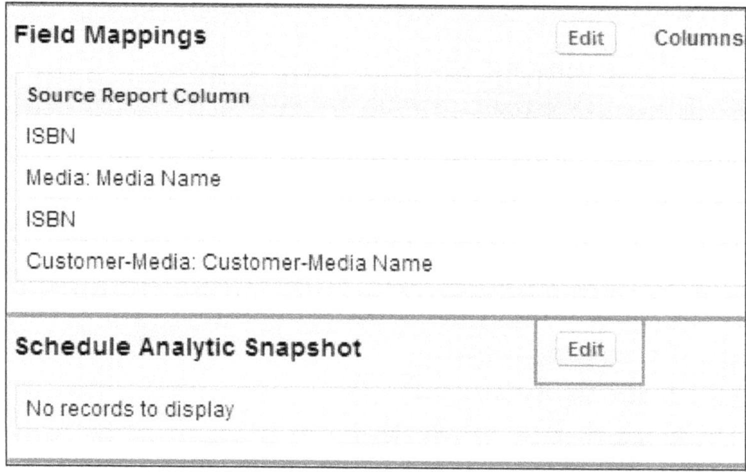

8. The scheduler is shown in the preceding screenshot; it is similar to the one used in reports and dashboards and has similar options. Hence, it won't be repeated again.

> We can save the analytic snapshot any time we want while creating it. If the snapshot isn't scheduled, it won't run. If we save it accidently while creating it, it can be scheduled from the snapshot page.

Now that we have a record of the historical data in the target object, we can run the report on it to analyze trends.

Summary

In this chapter, we learned about the analytics as a service offered by Salesforce. We can now create reports and dashboards that suit our requirements. We can analyze trends using the analytic snapshot. We can set up dashboards to visualize the entire company data on a single page.

In the next chapter, we will be entering the last phase of setting up a Salesforce organization; we will be creating users and designing applications for multiple users.

Test your knowledge

Q1 A manager wants to share specific fields of data with his subordinates that only he has access to. What is the best way to share specific fields of data? (Select any two)

1. Select the view dashboard as with his own name
2. Folder permission on a report
3. Run reports as scheduled reports and e-mail distribution
4. Folder permission on a dashboard

Q2 What are the features of a custom report type? (Select any two)

1. Define object relationships and fields for reports
2. Define anti-join relationships
3. Create analytic snapshot reports
4. Define up to four object relationships

Q3 A developer needs to create a trending report. What should they use to get the historical data?

1. Reports
2. Analytic snapshots
3. Roll-up summary
4. Report types
5. Audit history records

Q4 An application was designed without considering requirements for reports and dashboards. Which of the following statements is true?

1. The data model will support all the requirements of the application, including reports and dashboards
2. Reports are part of the application and the application design will take care of them
3. No special considerations for reports or dashboards are required as Salesforce can natively take care of the requirements
4. The data model and the application will not cater for reports and dashboards

Q5 Dashboard refresh can be monitored using:

1. Apex jobs
2. Scheduled jobs
3. Dashboard jobs
4. Report jobs

Q6 Which component in a dashboard gives you a grand total? (Select any two)

1. Table
2. Gauge
3. Chart
4. Metric

Q7 What is the best type of dashboard component to display a list of your top 10 customers?

1. Metric
2. Table
3. Gauge
4. Chart

7
Application Administration

So far, we have seen how to build and secure a Force.com application. In this chapter, we will take a look at ways to administer the application and the available tools that will help us achieve these.

We will cover the following topics in this chapter:

- Managing the access control
- An overview of Force.com licenses
- Restricting data access
- Understanding the stakeholders in the organization
- Understanding the security pyramid
- Managing profiles
- Setting up roles
- Sharing settings
- Managing different types of accounts

Now that we know how to build an application on Force.com, it is time to set up the platform to be used. We are going to bring everything we learned so far and put them together to be used by different people. So, let's begin.

Managing the access control

Any enterprise application is built for multiple users at different levels. Different types of users will require different types of access controls. Different departments will use different applications as their daily drivers. For example, the support call center users need the service cloud but have limited or no access to Leads and opportunities. Similarly, the cold calling team may not be able to see the cases and solutions but will be able to see only the leads. The application should simplify their job and not add complications to it.

In the Library Management System, the librarian has complete access to the entire library database, but the clerks who are dealing with check-in and checkout transactions do not need to access the books table to modify it. There will also be a few administrators and superusers who will customize the application based on their requirements.

Force.com licenses

Every user on the Force.com platform requires a primary user license and different feature licenses. We can add multiple feature licenses to a user but can add only one user license.

Let's find out how many licenses are available in your organization:

1. Go to **Setup** | **Administration Setup** | **Company Profile** | **Company Information**.
2. Below the **Company Profile** in the related list, the number of licenses available for use is shown in the following screenshot:

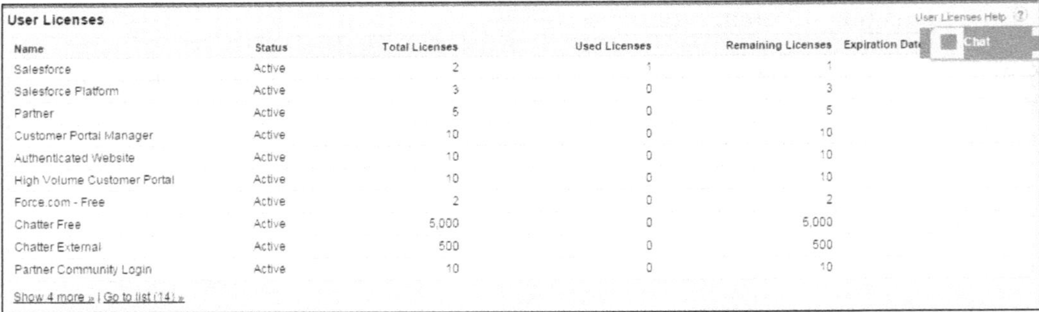

User Licenses

User Licenses Help

Name	Status	Total Licenses	Used Licenses	Remaining Licenses	Expiration Dat
Salesforce	Active	2	1	1	
Salesforce Platform	Active	3	0	3	
Partner	Active	5	0	5	
Customer Portal Manager	Active	10	0	10	
Authenticated Website	Active	10	0	10	
High Volume Customer Portal	Active	10	0	10	
Force.com - Free	Active	2	0	2	
Chatter Free	Active	5,000	0	5,000	
Chatter External	Active	500	0	500	
Partner Community Login	Active	10	0	10	

Show 4 more » | Go to list (14) »

To apply the user licenses, perform the following steps:

1. Go to **Setup** | **Administration Setup** | **Manage Users** | **Users**.
2. Create **New User** or **Edit** an existing user.

A user once created cannot be deleted. We can only make a user active or inactive. Creating an active user consumes a user license, which is directly linked to the billing of Salesforce usage. It is recommended that you practice this in a developer organization. Consult your administrator if you are creating a new user in the production organization.

3. Select the user license from the drop-down menu, as shown in the following screenshot:

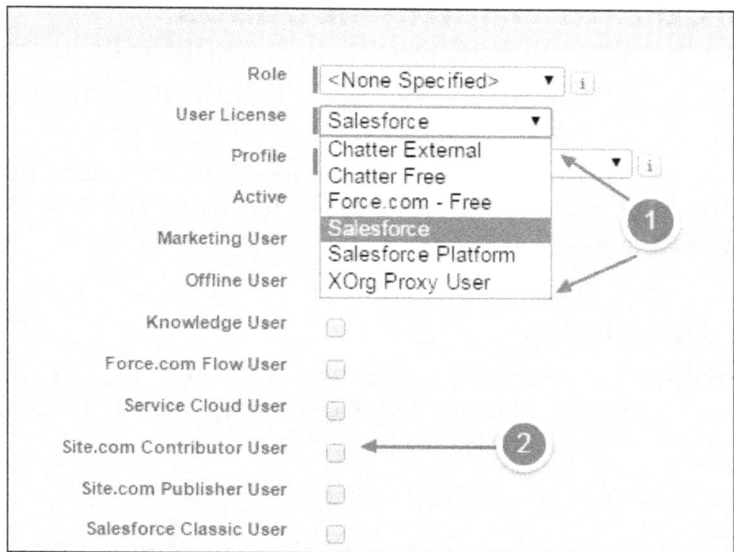

Let's take a look at the different license types that are available on Salesforce.

Types of licenses

Depending on the type of license, we get access to the different objects on Force.com. The following table summarizes the use of the main licenses:

Features	**Salesforce**	**Salesforce platform**	**Chatter - Free**	**Chatter- External**
Salesforce CRM	Yes	No	No	No
Chatter	Yes	Yes	Yes	Yes, only groups that are invited to participate
Custom Apps	Yes	Yes	No	No
AppExchange Apps	Yes	Yes	No	No

Salesforce and Chatter licenses

The basic Salesforce license provides access to the entire Salesforce application while the Salesforce platform license is used to deploy a custom app for users on Force.com.

A Chatter free license is used to invite your coworkers to use Chatter, but they do not get access to Salesforce while the Chatter external license is used to invite customers to particular groups.

Feature licenses

To extend the Salesforce application beyond basic CRM, we can use feature licenses. Most of the feature licenses come bundled with the CRM user licenses; however, additional licenses can be purchased for further use.

Let's see how many feature licenses are available for us to use:

1. Go to **Setup** | **Administration Setup** | **Company Profile** | **Company Information**.

2. Below the **Company Profile** in the related list, the number of feature licenses available for use is shown in the following screenshot:

Feature Licenses

Feature Licenses Help

Feature Type	Status	Total Licenses	Used Licenses	Remaining Licenses
Chatter Answers User	Active	25	0	25
Marketing User	Active	2	1	1
Apex Mobile User	Active	2	1	1
Offline User	Active	2	1	1
Knowledge User	Active	2	0	2
Force.com Flow User	Active	3	1	2
Service Cloud User	Active	2	1	1
Salesforce CRM Content User	Active	2	1	1
Site.com Contributor User	Active	1	1	0
Site.com Publisher User	Active	2	1	1

Feature licenses are used to access the special features of the Salesforce application. A user can utilize more than one feature license, for example, the Service Cloud Console and Sales Cloud Console license.

Using queues to balance workloads

In a customer service support team, different teams are available to support different types of issues. When a new case is created, we don't know which support representative has the necessary bandwidth, and hence, it should be assigned to a queue, which is basically a team of users. When a member of the queue accepts the ownership of the case, they will become the owner:

1. To create a custom object queue, go to **User Name** | **Setup** | **Administration Setup** | **Manage Users** | **Queues**:

New

Action	Label ↑	Queue Name	Queue Email	Supported Objects
Edit | Del	International - Escalations	InternationalEscalations	hi35@hi.com	Case
Edit | Del	International - Platinum/Gold	InternationalPlatinumGold	hi35@hi.com	Case
Edit | Del	International - Silver/Bronze	InternationalSilverBronze	hi35@hi.com	Case
Edit | Del	International Leads	InternationalLeads	hi35@hi.com	Lead
Edit | Del	Partner Relations	PartnerRelations	hi35@hi.com	Case
Edit | Del	US - Escalations	USEscalations	hi35@hi.com	Case
Edit | Del	US - Platinum/Gold	USPlatinumGold	hi35@hi.com	Case
Edit | Del	US - Silver/Bronze	USSilverBronze	hi35@hi.com	Case
Edit | Del	US Leads	USLeads	hi35@hi.com	Lead

2. Click on **New** and set the **Queue name** as **Incoming Cases**, as shown in the following screenshot:

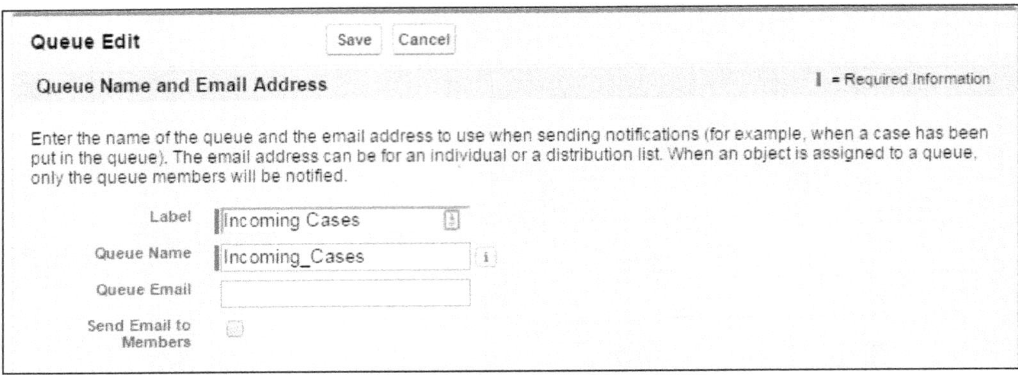

3. In the next step, select the objects that will be owned by this queue:

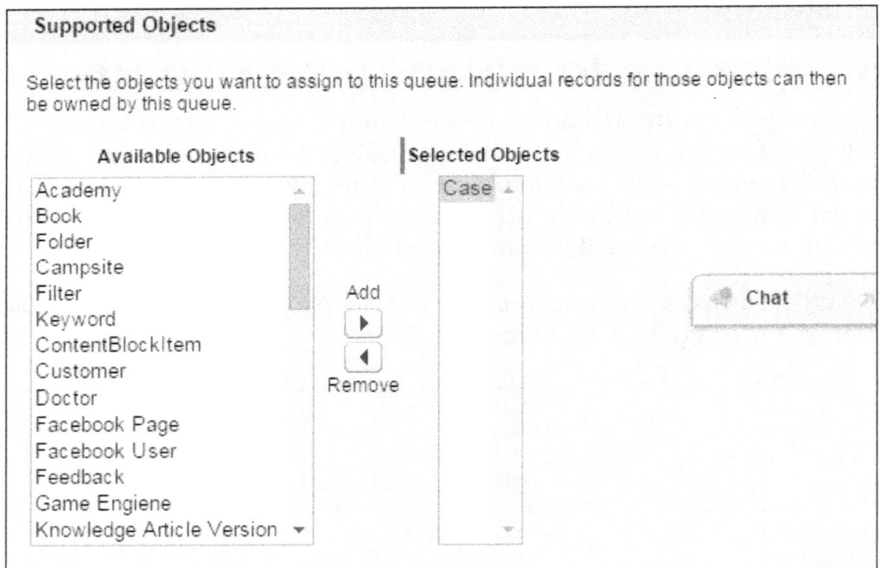

4. We can assign individual users or groups to be members of a queue. All the users get ownership access if the record is owned by the queue:

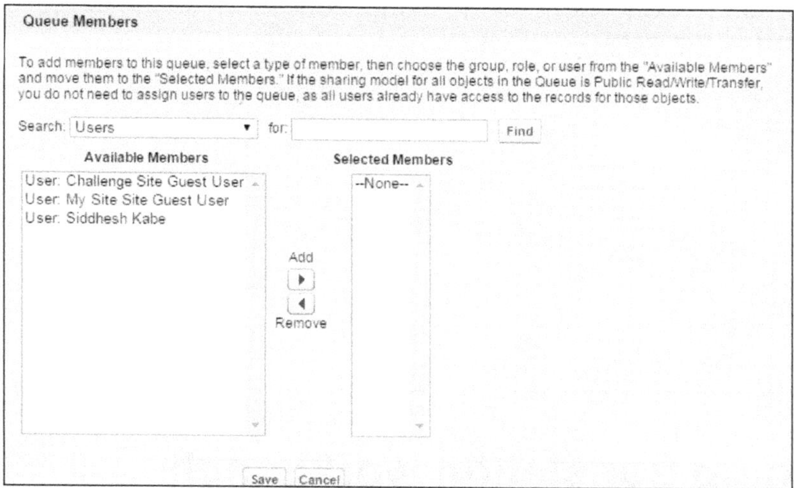

5. We can now use this queue to transfer the ownership of the case records. Any records that are owned by the queue will be shared among the members. They are then transferred to the one who picks it up first.

Localization with the translation workbench

Another aspect of administering Salesforce is translating it into the local language of the user. Salesforce fully supports 18 languages and 17 end user languages. We can easily translate the entire app into one of the supported languages; however, if we need to localize the app in a custom language not available in the list, we use the translation workbench to manually translate it.

The **Translation Workbench** allows us to specify languages that we want to translate, assign translators to languages, create translations for an app, and override labels and translations from managed packages. Everything from custom picklist values to custom fields can be translated into the language.

To open the **Translation Workbench**, go to **User name** | **Setup** | **Administration Setup** | **Translation Workbench**, as shown in the following screenshot:

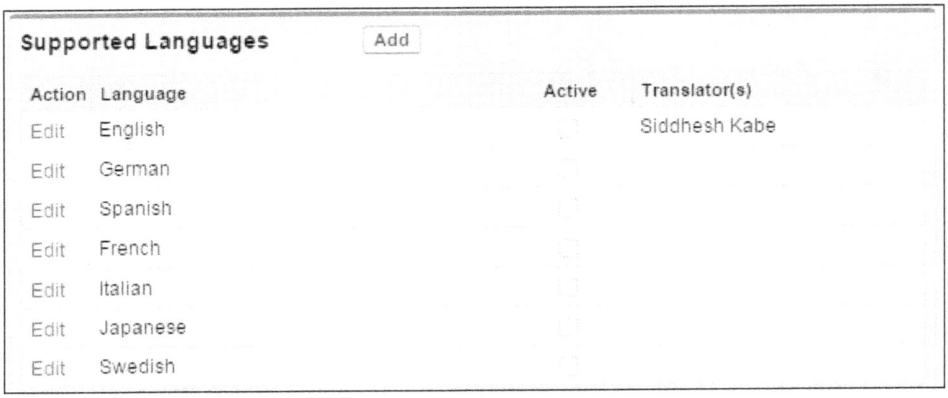

Supported Languages Add

Action	Language	Active	Translator(s)
Edit	English		Siddhesh Kabe
Edit	German		
Edit	Spanish		
Edit	French		
Edit	Italian		
Edit	Japanese		
Edit	Swedish		

Setting up translation workbench

To begin with the translation workbench, we first need to enable it. Enabling the workbench makes some significant changes in the organization. Once we enable the workbench, the following changes occur.

We cannot mass edit picklist values; however, we can mass add new values. When picklist values are sorted alphabetically, they are done according to the primary language of the organization.

The translation workbench only helps translate the constant data, such as labels and static picklist values; the user entered data is `NOT` translated. To enable the translation workbench, perform the following steps:

1. Go to **User name** | **Setup** | **Administration Setup** | **Translation Workbench** | **Translation Settings**.

2. The page will display the basic warning and general info with the **Enable** button at the bottom, as shown in the following screenshot:

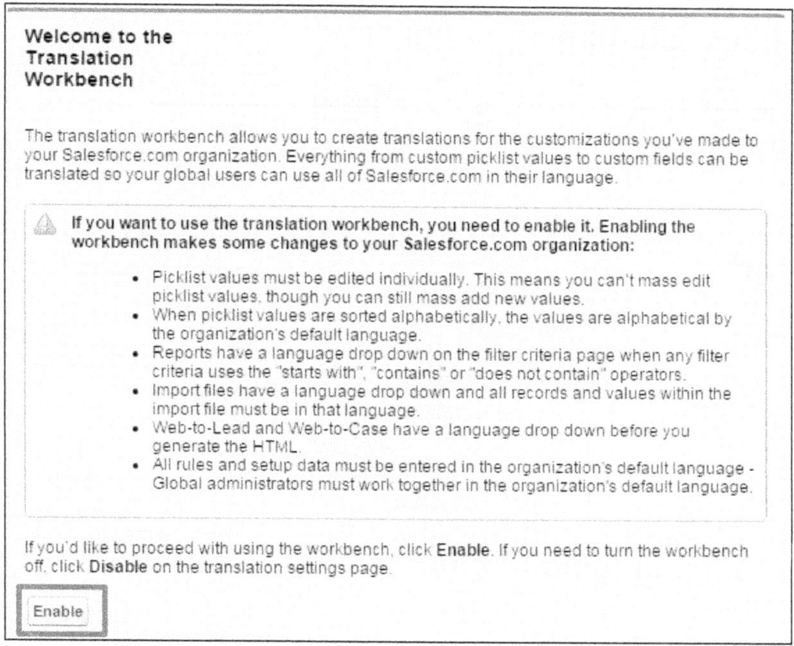

Welcome to the Translation Workbench
The translation workbench allows you to create translations for the customizations you've made to your Salesforce.com organization. Everything from custom picklist values to custom fields can be translated so your global users can use all of Salesforce.com in their language.
If you want to use the translation workbench, you need to enable it. Enabling the workbench makes some changes to your Salesforce.com organization:
Picklist values must be edited individually. This means you can't mass edit picklist values, though you can still mass add new values.
When picklist values are sorted alphabetically, the values are alphabetical by the organization's default language.
Reports have a language drop down on the filter criteria page when any filter criteria uses the "starts with", "contains" or "does not contain" operators.
Import files have a language drop down and all records and values within the import file must be in that language.
Web-to-Lead and Web-to-Case have a language drop down before you generate the HTML.
All rules and setup data must be entered in the organization's default language - Global administrators must work together in the organization's default language.
If you'd like to proceed with using the workbench, click Enable. If you need to turn the workbench off, click Disable on the translation settings page.
Enable

3. Once we enable the workbench on the settings page, we find another option to add a new language. Click on the **Add** button to add new languages:

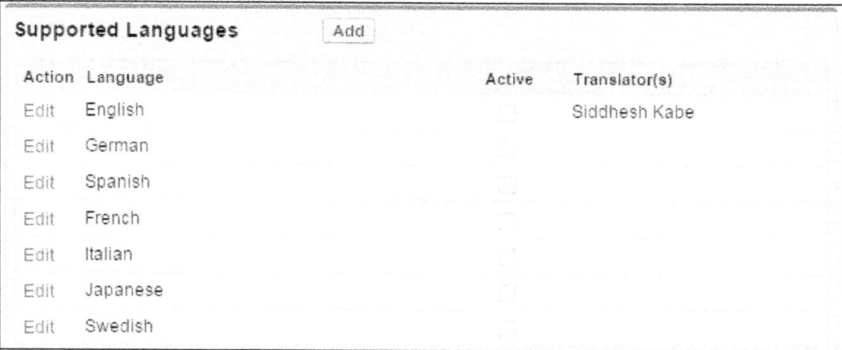

4. We can select the **Language** from the list of languages and the user to associate with the language, as shown in the following screenshot:

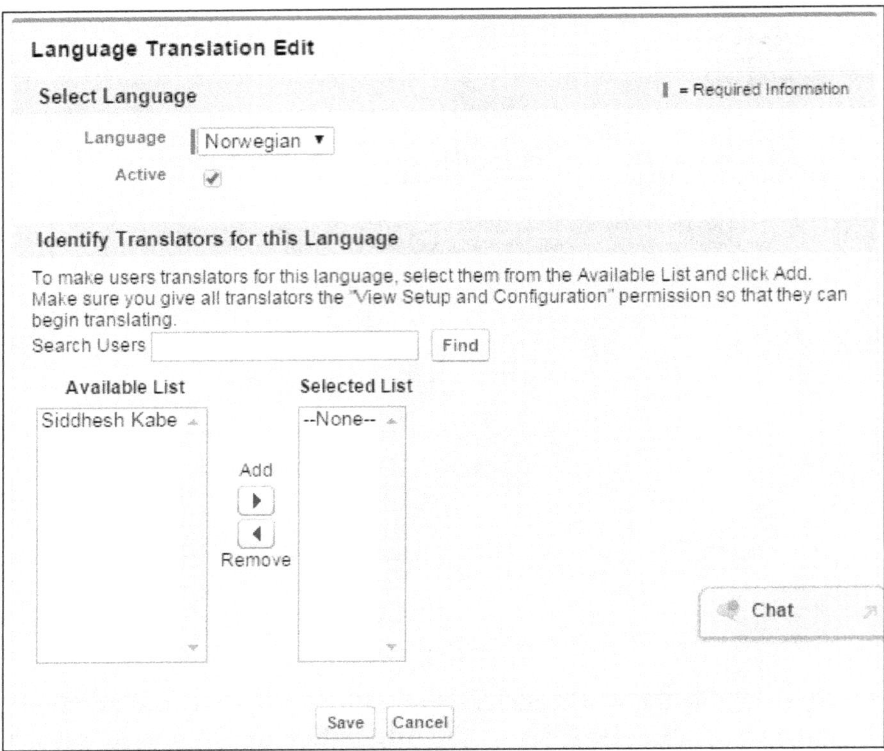
Language Translation Edit
Select Language
= Required Information
Language
Norwegian
Active
Identify Translators for this Language
To make users translators for this language, select them from the Available List and click Add.
Make sure you give all translators the "View Setup and Configuration" permission so that they can begin translating.
Search Users
Find
Available List
Selected List
Siddhesh Kabe
--None--
Add
Remove
Chat
Save
Cancel

5. If the user associated with the language has the **View Setup** and **Configuration** options in their profile, they can also help translate the application into their language.

Restricting data access

The most crucial part of any enterprise-level application (built on Salesforce or otherwise) is the control of data. The litmus test for the effectiveness of an enterprise-level application is the way in which we restrict unauthorized access to data.

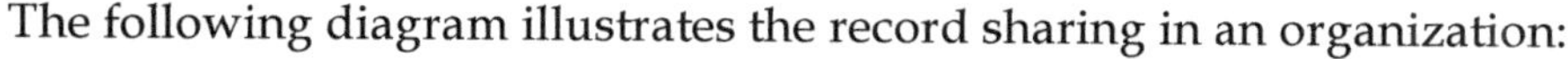

The following diagram illustrates the record sharing in an organization:

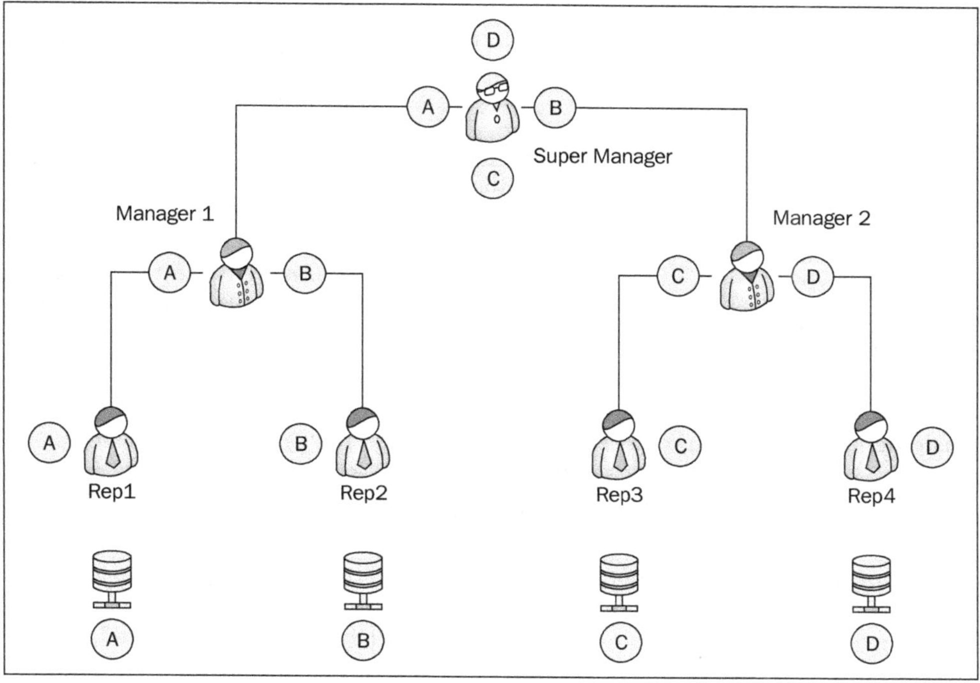

The four records `A`, `B`, `C`, and `D` are evenly distributed between the reps and the **Manager**. Rep `1` should only see record `A`, Rep `2` should only see record `B`, and so on.

At the top of the chain, the **Super Manager** can see all the records under him.

Before we design the application, we first need to consider the stakeholders of the application:

- Who will be using the application?
- What will these users do?
- Is the data sensitive or critical?
- Who will be customizing the application?
- Are there any global records that should not be edited by the users?
- Which set of users will be editing which data?

These are some of the questions that need to be addressed before we understand the security model of the application.

Exercise – defining actors

Let's revisit the problem statement of the Library Management System. The purpose of this exercise is to determine the actors in the system. Let's have a recap of the objects of the Library Management System:

Object name	Related to (relationship)	Comments
Media	`CustomerMedia` (the detail object of media)	The media object is the master table used to store the collection of media. Books and videos are separated by the record type to show different types of media.
Customer	`CustomerMedia` (the detail object of a customer) Book Penalty (the detail object of a member)	The Customer object stores the customer information. It also stores the total fine paid by the customer as a roll-up field.
CustomerMedia	Customer, Media (the master object)	The `CustomerMedia` object stores the customer and media in a junction object and is used during the checkout and `checkin` function of the library management system.
Book Penalty	Customer	This is a child object of a customer and stores the amount of late fees paid by the customer.

For the sake of simplicity, there will be two types of users that will be using the system:

- **Librarian(s)**: They will be responsible for the check-in and checkout of the books. They will be responsible for collecting penalties from the customers.
- **Admin**: Admin will update the book catalogue and add new members to the library.

In the next section, we will take a look at the Force.com security control.

The Force.com security pyramid

The security of the Force.com model is split into four parts:

- Organization-wide default
- Profile and role-based sharing
- Sharing rules
- Manual sharing

The four types of sharing can be visualized as a reverse pyramid with the maximum number of people accessing the data increasing as we move up the pyramid, as shown in the following diagram:

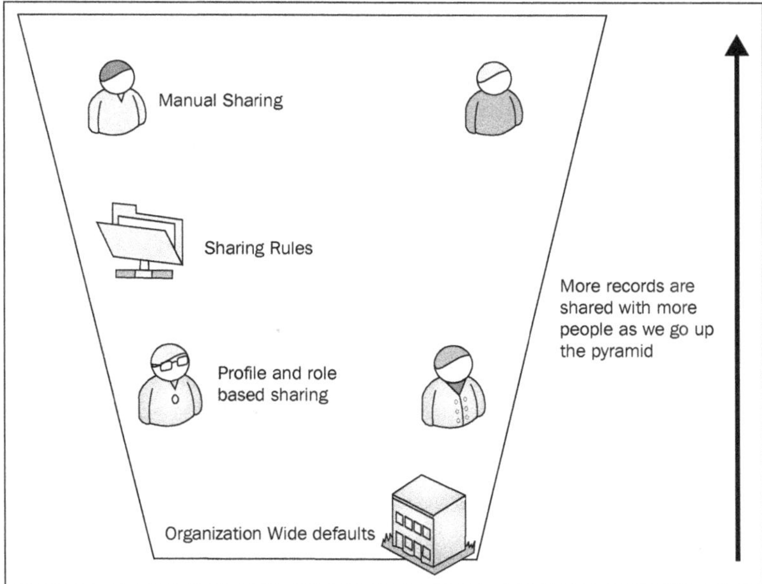

Let's climb to the top of the pyramid one by one and look at the different types of security offered by Force.com.

At any level, we can extend the sharing of the record to the other users. An important point to note here is that at no level can we restrict the record from the user if they can access it using the bottom-most rules.

For example, if a user sees a record due to **Organization-Wide** defaults and profiles, there is no way we can restrict the user from seeing the record using **Sharing Rules** or **Manual Sharing**. However, if the user cannot access the object due to **Organization-Wide** defaults, we can make it visible using **Sharing Rules** or **Manual Sharing**. The rule of thumb.

User security

As we have already seen in *Chapter 1, Getting Started with Force.com*, users need the combination of a username, password, and IP address or security token to log in to any Force.com application. As with any multiple users-based system, the most important aspect is not what the user sees, but what the user should not see.

Once the user is authenticated using any of the combinations mentioned earlier, the level of a user is determined. If the user has certain restrictions or special privileges, the data is displayed accordingly. The restrictions and privileges are stored by the system administrator in the profile.

The system administrator is usually the first user created by Force.com. The profile of system administrator has full access to the system and it is always recommended that you have a minimum set of administrators.

Based on the permission set in the profile associated with the user, the data, application, and logic is displayed. By default, Salesforce provides us with six standard profiles. These six profiles cannot be modified; if we wish to change some permission in any of them, we clone the profile and modify the clone:

- System administrator
- Authenticated website user
- Standard platform user
- Force.com user
- Contract manager
- Standard user

Custom profiles and roles

Roles and profiles are used to determine user access to data. The profile determines what objects the user can see, while the user role determines what records the user can see.

Let's explore both of them in more detail.

Understanding profiles

The profile determines the level of access the user has to the object. It also contains the setting to enable or disable access to a few applications on the platform. Using the profile, we can control the following:

- We can set which apps the user can see
- We can set which tabs the users are permitted to use
- We can determine which objects the user can see, create, update, and delete
- We can configure the default **RecordType** and the default page layout available for the user
- We can set which fields are enabled or restricted for the profile
- The Apex class and Visualforce pages are accessible to the user
- Whether the profile also configures the hours in which the user logs in as well as the IP address from which they can log in
- The system-level configurations that the users are permitted to change

Creating a custom profile

Force.com limits editing of the standard profile, and hence, it is recommended that you create a custom profile for special permission set users. In this section, we will create a custom profile for the librarian.

In contact manager, group, and professional edition organizations, we cannot create custom profiles or edit standard profiles. In enterprise, unlimited, and developer edition organizations, we can create, edit, and delete custom profiles.

To create a profile, perform the following steps:

1. Go to **Username** | **Setup** | **Administration Setup** | **Manage Users** | **Profiles**.
2. Click on the **New** button.
3. We need to select the base standard or existing custom profile to clone the new one. This will copy the existing permissions to the new one.
4. To create a **Librarian** profile, we need to clone the **system administrator** profile, as shown in the following screenshot:

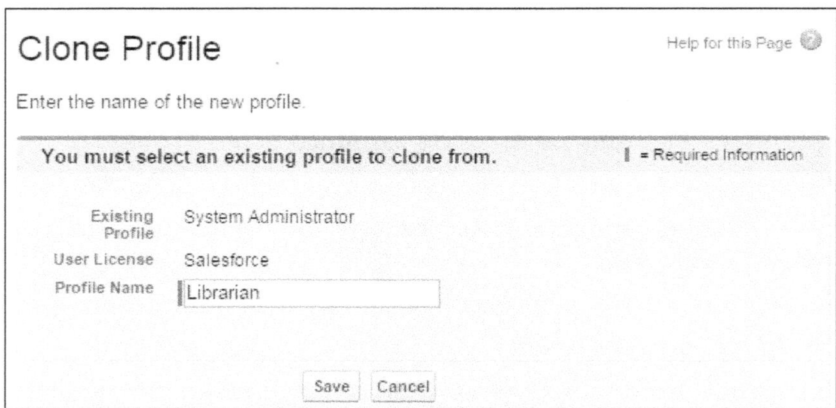

5. We will be redirected to the profile detail page. In the next section, we will take a look at the different and important aspects of the profile detail page.
6. The profile details page contains different sections that allow us to configure the different aspects of the platform, as shown in the following screenshot:

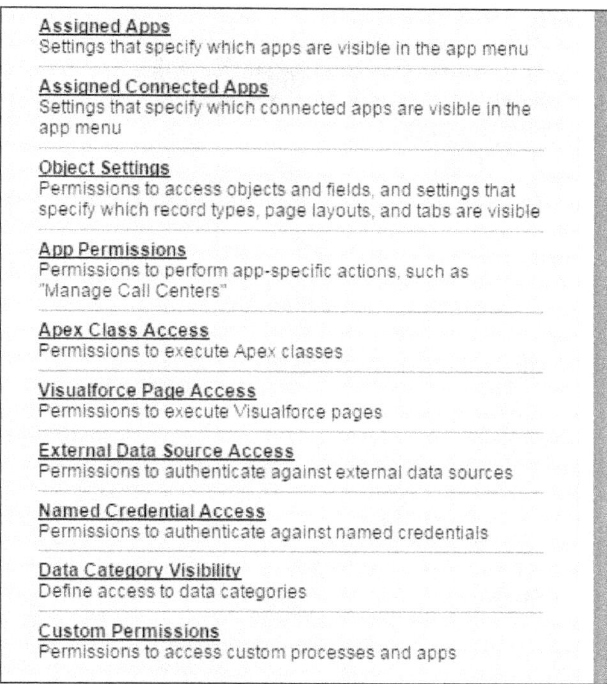

Assigned Apps
Settings that specify which apps are visible in the app menu
Assigned Connected Apps
Settings that specify which connected apps are visible in the app menu
Object Settings
Permissions to access objects and fields, and settings that specify which record types, page layouts, and tabs are visible
App Permissions
Permissions to perform app-specific actions, such as "Manage Call Centers"
Apex Class Access
Permissions to execute Apex classes
Visualforce Page Access
Permissions to execute Visualforce pages
External Data Source Access
Permissions to authenticate against external data sources
Named Credential Access
Permissions to authenticate against named credentials
Data Category Visibility
Define access to data categories
Custom Permissions
Permissions to access custom processes and apps

Let's take a look at some of the important sections in detail.

Assigned apps

The **Assigned Apps** section allows us to choose the **Apps** that the user can access. We can also set the **Default** app for the user:

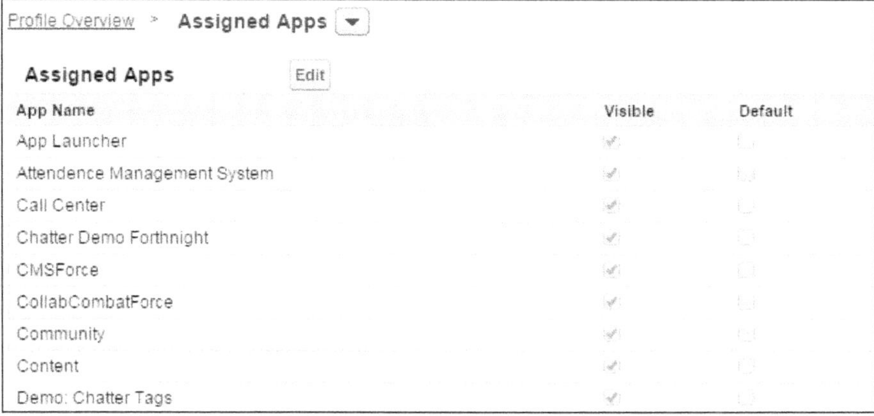

Profile Overview > Assigned Apps
Assigned Apps
Edit
App Name
Visible
Default
App Launcher
Attendence Management System
Call Center
Chatter Demo Forthnight
CMSForce
CollabCombatForce
Community
Content
Demo: Chatter Tags

Object settings

The **Object settings** section allows us to choose the object's permission for the user. In one layout, we can see all the objects a user has access to. We can view the **Object permissions** and **Tab settings** tabs:

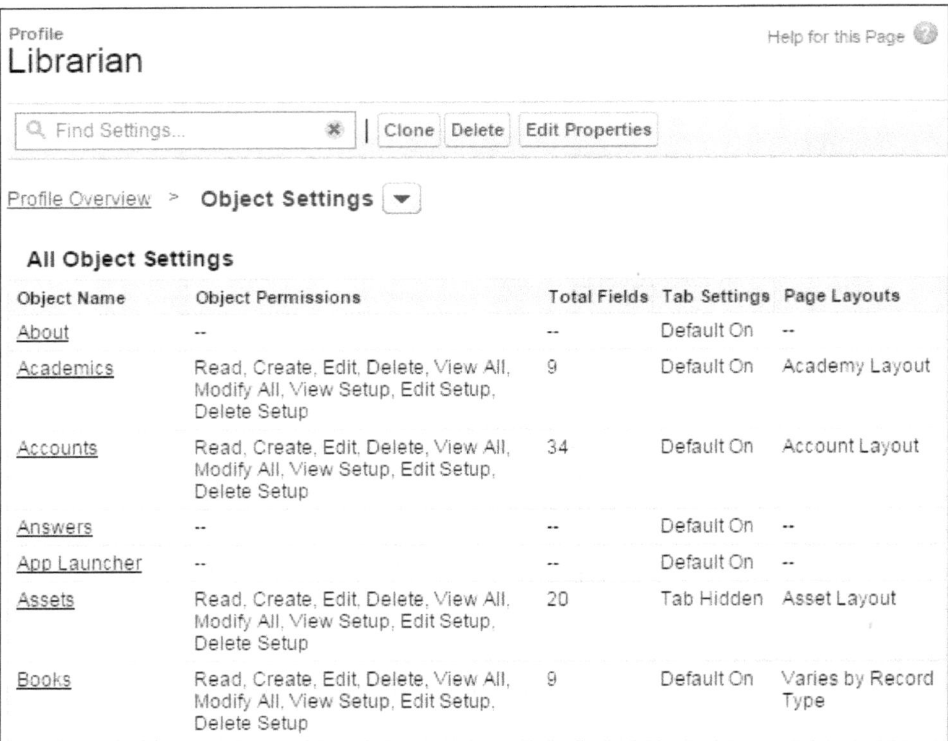

Profile
Librarian
Help for this Page
Find Settings...
Clone
Delete
Edit Properties
Profile Overview > Object Settings
All Object Settings
Object Name
Object Permissions
Total Fields
Tab Settings
Page Layouts
About
--
--
Default On
--
Academics
Read, Create, Edit, Delete, View All, Modify All, View Setup, Edit Setup, Delete Setup
9
Default On
Academy Layout
Accounts
Read, Create, Edit, Delete, View All, Modify All, View Setup, Edit Setup, Delete Setup
34
Default On
Account Layout
Answers
--
--
Default On
--
App Launcher
--
--
Default On
--
Assets
Read, Create, Edit, Delete, View All, Modify All, View Setup, Edit Setup, Delete Setup
20
Tab Hidden
Asset Layout
Books
Read, Create, Edit, Delete, View All, Modify All, View Setup, Edit Setup, Delete Setup
9
Default On
Varies by Record Type

Let's take a look at the **Books** object in detail:

The first section is the **Tab Settings** that determines the access level of the object tab.

There are three options that we can choose for the tab settings:

Default On	This makes the tab default to the user when they open the app
Default Off	This hides the tab from the user, but the user can personalize their app to add the tab again
Tab Hidden	This hides the tab from the user and the user cannot add it

If there are some sensitive tabs containing important data, the tab has to be specifically hidden from the user. The user can personalize his app and add new tabs to it as well. It is always recommended that you hide the tab separately along with the app:

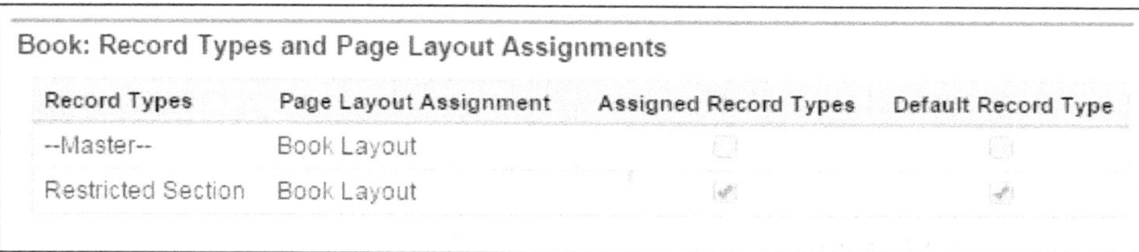

Book: Record Types and Page Layout Assignments
Record Types
Page Layout Assignment
Assigned Record Types
Default Record Type
--Master--
Book Layout
Restricted Section
Book Layout

The next section is the **Record Types** and **Page Layout Assignments** that determine which `Recordtype` the user can access. We can assign a **Page Layout** to every **Record Type**. We can also assign a `recordType` as default:

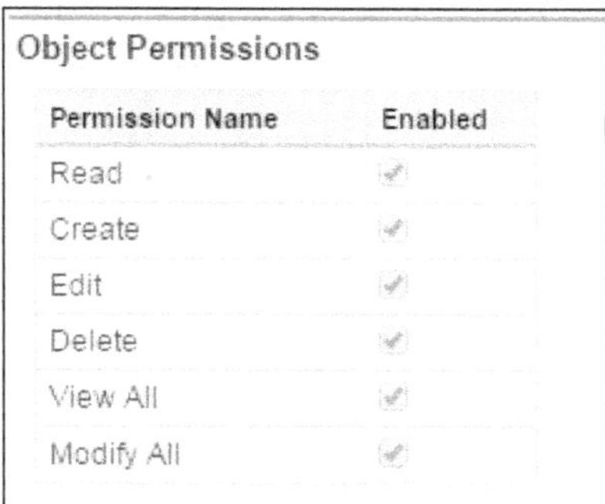

The **Object Permissions** section determines the level of access to the object. These permissions determine what access control the user has on the object that is specified. The **View All** and **Modify All** checkboxes make the object visible and shareable regardless of any other sharing settings.

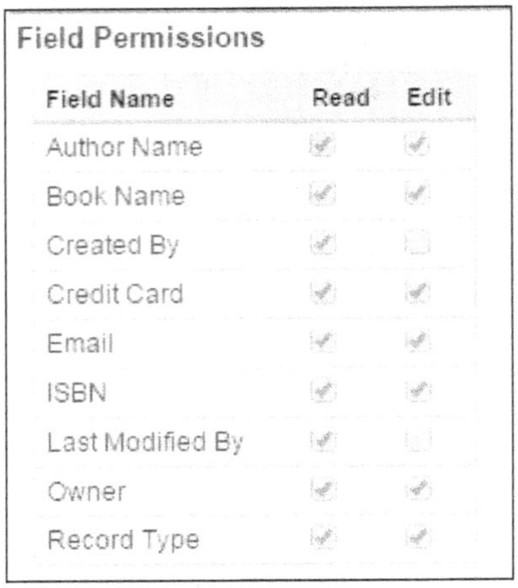

Field Permissions

Field Name	Read	Edit
Author Name	✓	✓
Book Name	✓	✓
Created By	✓	
Credit Card	✓	✓
Email	✓	✓
ISBN	✓	✓
Last Modified By	✓	
Owner	✓	✓
Record Type	✓	✓

The **Field Permissions** section allows us to select the individual **Read** and **Edit** permissions for each field of that object.

App permissions

The App permissions section gives us administrative capabilities for the Salesforce CRM applications and the platform. We can configure the standard applications, such as Call Center, as shown in the following screenshot:

▼ Call Center

Permission Name	Enabled	Description
Edit Case Comments	✓ i	Edit their own case comments but not other user's comments.
Edit Self-Service Users	✓ i	Enable and disable contacts for Self-Service and Customer Portal access.
Import Solutions	✓ i	Import solutions for the organization.
Manage Business Hours Holidays	✓ i	Create, edit, and delete business holidays.
Manage Call Centers	✓ i	Create, import, edit, and delete a call center configuration.
Manage Cases	✓ i	Administer case settings, including Email-to-Case and mass transfer of cases.
Manage Categories	✓ i	Define and modify solution categories settings.
Manage Macros Users Can't Undo	✓	Create, update, and run macros that include irreversible instructions.
Manage Published Solutions	✓ i	Create, edit, and delete publicly accessible solutions.
Manage Self-Service Portal	✓ i	Manage Self-Service portal settings and reports.
Run Macros on Multiple Records	i	Run macros on multiple records at the same time.
Transfer Cases	✓ i	Change a case's owner.

Other sections

There are other permissions, such as **Apex Class Access**, **Visualforce Access**, **External Data Sources Access**, **Named Credential Access**, **Data Visibility**, and **Custom Permissions**, that allow us to assign the respective metadata to the profile:

Apex Class Access
Permissions to execute Apex classes

Visualforce Page Access
Permissions to execute Visualforce pages

External Data Source Access
Permissions to authenticate against external data sources

Named Credential Access
Permissions to authenticate against named credentials

Data Category Visibility
Define access to data categories

Custom Permissions
Permissions to access custom processes and apps

System permissions

System permissions controls the access to the system and allows us to turn on/off the features of the Salesforce system, as shown in the following screenshot:

System Permissions
Permissions to perform actions that apply across apps, such as "Modify All Data"

Desktop Client Access
Permissions to access desktop clients, such as "Connect for Office"

Login Hours
Settings that control when users can log in

Login IP Ranges
Settings that control the IP addresses from which users can log in

Session Settings
Settings that control required session security level and timeout for inactive sessions

Password Policies
Profile Based password policies

For example, if we turn off the Author Apex permission, the user cannot access and see the custom code written on the platform.

You can refer to a complete list of user permissions at `https://help.salesforce.com/htviewhelpdoc?id=users_profiles_system_perms.htm&siteLang=en_US`.

Now, let's see how the user should see the data using roles.

Assigning roles

Roles are created according to the corporate hierarchy of the system. Roles determine how the data is shared with the user. While profiles determine which objects can be seen by which users, roles determine which records from the object can be seen by the user. The user can be separated on the basis of their work department, territory, or company hierarchy.

The following diagram illustrates a basic sample role hierarchy:

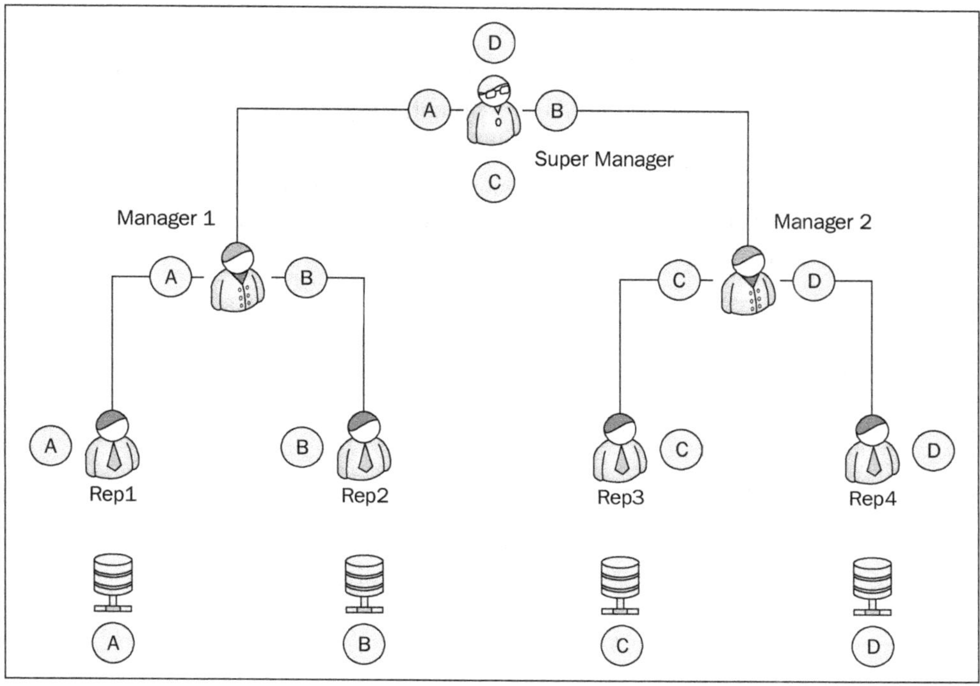

In the preceding diagram, **A**, **B**, **C**, and **D**, are records of the same objects owned by **Rep1**, **Rep2**, **Rep3**, and **Rep4**, respectively. While all the four reps have access to the same objects, they do not have access to each other's records. **Manager 1** can see the data and reports from **Rep1** and **Rep2** as they come under his hierarchy. He cannot, however, access the data for **Rep3** and **Rep4**. The **Super Manager** can see the entire organization's data as he is topmost in the hierarchy.

Role hierarchy prevents the data from being seen by people at the same level in the hierarchy, at the same time it grants full access to the people on top of the hierarchy. In the preceding example, **Manager 1** will get all access to the **Rep1** data.

To achieve this, we set up a role hierarchy.

Steps to set up role hierarchy

Perform the following steps to set up a role hierarchy:

1. Go to **Username** | **Setup** | **Administration setup** | **Manage Users** | **Roles**.
2. If it is your first time, it will show a splash page for roles with the **Set Up Roles** button. Click on the button to proceed.
3. As shown in the following screenshot, the default view is the tree view for the roles. The view can be changed in the top-right hand corner to the normal view or list view:

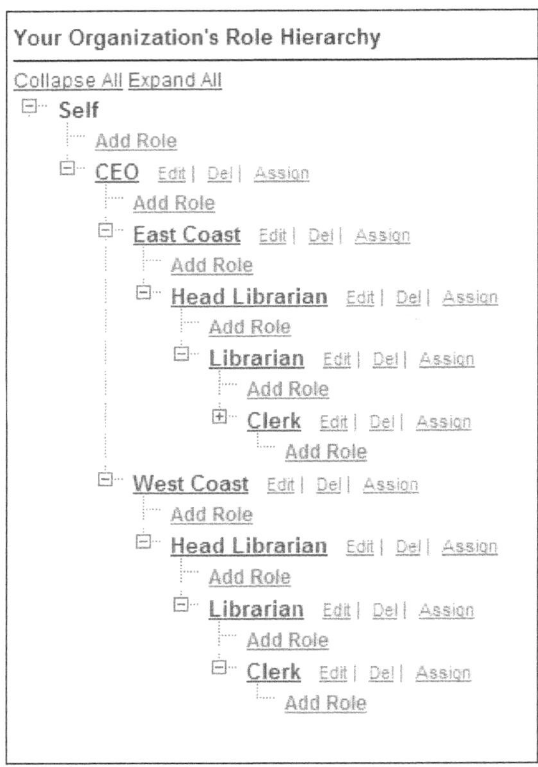

4. As shown in the preceding screenshot, with the **Add Roles** link, we can create roles at any level in the hierarchy.
5. Once we define the role, using the **Assign** link, we can assign users to the role.
6. In the next section, we will deal with the object-based security in Salesforce and understand the significance of role hierarchy in distributing the records.

Exercise – scaling the Library Management System

The general library now wishes to install this system across multiple locations. They have branches on the East coast as well as the West coast.

The structure of the organization is as follows:

- They have a separate head librarian for each coast who in turn gets reports from multiple sublibrarians
- Each branch has a clerk who handles the check-in and checkout of books and maintains the customer profiles

Permission sets

A user can have only one profile at a time but can have multiple permission sets. A permission set is a collection of settings and permissions. The permission sets are the same permissions that are found on profiles. The permission set extends the user functions without changing their profiles.

The permissions that are enabled in either the profile or the permission set are enabled for the user who has the right combination. For example, if the profile or the permission set has the **API Enabled** permission, the user with that combination will get the **API Enabled** permission.

We can use the permission set to create fuzzy grouping of users irrespective of their job roles. For example, if a few sections of users need to have the edit permission on the Media object, we can create a permission set for it and assign to it those users irrespective of their profiles or roles.

To create a permission set, perform the following steps:

1. Go to **User Name** | **Setup** | **Manage Users** | **Permission Sets** | **New**.
2. Add the **Label** and **API Name** to the permission set. Choose the correct license for the **Permission** set. We can set a specific license to the permission set to assign it to users of that license. If the permission set is for users with different license types, select `-- none --`:

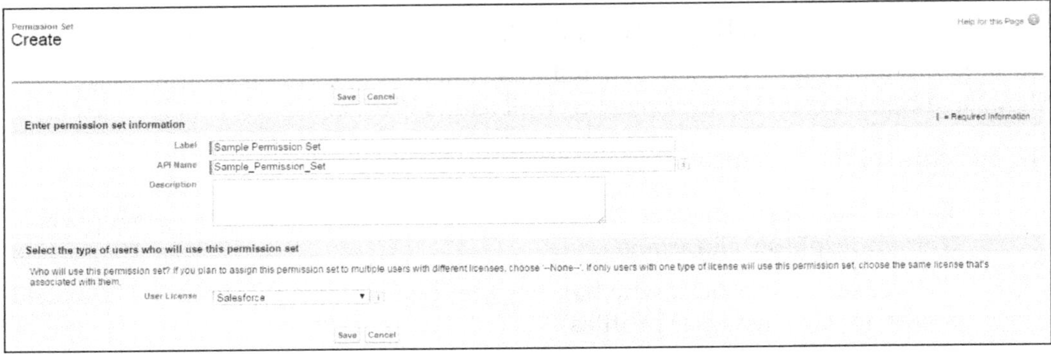

3. The layout of **Permission Set** is the same as the layout for profiles.

Organization-wide defaults

While roles and profiles are used to determine the user-based security, the organization-wide default determines the distribution of data with the user. We use the defaults in the object to determine which people across the role hierarchy can access which objects.

> Objects allowed to be viewed by the organization-wide defaults can be restricted using profiles and roles.

To set up **Organization-wide** defaults, follow these steps:

1. Go to **Username** | **Setup** | **Administrative Setup** | **Security Controls** | **Sharing Settings,** as shown in the following screenshot:

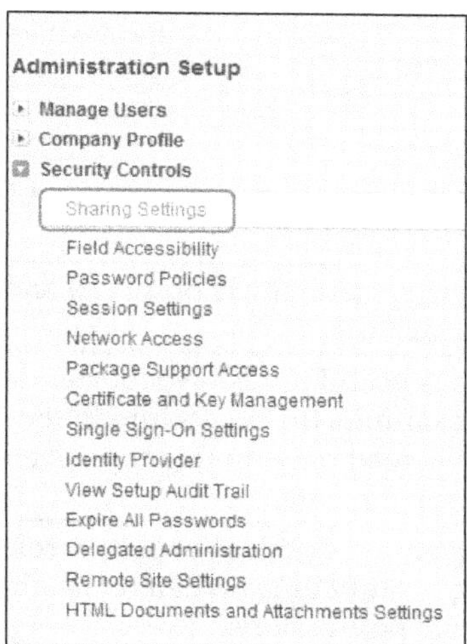

2. The general sharing diagram for the organization is shown in the following screenshot:

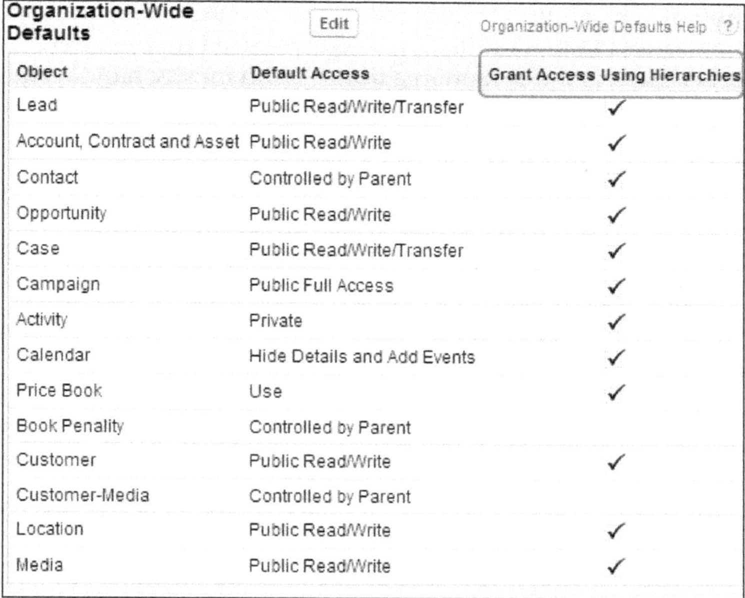
Organization-Wide Defaults Edit Organization-Wide Defaults Help ?

Object	Default Access	Grant Access Using Hierarchies
Lead	Public Read/Write/Transfer	✓
Account, Contract and Asset	Public Read/Write	✓
Contact	Controlled by Parent	✓
Opportunity	Public Read/Write	✓
Case	Public Read/Write/Transfer	✓
Campaign	Public Full Access	✓
Activity	Private	✓
Calendar	Hide Details and Add Events	✓
Price Book	Use	✓
Book Penality	Controlled by Parent	
Customer	Public Read/Write	✓
Customer-Media	Controlled by Parent	
Location	Public Read/Write	✓
Media	Public Read/Write	✓

3. Select the object to be configured for the organization-wide tabs. We get three options to choose from, as shown in the following screenshot:

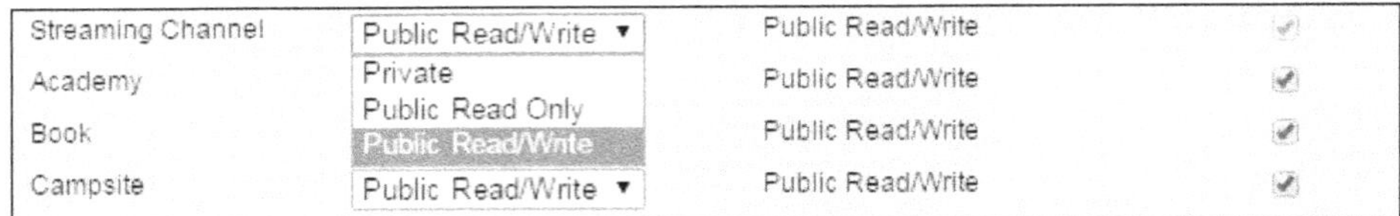

The following options determine the sharing settings of the object:

Private	The role hierarchy is observed and people cannot view their peer records.
Public Read Only	This is useful if we have master data that the people refer to, for example, the books info in the library. They can be kept as public read only. In this case, everyone across the hierarchy can see the data.
Public Read/Write	This option does not obey any role hierarchy and anyone can edit/modify or even delete the objects, depending on their profile permissions.

Organization-wide defaults summarized

To set up organization-wide defaults, follow the simple method:

1. First find out which user requires the least access to an object. Set the organization-wide default to all the objects based on this user. For example, the library clerk is the person in a library who mostly handles the issuing and the return of the books. They need the least access to the customer object (assuming that only the librarian can handle membership) set the customer object to private read only.
2. Most restrictive record access is defined using an organization-wide default. Access to additional records is made available through the role hierarchy, sharing rules, and manual sharing.
3. Changing organization wide default settings can delete manual sharing if that sharing is no longer needed.

Sharing rules

The organization-wide default sets us a base level for access to the object. We can open the access using role hierarchies and sharing rules. Sharing rules can create automatic exceptions to the organization-wide defaults. We can create sharing rules based on the record owner and field values. We can share the records with users for the objects that are set as **Private** and **Public Read Only** using sharing rules. Sharing rules can only expand the sharing of the records, if the records are marked as **Private** or **Public Read Only**. If the user can see the records with organization-wide defaults, we can restrict them using sharing rules.

Let's set up the sharing rules:

1. Go to **Username** | **Setup** | **Administrative Setup** | **Security Control** | **Sharing Settings**.
2. Below the organization-wide defaults, there are multiple sections of objects, as shown in the following screenshot:

3. We can set the sharing rules based on the criteria of the users, as shown in the following screenshot:

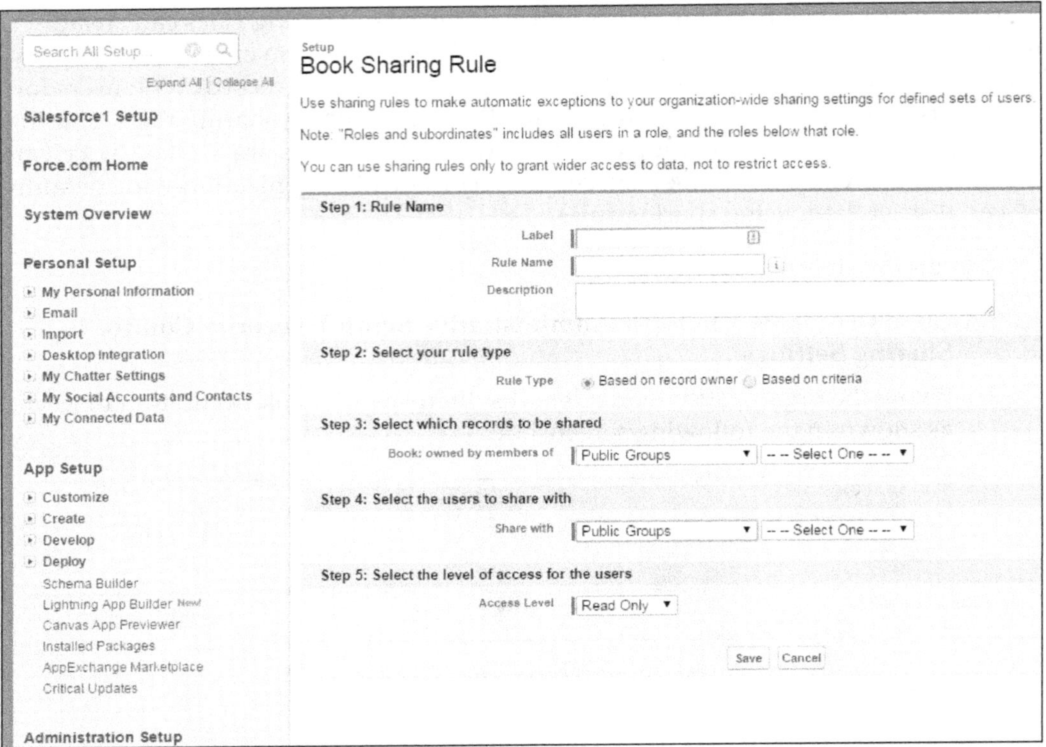

Some standard objects, such as leads, have different sharing settings. We can set the sharing rules as `Public Read/Write/Transfer` for **Lead** and **Cases**.

4. In step 2, we can choose the sharing based on the record owner or based on criteria. When we choose the sharing based on the record owner, we can set the rules to share records from a public group or role in step 3 to another public group or role in step 4, as shown in the preceding screenshot:

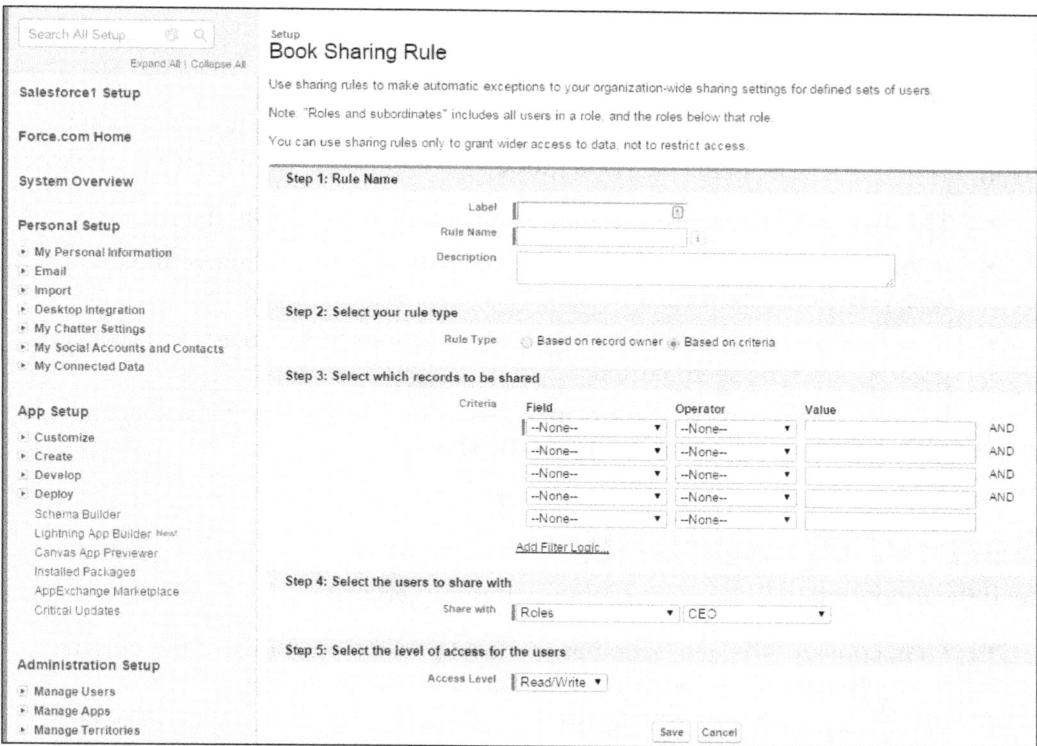

Manual sharing

Finally, the last option in sharing is the manual sharing option given to the individual users with full access to a record. It is used if the organization-wide default access for the object is set to Private. This is generally done by a record owner for a single record. Only the record owner and users above the owner in the role hierarchy are granted full access to the record. It is not possible to grant other users full access.

Users with the **Modify All** object-level permission for the given object or the **Modify All Data** permission can also manually share a record. User-managed sharing is removed when the record owner changes or when the access granted in the sharing does not grant additional access beyond the object's organization-wide sharing default access level.

Quick bites

Sharing can be a bit complex because we need to fix the complex business problems using different tools, so here is a quick guide to understand sharing:

- The owner of the record can view/edit/modify and delete the record
- If the organization uses sharing and security, the person above the owner can also view/edit the record
- If there is any object that has the sharing settings public read/write or greater, it can be seen/edited
- If the record is private, a user can access it only when there is a sharing rule giving them access or if it is manually shared

Setting up security

Keep the following points in mind while setting up security:

- First, consider the user who has the least possible visibility of the objects. Set up the organization-wide defaults based on them.
- Then, prepare the matrix for the users who have access to other objects. Prepare their profiles and permission sets based on that.
- Finally, set up the role hierarchies to enable mutual sharing of the objects.
- The remaining odd records can be shared using sharing rules.

Exercise – creating a user

Now that we have set up the roles and profiles, it's time to add our users.

The Library Management System is now in place and users can't wait to try it out. Create a user with a **Standard User** profile so that they can access the system:

1. To create a user, go to **Username** | **Setup** | **Administration Setup** | **Manage Users** | **Users**.
2. Click on **New User**.

   If required, we can also add multiple users in a fresh organization.

3. The **Add New User** page is self-explanatory; we will take at look at the important aspects only. Assign the **Standard User** profile to the user.

> Profiles are directly associated with the license type. The standard user profile and the other six user profiles are available as part of Salesforce licenses.

4. The checkboxes on the right-hand side determine the functionality and other desktop applications used. For instance, if the user is allowed to access Salesforce from a mobile application, select **Mobile User**. Similarly, if the user can access the service cloud console, select **service user**.
5. Fill in the contact information for the user. The user can change it later themselves.
6. Local settings determine the language and the time zone for the user when they log in.
7. Finally, if the user is to be notified, there is a separate checkbox at the bottom of the page. If the user is created for testing purposes, there shouldn't be a need to notify the user at the time. Checking this box will send the user a temporary one-time expiry password, which the user has to change at the first login.
8. Save the record.

There is one important step skipped purposely in the form that is adding of the role, which we will see in the next section.

Password policies

Another important step in user security settings is the password policy for the users. Password policies help maintain a strict and complex pattern in a password with the automatic expiry.

By default, Salesforce passwords expire in 90 days and the user cannot use three previous passwords. They are eight characters in length and should be a combination of alphanumeric characters. These policies can be changed using the **Password Policies** settings.

To change the **Password Policies** settings, perform the following steps:

1. Go to **User Name** | **Setup** | **Administration Setup** | **Security Controls** | **Password Policies**.
2. Change the policies according to the requirements, as shown in the following screenshot:

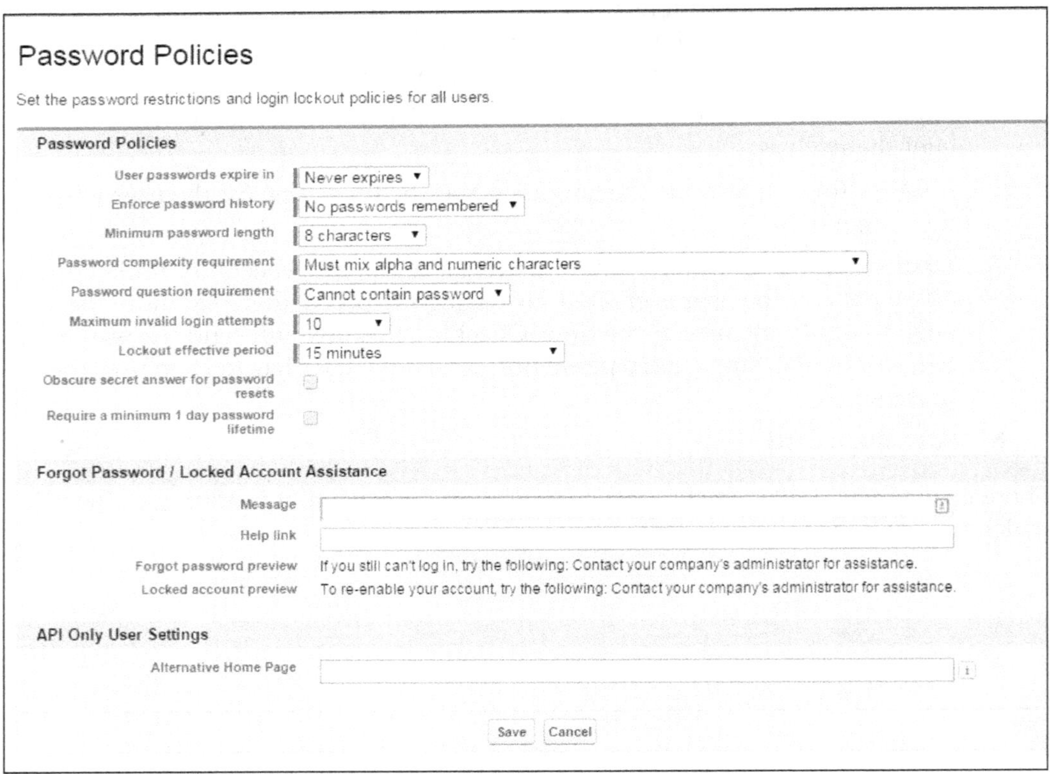

3. The message and help link can be provided to the users in case they forget the password. If the system administrator forgets the password, we can reset it using the reset link sent to the e-mail.

Managing Customers

Salesforce helps us manage our business and personal accounts. We can capture the information of the customers in the **Account object** provided by default in Salesforce. The accounts are Public by default; however; we can make them private if the company works with sensitive clients. We can capture the employees and important contacts with the account in the **Contact object**.

If it is a business to Customer Company, then we can set up a personal account that creates a single link between the account and contacts. A single contact record is merged with the account when we enable the personal account.

Along with the customers, we can capture opportunities, business deals, and contracts on the account.

For more information on the Accounts and Contact, go to `https://developer.salesforce.com/trailhead/en/module/admin_intro_accounts_contacts`.

Social features

Social accounts allows us to connect your Twitter and Facebook accounts to the Salesforce account and contact. We can connect the social media accounts to the contact records and stay updated with their latest activities. We can connect the following social networks with Salesforce to the Contact, Lead, and account.

Social Network	**Description**
Twitter	We can see bios, recent tweets, and the people who are following and being followed by our Salesforce accounts, contacts, and leads by connecting to their Twitter account.
Facebook	Facebook helps us find common interests. For contacts, leads, and person accounts, we can see profiles, status updates, and the number of mutual friends we share. For business accounts, we can see customers' corporate social media presence such as their company profile and wall posts.

Social Network	Description
Klout	We can use Klout to see the influence of our accounts, contacts, and leads on social media, who they influence, who influences them, and the topics they talk about.
YouTube videos	YouTube helps us find and view videos related to your accounts, contacts, and leads.

For more information on the social features, go to `https://help.salesforce.com/apex/HTViewHelpDoc?id=social_networks_enable.htm`.

Summary

In this chapter, we looked at the security of the Force.com application. We now understand the difference between the different Force.com licenses. We learned how to make the matrix sheet before designing the application. We climbed the sharing pyramid and learned how users are granted sharing access.

With this chapter, we come to the end of application development on the cloud-based Force.com platform. We now know how to build applications on Force.com without using code. We can create objects, make pages for them, and also solve business problems using clicks.

Using the powerful logic as a service, we can now manage to migrate the approval processes and workflows trigger on the cloud. By now, your sample Library Management System should be ready.

Finally, we are set to add our customer data in the organization and create users. Thus, we are ready to go live with the application.

Test your knowledge

Q1 A company wishes to deploy a custom build application on the Force.com platform. What license would the users need to access the application?
(Choose any that apply)

1. Chatter
2. The Salesforce platform
3. Salesforce
4. The Force.com free edition

Q2 A company is using Chatter for their internal communication. They wish to give a user access to the account object. If he is a Chatter user, what things should be done to give him access?

1. Assign a separate profile for him
2. Make the normal user his manager
3. It cannot be done

Q3 The users with the Salesforce platform license can access the CRM application.

1. True
2. False

Q4 If the actors who will be using the applications are not determined before the creation of application, which of the following will happen? Select any two choices.

1. We will be unable to create reports and dashboards
2. Unauthorized users can access sensitive data
3. There will be no room for scaling the application to large users

Q5 The library needs to make all records of an object visible to all users when it is in *Approved* status. The records are created with *New* status and are only visible to a select set of users. How will a user implement this?

1. Set the object level sharing to private and add a workflow rule to update the sharing rule when status changes
2. Set the object level sharing to public read-only; restrict the sharing when status is *New*
3. Set the object level sharing to private, create a public group with appropriate users, and modify manual sharing to the public group based on status
4. Create a role hierarchy and modify the user profiles when the status changes

8

Exam Guide and Practice Test

We have covered all the topics of Force.com that are part of the Salesforce Certified Platform App Developer Exam. This chapter will help you understand the exam and answer the frequently asked questions. This chapter also includes a practice test that will help you refresh the skills we have learned throughout the book.

We will cover the following topics in this chapter:

- An overview of the exam
- Certification and maintenance releases
- A sample test
- Additional resources

This chapter will give you an overview of the exam and help you mentally prepare for what is coming.

An overview of the Salesforce Certified Platform App Developer Exam

The Salesforce Certified Platform App Developer Exam is a multiple choice question exam. The exam consists of 60 multi-choice questions to be completed in 90 minutes. The passing score for the exam is 63 percent, so roughly at least 40 questions should be answered correctly.

The exam is proctored and no reference material should be referred to while sitting the exam. You can take the exam at an exam center or as an online proctored exam.

Anyone with a good knowledge of the Salesforce.com and Force.com platforms can take the exam. Salesforce also has classroom training for the exam. More information on the classroom training can be found at `http://certification.salesforce.com/app-builders`.

Once you finish the exam, the result is displayed instantly on the screen. The result shows only a Pass or Fail and the Certificate is delivered to the registered e-mail. No grades or percentages are displayed in the result.

Certification maintenance and releases

Once the exam has been taken, the candidate has to complete release-specific exams every three months (roughly). The release-specific exams are additional questions that cover the upgrades to the platform in the releases.

Release exams are published three times a year for each of the platform upgrades released throughout the year. An annual maintenance fee of $100 is charged to the candidate on the anniversary of the certification, which includes three release exams. Salesforce certified professionals are notified automatically when new release training materials and exams become available.

A practice test

The following is a practice test that will help you do a mock revision of all the things that we have learned so far. This can be used for proper time management as well. Set the timer to 90 minutes and solve this test.

Q1 A developer has completed work in the sandbox and is ready to send it to a related organization. Which deployment tool should be used?

1. The Force.com IDE
2. Unmanaged packages
3. Change sets
4. The Force.com Migration Tool

Q2 You have created a workflow rule to send an e-mail to your configuration sandbox. For some reason it's not working. What should you double check? (Select any two)

1. HTML does not work in the sandbox, so make sure that your e-mail has no HTML
2. Check the deliverability settings
3. Look at the system audit trail
4. Check whether you have the correct e-mail address

Q3 Universal Container installs an unmanaged package. Which of the following are true? (Select any two)

1. Components of unmanaged packages can be edited
2. Unmanaged packages can be upgraded
3. Unmanaged packages have a namespace prefix
4. Unmanaged packages don't have a version number
5. Tests are executed during deployment

Q4 Which deployment tools will you use to deploy metadata from one organization to another organization?

1. Change sets
2. Unmanaged packages
3. The Force.com IDE

Q5 Which tools do you need to use to migrate metadata to two different production organizations? (Select any three)

1. The Force.com Migration Tool
2. The Force.com IDE
3. Change sets
4. Data loader
5. Unmanaged package

Q6 Identify the standard Lightning components. (Select any three)

1. The Visualforce page
2. Reports
3. List View
4. Dashboards
5. Rich Text

Q7 You can create global actions to let users create which of the following records? (Select any three)

1. Opportunity
2. Question
3. Users
4. Chatter posts
5. Event (without invitees)
6. Products

Q8 What standard Chatter actions appear on the user profile page, regardless of the actions in the User page layout? (Select any three)

1. Post
2. Create
3. Poll
4. File
5. E-mail

Q9 Which a user creates a record using an object-specific create action, what feed item for that record appears?

1. The first entry in the feed for the new record
2. The feed for the record on which the new record was created
3. The user profile feed for all users who can view the record
4. The Chatter feed of the first user who follows the record on which the record was created
5. The Chatter feed of the user who created the record

Q10 How do you enable the Publisher Actions area on Page Layouts:

1. Setup | Customize | Feeds | Settings
2. Setup | Customize | <Objects> | Settings
3. Setup | Customize | Chatter | Chatter Settings
4. Setup | Customize | Actions | Settings

Q11 What is a Lightning page?

1. A page you can access via a customer community
2. The new name for a Salesforce page layout
3. A custom layout used to create pages in Salesforce1
4. A compact, configurable, and reusable element

Q12 What can you build with the Lightning App Builder?

1. At a glance, dashboard-style apps
2. Apps optimized for a particular task
3. Simple, single-page apps with drill-down capability
4. All of the above

Q13 Actions on a Lightning page allow you to do which of the following?

1. Send an e-mail, create a task, and create or update records
2. Send e-mails and delete or clone records
3. Clone records, add users, and assign permissions
4. Send e-mails, send outbound messages, and launch a flow

Q14 Which components can be added to a Lightning app on a custom object? (Select any three)

1. Visualforce
2. The Standard Lightning component
3. The Custom Lightning component
4. Object-specific actions on the custom object
5. Global actions

Q15 In order to create an App Launcher component in Lightning, what must an admin do?

1. Contact Salesforce to have the component activated for the Lightning App Builder
2. Navigate to **Setup** | **Customize** | **User Interface** to enable the component for the **Lightning App Builder**
3. Purchase a license for the Lightning App Builder
4. Join the pilot Lightning App Builder team

Q16 What is true when a field update is set to re-evaluate the workflow rule? (Select any three)

1. In a batch update, a workflow is only retriggered on the entities where there is a change
2. Only workflow rules that didn't fire before will be retriggered
3. Cascade of the workflow rule re-evaluation and triggering can happen up to ten times after the initial field update that started it
4. Only workflow rules on the same object as the initial field update will be re-evaluated and triggered
5. Any workflow rules whose criteria are met as a result of the field update will be ignored

Q17 Identify the field update limitations. (Select any three)

1. Field updates that are executed as approval actions don't trigger workflow rules
2. Read-only fields, such as formula or auto number fields, aren't available for field updates
3. The results of a field update can't trigger additional rules, such as validation, assignment, auto response, or escalation rules
4. In a batch update, workflow is retriggered on all entities where there is a change

Q18 Which is true about social accounts?

1. You can use social accounts data even when you are not logged in to the social account
2. You need a personal social account in order to see the social account data
3. You can use social accounts to import data into Salesforce
4. A connection to a social account is established through a company-wide *named principle*

Q19 A salesperson at AW computing only sees the social contact's link for Twitter and not Facebook on his records. Why would this be happening?

1. The administrator hasn't enabled Social Contacts for Facebook
2. Facebook is no longer supported by Social Contacts
3. The salesperson's login with Facebook has expired
4. None of his Facebook contacts have confirmed the nature of their relationship

Q20 Which social networks are available in Lightning Experience and Salesforce1? (select all that apply)

1. Facebook
2. Twitter
3. LinkedIn
4. Klout

Q21 What determines whether a user can create a new record using a specific record type?

1. Profile
2. Field-level security
3. Page layout
4. Sharing

Q22 Which statement about record types is true? (Select any two)

1. Users cannot view records assigned to a record type that their profile does not have access to
2. Record types can be used to define picklist values available for a given field
3. The ability to create records of a specific record type is determined by the profile
4. Record types can only be assigned to one profile at a time

Q23 Which functions are available when creating a roll-up summary field? (select any four that apply)

1. SUM
2. COUNT
3. MIN
4. AVG
5. MAX

Q24 Which statements are true regarding roll-up summary fields? (select all that apply)

1. Validation errors can display when saving either the detail or master record
2. Advanced currency management has no effect on roll-up summary fields
3. Once created, you cannot change the detail object selected or delete any field referenced in your roll-up summary definition
4. Automatically derived fields, such as the current date or current user, are allowed in a roll-up summary field
5. Because roll-up summary fields are not displayed on edit pages, you can use them in validation rules

Q25 Describe the ramifications of field updates and the potential for recursion for the following scenario: when a field update for Rule1 triggers Rule2 and a field update for Rule2 triggers Rule1.

1. When the second trigger is saved, an Imminent Loop Error message will be displayed and the workflow rule update will not save
2. The updates create a loop and the org limits for the workflow time triggers per hour will probably be violated

3. The updates create a loop and the org will be blocked until the admin resolves the issue
4. The loop is allowed to run 25 times within one hour. If it does not end on its own, the process will be stopped by R and D

Q26 Acme Corporation wants to store an area code and wants to be able to search for it in searches. Which are possible fields to store the data? (Select any two)

1. Phone
2. E-mail
3. Text
4. Multi Picklist
5. Number

Q27 You want to use an External Data Object Table from Heroku carrying Product Category information. The data needs to be included in Salesforce and be searchable. What do you have to do before you can use the connection? (Select any two)

1. Choose the *Include in Salesforce searches* option
2. Choose *Include as Index Field*
3. Choose the URL
4. Press *Validate and Sync*

Q28 Acme Corporation has included its orders as an external data object in Salesforce. You want to create a relationship between Accounts and the Orders Object (a one-to-many relationship) leveraging a key field for account on both the external object and Account. Which relationship will you create?

1. A lookup relationship
2. An indirect Lookup relationship
3. A master-detail relationship
4. A hierarchical relationship
5. An external Lookup relationship

Q29 Which of the following fields are not available for record types?

1. Opportunity Stages
2. Case Status
3. Solution Status
4. Lead Status
5. All of the above

Q30 Describe the capabilities of this core CRM object in the Salesforce schema: Person accounts (Select any two)

1. Uses space in both the account and contact table
2. Has the same icon as business accounts
3. Can only be merged with other person accounts
4. Are enabled by default
5. Are enabled via a feature license

Q31 Acme Corporation wants to roll out new product bundles with several pricing options. Pricing options include product price bundles, account-specific pricing, and more. Which product satisfies these needs?

1. Custom AppExchange app for product pricing
2. Workflow on Opportunity/Opportunity Product
3. Formula fields on Opportunity/Opportunity product
4. The Lightning Process Builder

Q32 Acme Corporation has a custom object, Service, which has a lookup relationship with Account. Acme Corporation wants to enhance Salesforce1 with an action that allows account managers to enter a new service to an Account while looking at the Account. How can Acme Corporation accomplish this?

1. Enter an object-specific action into Service and put it in the Account Layout
2. Enter an object-specific action into Service and put it in the Service Layout
3. Enter an object-specific action into Account and put it on the Account layout
4. Enter an object-specific action to Account and put it in the Service Layout

Q33 Acme Corporation is using assignment rules to distribute cases to regional teams. Which of the following are true?

1. It is possible to have multiple active assignment rules
2. Cases may be assigned to public groups (if configured)
3. Cases may be assigned to queues (if configured)
4. A workflow field update can be used instead

Q34 When should a system administrator consider using the Salesforce AppExchange? (Select any two)

1. When the standard Salesforce functionality needs to be extended
2. To find answers to Salesforce application questions
3. When looking for pre-built custom applications and tools
4. To submit ideas for Salesforce application enhancements

Q35 Which permission is required to install and uninstall packages from Salesforce AppExchange?

1. Upload AppExchange packages
2. Manage Package licenses
3. Download AppExchange packages
4. Create AppExchange packages

Q36 Which developer tool can be used to create a data model? (Select any two)

1. The Force.com data loader
2. The Schema Builder
3. The Application Data Model Wizard
4. The Force.com IDE

Q37 Which API cannot be used to create the data model? (Select any three)

1. The Force.com Metadata API
2. The Force.com Single Sign-on API
3. The Force.com API
4. AJAX Toolkit for Force.com

Q38 Acme Corporation has a custom object that has a N:M relationship with `opportunityLineItem` carrying the price and amount information. In order to compute total amounts and total prices per Opportunity using roll-up summary fields, which field type would you need to choose?

1. Junction
2. Master-Detail
3. Lookup
4. Cross-object

Q39 When considering Field Type Conversion, which of the following are true? (Select any two)

1. Data can be lost when converting from a simple picklist to a multi picklist
2. Data can be lost when converting from auto number to text
3. Data can be lost when converting from number to currency (assuming that field lengths are identical)
4. Information can be lost when converting from text area (rich) to text area (long)

That's it. You are done. Turn to the Appendix to check your answers.

Additional resources

This section lists some good official and community blogs and podcast videos that will provide even more information on the certification exam. The best way to find more resources is to Google them.

Official Salesforce resources

- The Developer Force blog is the primary resource of all things Force.com (`http://blogs.developerforce.com/`).
- The Certification Home contains all the information about Salesforce certification exams (`http://certification.Salesforce.com/Home`).
- The App Builders Track contains all information about classroom training and a guide for the Salesforce Certified App Builders exam (`http://certification.salesforce.com/app-builders`).
- Force.com Books contains additional books, workbooks, and cookbooks about creating applications on Force.com (`http://wiki.developerForce.com/page/Force.com_Books`).

Summary

Every journey has an end and thus we have reached the end of the book. We have covered all the topics that will help you become a Salesforce certified app builder. For further reading, you can visit some of the community resources provided in the previous section. Some of the best help is available on the Salesforce success forums or using `#AskForce` on Twitter.

All the best for your exam.

May the Force be with you.

Self-Test Answers

Chapter 1, Getting Started with Force.com

Question	Answer
Q1	2 and 3
Q2	3
Q3	2
Q4	1,3, and 4
Q5	2 and 3
Q6	1 and 2
Q7	1

Chapter 2, Creating a Database on Force.com

Question	Answer
Q1	2,3, and 4
Q2	2,3, and 4
Q3	2
Q4	2 and 3
Q5	1,2,5, and 6
Q6	5
Q7	2

Question	Answer
Q8	4
Q9	2
Q10	1

Chapter 3, User Interface

Question	Answer
Q1	1,3,4, and 5
Q2	1 and 3
Q3	1 and 3
Q4	1,2,4, and 5
Q5	1 and 2
Q6	2
Q7	1,3, and 4

Chapter 4, Implementing Business Logic

Question	Answers
Q1	3
Q2	2,3, and 4
Q3	1
Q4	1 and 4
Q5	1
Q6	3
Q7	1 and 4
Q8	1 and 3
Q9	2
Q10	1
Q11	1
Q12	3

Chapter 5, Data Management

Question	Answer
Q1	1,2, and 4
Q2	3
Q3	1
Q4	2
Q5	2
Q6	4
Q7	1

Chapter 6, Analytics and Reporting

Question	Answer
Q1	1 and 3
Q2	1 and 4
Q3	2
Q4	4
Q5	2
Q6	2 and 4
Q7	2

Chapter 7, Application Administration

Question	Answer
Q1	2 and 3
Q2	3
Q3	2
Q4	2 and 3
Q5	3

Chapter 8, Exam Guide and Practice Test

Question	Answer
Q1	3
Q2	2 and 4
Q3	1 and 4
Q4	3
Q5	1,2, and 5
Q6	1,3, and 5
Q7	1,2, and 5
Q8	1,3, and 4
Q9	1,2, and 5
Q10	3
Q11	3
Q12	4
Q13	1
Q14	2,3, and 5
Q15	1
Q16	1,2, and 4
Q17	1,2, and 3
Q18	2
Q19	1
Q20	2
Q21	1
Q22	2 and 3
Q23	1,2,3, and 5
Q24	1,3, and 5
Q25	2
Q26	1,3, and 5
Q27	1 and 4
Q28	2
Q29	5
Q30	1 and 3
Q31	4
Q32	3

Question	**Answer**
Q33	3
Q34	1 and 3
Q35	3
Q36	2 and 4
Q37	2,3, and 4
Q38	2
Q39	2 and 4

Index

Symbols

A

B

C

D

E

F

G

J

K

L

M

T

U

V

W

www.ingramcontent.com/pod-product-compliance
Lightning Source LLC
Chambersburg PA
CBHW080935220326

41598CB00034B/5783

* 9 7 8 1 7 8 5 2 8 3 6 9 7 *